OXFORD
UNIVERSITY PRESS

Oxford International Primary Maths

Teacher's Guide

NEW! Increased support for your classroom

Tony Cotton

Caroline Clissold

Linda Glithro

Cherri Moseley

Janet Rees

Language consultants:
John McMahon
Liz McMahon

6

Oxford International Primary for enquiring minds

OXFORD

OXFORD
UNIVERSITY PRESS

Great Clarendon Street, Oxford, OX2 6DP, United Kingdom

Oxford University Press is a department of the University of Oxford.
It furthers the University's objective of excellence in research,
scholarship, and education by publishing worldwide. Oxford is a
registered trade mark of Oxford University Press in the UK and in
certain other countries

British Library Cataloguing in Publication Data
Data available

978-0-19-841807-8

10 9 8 7 6

Paper used in the production of this book is a natural, recyclable
product made from wood grown in sustainable forests.
The manufacturing process conforms to the environmental regulations
of the country of origin.

Printed in Great Britain by CPI Group (UK) Ltd, Croydon CR0 4YY

Acknowledgements
The publishers would like to thank the following for permissions to
use their photographs: Cover photo: Patryk Kosmider/Shutterstock

Although we have made every effort to trace and contact all copyright
holders before publication this has not been possible in all cases.
If notified, the publisher will rectify any errors or omissions at the
earliest opportunity.

6 Contents

Further support can be found on the website. Access the website here:

www.oxfordprimary.com/OIPMteacher

Teaching techniques

A problem solving approach to teaching mathematics often requires the teacher to adopt a new approach if students are to develop their mathematical understanding. Whilst mathematical facts are important, it is unlikely that simply giving the students the information they need will result in them understanding the mathematics and being able to apply their learning in new situations. This is often described as a move from 'surface learning' to 'deep learning'.

Many people remember mathematics lessons as places where the teacher stands at the front of the class writing on the board. The students copy the information down, maybe work through a couple of examples with the teacher and then proceed to complete a series of exercise to practise the skill that they have been taught. This can be described as a *didactic* approach and it relies on the idea that direct instruction is the appropriate strategy to adopt. The authors of this series would argue that *heuristic* strategies encourage students to explore the mathematics for themselves supported by the teacher. This results in a deeper understanding for the student.

A problem solving approach requires a teacher to think carefully about differentiation as, on many occasions, learners will all be offered the same starting point but will proceed at different rates so individual learning outcomes may differ. This requires a different approach to grouping students. Both of these issues are discussed in more detail here.

Similarly assessment takes a different form as teachers will need to continually assess students throughout the lesson to ensure they know when learners should move to the next stage. This form of assessment is often called *assessment for learning* (AfL), and strategies to support AfL are described in this Introduction.

Differentiation

There are several ways that you can differentiate learning in the classroom. These include:

- Differentiation by task
- Differentiation by outcome
- Differentiation by support
- Differentiation by grouping.

It has been traditional in some schools to offer up to three different tasks for each lesson. This is differentiation by task. However, the mastery approach, pioneered by Shanghai and Singapore, and currently being adopted in many schools around the world, suggests that it is important all students are engaged on the same task to ensure that key mathematical objectives are met. This suggests that differentiation by task does not support deep learning for all students. It is important that all students are exploring the same area of mathematics as they can collaborate and discuss their mathematics in a way that is not possible if learners are engaged on different activities. The Education Endowment Foundation teacher's toolkit suggests that collaborative learning can result in a five month acceleration in student learning. (See https://educationendowmentfoundation.org.uk/resources/teaching-learning-toolkit.)

The expectation in this series is that all students will be offered the same starting point. All students start at the same point. The activities are carefully designed to be accessible to all students in your class and the teacher's notes for the activity offer differentiated outcomes for students. It is also important that you offer differentiated support to different students. You will mainly do this through the sort of questioning that you engage in. You will ask challenging questions to stretch some students and supporting questions to help other students access the task. For example, when engaging in a simple counting activity with some learners you may model the action of counting by placing a finger on each object as you count and emphasise the last number you say to model that the last number you say gives the number of objects in the set. For other learners engaged in the same activity you may ask them to compare two sets, or to find one more or one less than the set they are counting.

Ways of grouping

When engaging in learning mathematics it is expected that you will use a variety of groups. This may be a change for some teachers who have previously grouped students by prior attainment in their classroom. Research has shown that grouping students 'by ability' which usually means grouping learners using test results, can have a negative impact on their future attainment. It is more effective to use a range of ways of grouping learners. You will decide on the most appropriate way of grouping students depending on the activity. You are also given advice in the teacher's notes when a particular form of grouping is most appropriate. It is important that the teacher is active in deciding which form of grouping is appropriate. It is also important that students learn how to operate in a range of different groups and with a range of different learners.

There are four main ways of grouping students:

- Friendship
- 'Ability'
- 'Prior experience'
- Mixed-attainment.

Friendship groups are most appropriate for activities in which the students have been given some element of choice. Perhaps they are carrying out some research for a data handling project or exploring data on animals to develop their understanding of measurement. This grouping is the default if teachers do not actively group students.

'Ability' groups, or groups based on the prior experience of students, may be helpful if the activity requires a very specific prior knowledge. You can group learners who you know have this knowledge together to allow you to focus your teaching appropriately, or to use any classroom support that you have effectively.

Mixed-attainment groups are the grouping that is encouraged for the majority of the activities. This kind of grouping is particularly helpful for students new to English. All-attainment groups allow students who are less confident in English to hear their more confident peers using mathematical vocabulary. Research has shown that mixed-attainment groups benefit both high attainers, who become more secure in their mathematics knowledge through explaining their thinking to peers and to those less secure in their mathematical knowledge as peer teaching has been shown to be effective.

Whatever form of grouping you choose it is helpful to assign roles to individuals in the group. Some teachers use 'role cards' to remind members of the group of the role they should play. Examples of these roles are:

- Leader: You should make sure everyone has a chance to speak and focus the discussion around the task.
- Time keeper: You should encourage the group to stay on task. Announce when the time is half way through and when time is nearly up.
- Recorder: You should write down the group member's ideas or draw a collective graphic. You will write on the board during the presentation.
- Presenter: You will present the groups findings to the while class at the end of the session.
- Resource organiser: You will make sure the group has all the resources they need during the task.

Assessment for learning

Dylan Wiliam has suggested that there are five key strategies for assessment for learning. These are outlined below with suggestions of how you can do this in your classroom.

1 Being clear about learning objectives and success criteria with the students.

Each activity has at least one learning objective. When there is more than one objective a key objective is highlighted. At the beginning of a lesson share this with the students. This should be more than simply stating the objective. You should make sure that students understand the objective and how you will measure success. For example, you might say: *I know that you can all count 10 objects* and all count to 10 as a class. Then you point to '20' on a number line and ask: *Does anyone know what this number is?* If a student knows it is 20 praise them, if no-one knows, tell them it is twenty and say: *By the end of the lesson I will be able to listen to you count to twenty.*

2 Planning student discussions that give you evidence of their learning.

Every activity plan in the teacher's guide offers the opportunity for small group or whole class discussion. There are also examples of probing questions that you can ask to assess the student's current understanding. For example, if a group has been counting two sets of objects you can ask: *Were there more or less in the second group? How do you know?*

3 Giving students feedback that helps them move forward.

This allows students to know whether or not they are meeting the success criteria and what they can do next to move their learning on. Developing the example above, if a group has been comparing two sets and understands the concept of 'more' and 'less' you could ask them to make sets that are 'one more' and 'one less' or even 'two more and two less'.

4 Activating students to act as instructional resources for each other.

Collaborative group work in all-attainment groups is the best way of ensuring that students can act as peer teachers.

5 Activating students as owners of their own learning.

The key point here is to listen carefully to the students and adapt your questioning to support individual development and to follow individual interests.

Questioning is key

The most skilled mathematics teachers can ask open questions to elicit students' current understandings. Skilful open questioning also allows students to articulate their current understanding carefully and through this process either consolidate their understanding or come to realise where they have made a mistake. The list below offers a series of open questions that can be used whatever mathematics you are teaching:

- *How are these the same/different?*
- *About how many/how long/many more …. do you think there will be?*
- *What would happen if …?*
- *How else could you have done that?*
- *Why did you ….?*
- *How did you …?*
- *How do you know that is correct?*

If you want students to check their solutions and consolidate their learning it is helpful to ask them to explain how they reached their solution to a partner. Similarly, to support students in reflecting on their learning you might ask:

- *What mathematics did you use to solve the problem?*
- *What new mathematics did you learn?*
- *What key words did you use?*
- *What was the most challenging part of the activity?*
- *What did you do when you got stuck?*
- *What other questions could you ask?*
- *Did this remind you of any other areas of mathematics?*

If you get in the habit of asking these questions regularly your students will become very skilled at answering them in some depth, and you will find out a lot about their current mathematical understandings.

Word problems

Many teachers find teaching word problems a challenge. This area is particularly challenging for learners with a limited English vocabulary as word problems are tightly bound to linguistic ability. We have to decode and understand what the problem is asking us to do before we can begin to apply our mathematical knowledge. Some teachers have found the following acronym helpful when working with students on solving word problems.

R: Read the problem carefully.

U: Understand what the problem is asking you to do.

C: Choose the mathematics or arithmetical operations that you need to use to solve the problem.

S: Solve the problem.

A: Answer the problem.

C: Check the answer is accurate and reasonable.

It is often helpful for students to underline key facts and write down the operations they are going to use before they solve the problem. For example:

> Tony rode his bicycle <u>7 miles</u> to school with his friend. On his way home he took a short cut which was only <u>5 miles</u>. <u>How far</u> did he cycle <u>altogether</u>?
>
> *This will be an addition calculation.*

It is a useful activity for students to annotate word problems and write down the operation(s) they will use without carrying out the calculation as this focuses on the skill of understanding the problem and choosing the operations appropriately.

Another activity which helps students become skilled at solving word problems is asking them to write their own word problems based on a picture or a set of objects. For example:

- How many black cubes are there? (3)
- Two friends took three cubes each. How many were left? (2)
- If I take out the black cubes, how many are left? (5)
- If I share the cubes equally between two people, how many do they each get? (4)

Language Support Introduction

The challenges

Ministries of Education at both local and national level are increasingly adopting the policy of English Medium Instruction (EMI), for either one or two subjects or across the whole curriculum. The rationale for doing so varies according to the local context, but improving the levels of achievement in English is an important factor.

In international schools an additional reason is likely to be that students do not share a mother tongue with each other or perhaps the teacher. English is, therefore, chosen as the medium for instruction so that all students are in the same position and to provide the opportunity to develop proficiency in an international language.

This does not mean that the maths teacher is now being asked to replace the English teacher, or to have the same skills or knowledge of English (though in many primary schools one teacher may indeed teach both). What it does mean, however, is that the maths teacher has to view his/her role differently: he/she has to become much more language aware. It is this recognition of the need to ensure that *the delivery of the content is not negatively impacted by the use of the second language* that informs the planning and methodology of EMI.

This raises significant challenges, including:

- the teacher's knowledge of English
- students' level of English (which may vary considerably in international schools)
- resources which provide appropriate language support
- assessment tools which ensure that it is the content and not the language which is being tested
- differentiation which acknowledges different levels of proficiency in both language and content.

Meeting the challenges positively

Perhaps lack of confidence in their own English proficiency is one of the most common concerns among teachers. However, while it is a factor, success in EMI is not necessarily linked to the teachers' proficiency in the second language. Teachers who have English as their mother tongue may well lack the sensitivity to, or awareness of, the language that a non-native speaker has acquired through learning and studying the second language. *Developing this awareness and demonstrating it in both materials and method is the key to effective EMI.*

Classroom language/Teacher Talk

Often non-native-speaker teachers are more concerned about their ability to run and manage the whole class in English than they are about the actual teaching of the maths concepts, as the resources or textbook should help them with the latter. However, this use of English in the class is very important as it provides exposure to the second language, which plays a valuable role in language acquisition. It is also true that the Teacher Talk for purposes such as checking attendance and collecting homework does not have to be totally accurate or accessible to the learners. *When teaching the maths concepts, however, it is essential that the Teacher Talk is comprehensible.* Some basic strategies to ensure this include:

- simplification or grading of your language
- use short simple sentences and project your voice
- paraphrase as necessary
- use visuals, the board, gestures and body language to clarify meaning

- repeat as necessary
- plan before the lesson
- prepare clear simple instructions and check understanding.

Creating a language-rich environment

Primary teachers often excel at providing a colourful and engaging physical environment for students. In the EMI classroom this becomes even more important. Posters, 'Word walls', lists of key structures, students' work, and English signs and notices all provide a backdrop which provides the opportunity for exposure and language acquisition.

Planning

When planning, look carefully at each stage of the unit and identify what the Language Demands are. This means thinking about what language students will need to *understand* or *produce*, and deciding how best to scaffold the learning to ensure that language does not become an obstacle to understanding the concept. This involves providing Language Support and goes beyond the familiar strategy of identifying key vocabulary.

Support for listening and reading

Listening and reading are *receptive* skills, requiring understanding rather than production of language. Here are some suggestions for approaching such tasks. If you are asking your students to listen to or read texts in English, ask yourself the following questions when you are planning the unit:

1 Do I need to teach any vocabulary before they listen/read?

2 How can I prepare them for the content of the text so that they are not listening 'cold'?

3 Can I provide visual support to help them understand the key content?

4 How many times should I ask them to read/listen?

5 What simple question can I set before they listen/read for the first time to focus their attention?

6 How can I check more detailed understanding of the text? Can I use a graphic organiser (e.g. tables, charts and diagrams) or gap-fill task to reduce the Language Demands?

7 Do I need to differentiate the task for those students who find reading/listening difficult?

8 Could I make the tasks interactive (e.g. jigsaw reading, when students access different information before coming together, and information share)?

9 How am I going to check their answers and give feedback?

Support for speaking and writing

Speaking and writing are *productive* skills and, as such, may need more language input from the teacher, who has to decide what language students will need to complete the task in the second language and how best to provide this.

When you plan to use a task which requires students to *produce* English (speak or write), you need to think about how to help them do this.

This means that you have to think in detail about *what language* the task requires (Language Demands, LD) and what strategies you will use to help them use English to perform the task (Language Support, LS).

You need to ask yourself the following questions:

1   What *vocabulary* does the task require? (LD)

2   Do I need to teach this before they start? How? (LS)

3   What *phrases/sentences* will they need? Think about the language for learning maths, e.g. predicting and comparing. What structures do they need for these language functions? (LD)

4   Will they be able to produce these sentences or should I provide some *scaffolding* [e.g. sentence starters/sentence frames/gapped sentences/substitution table (see below)]? (LS)

A

square

sides

triangle 3

rectangle has 4

quadrilateral 5

pentagon

5   While I am *monitoring* this task is there any way I can provide further support for their use of English (especially for the weaker students)? (LS)

6   What language will students need to use at the *feedback* stage (e.g. when they present their task)? Do I need to scaffold this? (LD, LS)

Teaching vocabulary and structures

Vocabulary

Learning the key maths vocabulary is central to EMI and 'learning' means more than simply understanding the meaning. Knowing a word also involves being able to *pronounce* it accurately and *use* it appropriately. Below is a list of strategies which could be useful:

*   Avoid writing the list of vocabulary on the board at the start of the unit and 'explaining' it.

The vocabulary should be introduced as and when it arises in the unit. This helps students associate the word or phrase with the concept and context.

*   Record the vocabulary clearly on the board and check that you are confident with the pronunciation and spelling.
*   Give students a chance to say the word once they have understood it. The most efficient way to do this is through repetition drilling.
*   Use visuals whenever possible to reinforce students' understanding of the word.
*   Ensure students are recording the vocabulary systematically in their glossaries and, if possible, use a 'Word wall' which lists the vocabulary under unit/topic headings.
*   Remember to recycle and revise the vocabulary.

Structures

In order for students to talk or write about their maths they will need to go beyond vocabulary: they will also need to use those phrases and sentence frames which a particular task requires.

For example, they may need the following expressions in maths:

> *X is the same as Y.*
>
> *The sides are the same length.*
>
> *The next number in the sequence.*
>
> *I predict that X will happen.*
>
> *If X happens, then Y happens.*
>
> *The next step is …*

You need to build up these banks of common maths phrases and encourage students to record them. This is an important part of identifying the Language Demands and providing the necessary support. The teacher does not have to focus on grammar here as the language can be taught as 'chunks' rather than specific grammatical structures.

Using the teacher's guides

Every activity has a step-by-step guide in the teacher's guide to lead you through the activity.

Engage activities are one-page discussion activities at the start of a unit. You can use these to introduce a new topic to the class.

Discussion and Explore activities are all two-page activities that contain everything you need to teach a particular aspect of the curriculum.

Learning focus: For every activity, there are specific learning objectives and at least one problem solving objective. Often you will find several objectives listed for the activity. If this is the case one objective will be highlighted. This should be the main mathematical focus for the activity. Other objectives may be referred to allow the teacher to make connections between different areas of mathematics.

Key vocabulary: This is the vocabulary you should focus on within the activity, taking care to model the correct pronunciation. There is a full glossary for reference on page 219.

Resources and links to Student Books, Workbooks and Digital Resource Packs: All the key resources are listed here. This includes links to Workbooks and digital resources.

Language support: This section of the teaching notes provides specific language support. A range of strategies are suggested, including card sorts and card games, word walls, team games to define or explain words, use of similar words to explain meaning and exploration of the origins of words.

The key principles underpinning the language support are:

- Words should be introduced and explained carefully.
- The word should be explained in context.
- Repetition is vital.
- Words should be linked to pictures or actions.
- Students should develop their own glossaries.
- The learning of mathematics vocabulary should be fun.
- Language should not be a barrier to effective learning of mathematics.

Activity plan: The activity plan is outlined in detail including probing questions for formative assessment which are italicised. Icons are used to suggest to teachers the groupings that should be used at each point of the activity.

Differentiation: Whilst all students should start at the same point in order not to place a limit of student achievement, the teacher's guide offers differentiated outcomes. These outcomes are listed in the form of:

All students should …

Most students will …

Some students may …

The activity guide also offers strategies for you to **support** those students who may have difficulty accessing the task; to **consolidate** the learning for those students who need a little more practice; and to **extend** the learning for those who need more challenge.

Assessment for learning: Assessment is built into the activity plan through the italicised probing questions. The learning review activity is also a point at which formative assessment will take place. At the end of each unit there are summative assessment activities. There is also an assessment activity on a resource sheet (see www.oxfordprimary.com/OIPMteacher). This activity is a mixture of multiple choice questions and short answers.

A full set of answers for each activity is given at the end of the notes for the activity.

Unit 1   Number and Place Value

Overview

Big Idea

The two Big Ideas for this unit are place value, and recognising and extending number sequences. In the decimal number system, the value of a digit depends on its place, or position, in the number. It is important to know that each place has a value of 10 times the value of the place to its right.

Clear mental images of the number system help students to understand number sequences. The use of 100-squares, number lines and empty number lines enables students to notice and describe number sequences and properties.

Possible misconceptions

Students may say that to multiply by 10 you 'add a zero'. This strategy gives the correct answer for the multiplication of integers (for example $257 \times 10 = 2570$). However, this strategy gives incorrect answers for the multiplication of decimals (for example 24.31×100 does not equal 24.3100). The activities in this unit show students that, when multiplying or dividing by 10 or 100, the digits change position on the place value grid.

For the 'counting on' and 'counting back' activities in this unit, students need to count back across zero. Students may think that you cannot subtract a larger number from a smaller number. For example, students may think that $25 - 75$ 'doesn't work', not that $25 - 75 = -50$. It is important to use a number line with negative numbers to support these activities.

Key vocabulary and language structures

Ten thousand, hundred thousand, million; 4-digit number; number system, script; factor; multiple; prime number; prime factor; composite number; common multiple; > greater than, more than, larger than, bigger than; < less than, fewer than, smaller than; ≥ greater than or equal to; ≤ less than or equal to; half-way between estimate; about the same as; is approximately equal to just over, just under round to the nearest; sequence; extend, predict, term, continue the sequence, predict the next number in the pattern, the rule for the pattern

Coverage in lessons

Learning focus	Learning outcomes
The number system	Can I explain the historical origins of the number system we use?
Place value	Can I identify what each digit represents in whole numbers up to a million?
	Can I identify what each digit represents in one-place and two-place decimal numbers?
	Can I explain the effect of multiplying and dividing numbers by 10, 100 and 1000?
Number properties	Can I find factors of two-digit numbers?
	Can I find common multiples?
	Can I explain what prime numbers are?
	Can I represent 'greater than' and 'less than' with mathematical signs?
Estimation and rounding	Can I round numbers to the nearest 10, 100 or 1000?
	Can I estimate where 4-digit numbers lie on an empty 0–10 000 line?
Number sequences	Can I recognise number sequences?
	Can I extend number sequences?

1 Number and Place Value

Engage

Specific learning foci

- Know what each digit represents in numbers up to a million.
- *Make and justify estimates and approximations of large numbers.*

Problem solving focus

- Explain why they chose a particular method to perform a calculation and show working.

Key vocabulary

ten thousand, hundred thousand, million

Resources

- Metre rules and measuring tapes
- Cuboid containers of various sizes
- Dried chickpeas or similar
- Calculators

Links to Student Book

See page 1 in Student Book.

Language support

Listen to how students say large numbers. Encourage them to say the number in full and not to say each digit separately. For example: 876 426 is 'eight hundred and seventy-six thousand, four hundred and twenty-six' not 'eight seven six four two six'. Model this in your discussions with students.

Introductory activity

Ask students: *How long would it take you to count to one **million**?* Some students may assume that you can count each number in one second and calculate how long one million seconds is in days and hours. To challenge this assumption, ask: *How long does it take you to say a number like 876 426 out loud?* Students need to understand what each of the digits in a six-digit number represent.

Main activity

Students should work in mixed-attainment groups of four to six students. Ask students: *How many chickpeas would fill the classroom?* After their suggestions ask: *How could you calculate this?* Give students time in their groups to decide how to solve this problem. You can simplify the problem by using a much smaller container and asking: *How many chickpeas would fill this container?* and then ask: *How many small containers would fill a 1 cubic metre container?* Then you can calculate the size of the classroom in cubic metres to solve the problem.

Differentiation

Supporting: Encourage students to take an active role in the discussions and contribute to the group activity.

Consolidating: Ask students to support one another in deciding on appropriate calculations and to explain the strategies they are using.

Extending: Ask students to check the accuracy of their answers and to justify them.

Learning review

Ask groups to share their solutions with the whole class. Each group should tell the presenting group two things that they like in the solution ('We like …') and one target for future problem-solving activities ('In future you could …').

Additional activities

Students can work on other activities with large numbers. For example: *How many times would the total number of students in this school fit into the National Stadium?* or *How long would it take to walk from your school to the capital city (or a capital city of a neighbouring country)?*

1A The number system

Discover

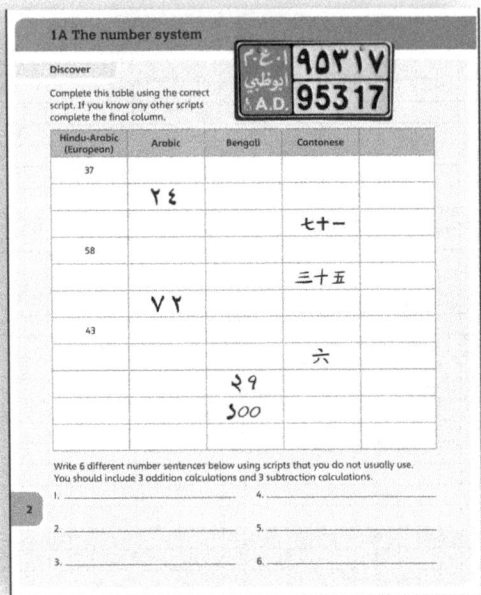

Specific learning foci

- *Recognise the historical origins of the number system and begin to understand how it developed.*
- Know what each digit represents in whole numbers up to a million.

Problem solving focus

- Use logical reasoning to explore and solve number problems and mathematical puzzles.

Key vocabulary

Number system, script

Resources

- 100-squares in different scripts (see Resource sheets 1a–1c from www.oxfordprimary.com/OIPMteacher) – cut into 6 pieces to form jigsaws. You need enough so that each student can have one piece. Each square should be copied in a different colour so the students can find others in their group.
- Mini whiteboards and markers

Links to Student Book

See page 2 in Student Book.

Links to Workbook

Workbook pages 6 and 7

Language support

As students are completing the jigsaws of different scripts, ask them to explain their thinking. Focus on the language of place value, looking for 'hundreds', 'tens' and 'units'. Support students in using the English words for the numbers.

Introductory activity

Give each student a piece of jigsaw. Form groups of six students and ask them to complete the jigsaw. Ask the students to explore the 100-squares carefully. They should discuss what they notice. Which numerals did they recognise? How did they use their knowledge of 100-squares to 'translate' the numerals? Ask students if any of them know a **number system** in another language. If they do, take this opportunity to learn this number system to 20 as a class, asking the students who suggested the number system to teach other students.

Point out that the Hindu-Arabic system was developed by the Persian mathematician Al-Khwarizmi in about AD 825, drawing on earlier work by Indian mathematicians.

Main activity

Drawing on the discussion in the Introductory activity, students should work in pairs to complete the table on page 2 of the Student Book. If students know the words for the numerals in any of the languages, encourage them to say the numbers aloud. If you have been able to learn another language, use this to complete the final column. The pairs should then take it in turns to set a calculation for their partner. This should be written in one of the **scripts** that are unfamiliar to the students.

Differentiation

Supporting: Ask students to describe similarities and differences between the scripts.

Consolidating: Ask students to describe the patterns they notice in the 'new' number script.

Extending: Ask students to carry out calculations in a new script.

Differentiated outcomes	
All students	should use their understanding of place value to complete the jigsaws.
Most students	will notice the patterns in a 100-square.
Some students	will carry out calculations in a new script.

Learning review

Ask individual students to come to the front and write one of their calculations on the board. The pairs should write the answer in the appropriate script on their mini whiteboards. The student at the front should check the responses. Repeat several times using the different scripts.

Additional activities

Students can teach their parents or guardians the scripts that they have been working with and set questions for the adults to attempt. They can see if there are any home languages which use a range of number scripts.

Students can complete Workbook pages 6 and 7.

Answers

Student Book page 2

Check that students' number sentences use their chosen scripts correctly and are mathematically correct.

Hindu-Arabic (European)	Arabic	Bengali	Cantonese
37	٣٧	৩৭	三十七
24	٢٤	২৪	二十四
71	٧١	৭১	七十一
58	٥٨	৫৮	五十八
35	٣٥	৩৫	三十五
72	٧٢	৭২	七十二
43	٤٣	৪৩	四十三
6	٦	৬	六
27	٢٧	২৭	二十七
100	١٠٠	১০০	一百

Workbook pages 6 and 7

	Millions	Hundred thousands	Ten thousands	Thousands	Hundreds	Tens	Ones	.	tenths	hundredths
1.			3	9	7	7	5	.	7	1
2.	1	6	6	5	6	7	1	.	0	0
3.	5	6	2	5	4	2	9	.	0	0
4.	6	2	2	7	6	7	8	.	0	0
5.		4	1	5	1	5	1	.	0	0
6.							9	.	5	8

Explore

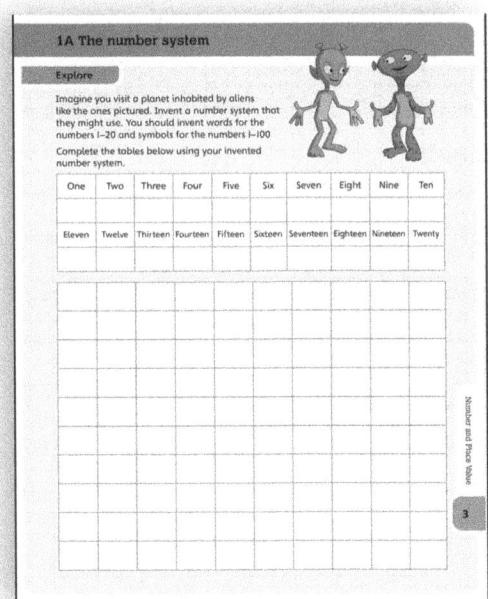

Specific learning foci

- *Recognise the historical origins of the number system and begin to understand how it developed.*
- Know what each digit represents in whole numbers up to a million.

Problem solving focus

- Use logical reasoning to explore and solve number problems and mathematical puzzles.

Key vocabulary

Number system, script

Resources

- 100-squares in different scripts to use for ideas
- Mini whiteboards and markers

Links to Student Book

See page 3 in Student Book.

Links to Workbook

Workbook pages 6 and 7

Language support

As students invent their number systems, focus on the language of place value, looking for 'hundreds', 'tens' and 'units'. Support students in using the English words for the script they are inventing.

 Introductory activity

Ask students in pairs to look at the image on page 3 of the Student Book. Ask them to discuss how a **number system** might have developed for these 'aliens'. They may think that the aliens with 3 fingers on one hand might count in sets of 3 or 6 – just as our number system works in sets of 10. The aliens with 4 fingers might count in sets of 4 or 8. Allow any answers. The idea is for the students to come up with creative ideas. Creating new number systems supports students in coming to a clearer understanding of the structure of the number system they use.

 Main activity

Drawing on the discussion in the Introductory activity, students should work in pairs to invent their own number systems and complete page 3 of the Student Book. Encourage students to develop noticeable patterns in both the words and symbols, pointing out the patterns that exist in the languages they are familiar with.

Differentiation

Supporting: Ask students to explain the meanings of their new numbers.

Consolidating: Ask students how their numbers reflect the place value of their new system.

Extending: Encourage students to develop systems which are not base 10.

Differentiated outcomes	
All students	should invent a new number system.
Most students	will reflect place value in the **script** they invent.
Some students	will work in a base which is not base 10.

 Learning review

Ask one student from each pair to set a calculation for their partner, using their script. Repeat this, with students swapping roles. Select one of the pairs to 'teach' their invented system to the rest of the class. Select a pair who have developed a clear pattern in both the words and the symbols.

Additional activities

Students can teach their parents or guardians the scripts that they have invented and set questions for their parents to attempt.

Students can complete Workbook pages 6 and 7.

Answers

Student Book page 3

Answers will vary as students choose their own number systems and their own number names for the aliens. Whilst students are working, ask them to explain how their number systems work and how they know how their number system would show 37 in our number system.

Workbook pages 6 and 7

	Millions	Hundred thousands	Ten thousands	Thousands	Hundreds	Tens	Ones	.	tenths	hundredths
1.			3	9	7	7	5	.	7	1
2.	1	6	6	5	6	7	1	.	0	0
3.	5	6	2	5	4	2	9	.	0	0
4.	6	2	2	7	6	7	8	.	0	0
5.		4	1	5	1	5	1	.	0	0
6.							9	.	5	8

Discover

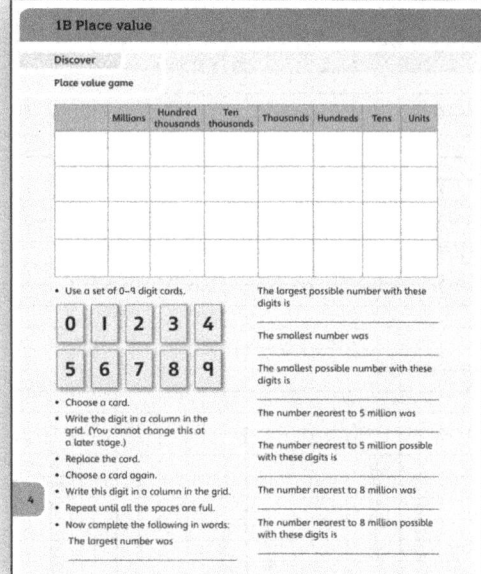

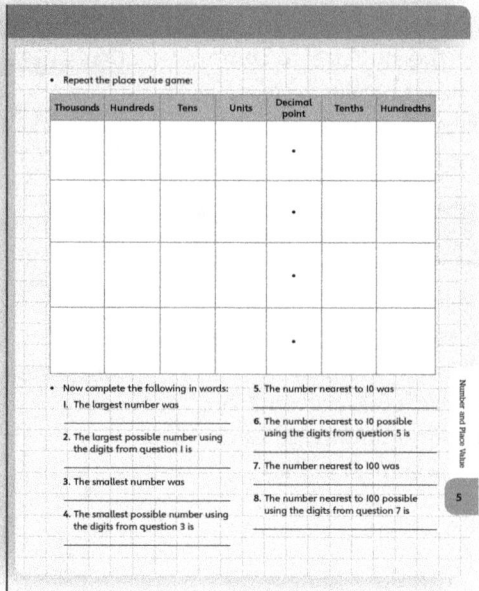

Specific learning foci

- Know what each digit represents in whole numbers up to a million.
- Know what each digit represents in one- and two-place decimal numbers.

Problem solving focus

- Use ordered lists or tables to help solve problems systematically

Key vocabulary

Ten thousand, hundred thousand, million, tenths, hundredths

Resources

- The digits 0–9 written on sheets of A4 card
- Mini whiteboards and markers

Links to Student Book

See pages 4–5 in Student Book.

Links to Workbook

Workbook pages 6 and 7

Links to Digital Resource Pack

Digital Resource Pack 6 contains two activities which can be used to support students' understanding of the place value of large numbers. On the home page, select 'Number and Place Value'.

Language support

Listen to each student speaking the numbers out loud. Ask, for example:

- *How many digits does this number have?*
- *What do you know about a five/six-digit number?*

Use the vocabulary of place value: ten thousand, hundred thousand, million, tenths, hundredths, decimal point, etc.

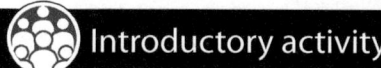

Introductory activity

Ask seven students to come to the front of the classroom. Let each student take a digit from the A4 cards you have prepared. Ask these students to make a line facing the rest of the class. They should make this line one student at a time. As each student joins the line, ask the rest of the class: *What number is this?* (Or ask individual students.)

- One student with the number 7 – The class say 'seven'.
- Two students with the number 3 and the number 7 – The class say 'thirty-seven'.
- Three students with the numbers 5, 3 and 7 – The class say 'five hundred and thirty-seven'.
- Four students with the numbers 6, 5, 3 and 7 – The class say 'six thousand, five hundred and thirty-seven' and so on.

Repeat this as many times as you think is necessary.

 ## Main activity

Ask students to work in pairs to complete the activities on pages 4 and 5 of the Student Workbook. While students work, ask them to say the numbers out loud to you so that you can check their understanding. Ask them questions. For example: *How did you decide that this was the biggest possible number? Are you sure that you can't find a smaller number than that?*

Differentiation

Supporting: Ask students to show you the largest and smallest numbers and explain their reasoning.

Consolidating: Ask students to justify their responses to the questions on pages 4 and 5 of the Student Book.

Extending: Ask students to create 8-digit numbers or numbers with three places of decimals and to order these numbers smallest to greatest and vice versa.

Differentiated outcomes	
All students	should order numbers up to 7 digits.
Most students	will recognise numbers closest to **millions** quickly and order up to 2 places of decimals.
Some students	will extend to beyond 7 digits and two places of decimals.

 ## Learning review

Give out mini whiteboards and markers. Say to students: *Write the following numbers on your whiteboards.* Read out a series of five-, six- and seven-digit numbers. Give students five seconds to write the numbers. Then say: *Show me your numbers.* This helps you assess individual understanding. Include some numbers with zeros as place-holders, for example 'three hundred and two thousand one hundred and seven' (302 107). Repeat for a group of numbers with two decimal places.

Additional activities

You can give students some newspapers and magazines and say: *Find examples of large numbers and decimals.* Then ask them to write the numbers in words.

Students can complete Workbook pages 6 and 7.

Answers

Student Book pages 4 and 5

Answers will vary as students use digit cards to make their numbers. Check that their answers to the questions are correct for the numbers they have made. Note who has a good understanding of the place value of large and decimal numbers and the size of numbers, and who requires more practice in working with these numbers.

Workbook pages 6 and 7

	Millions	Hundred thousands	Ten thousands	Thousands	Hundreds	Tens	Ones	.	tenths	hundredths
1.			3	9	7	7	5	.	7	1
2.	1	6	6	5	6	7	1	.	0	0
3.	5	6	2	5	4	2	9	.	0	0
4.	6	2	2	7	6	7	8	.	0	0
5.		4	1	5	1	5	1	.	0	0
6.							9	.	5	8

Explore

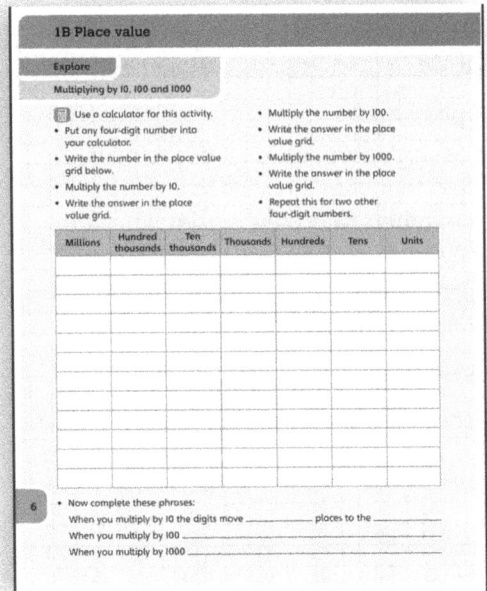

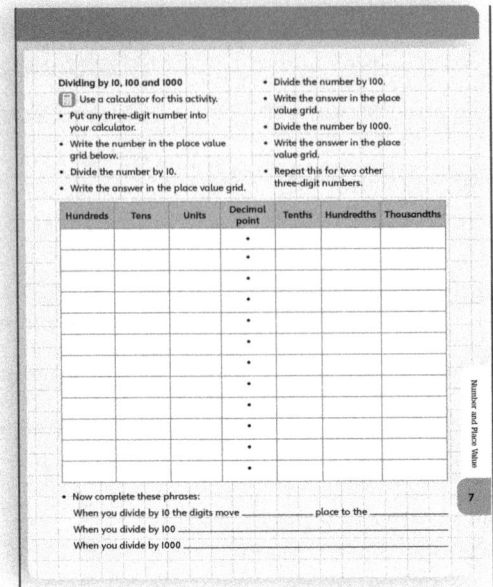

Specific learning focus

- Multiply and divide any whole number from 1 to 10 000 by 10, 100 or 1000 and explain the effect.

Problem solving focus

- Use ordered lists or tables to help solve problems systematically.

Key vocabulary

Ten thousand, hundred thousand, million, tenths, hundredths

Resources

- The digits 0–9 written on sheets of A4 card
- Mini whiteboards and markers

Links to Student Book

See pages 6–7 in Student Book.

Links to Workbook

Workbook pages 6 and 7

Links to Digital Resource Pack

Digital Resource Pack 6 contains two activities which can be used to support students' understanding of the place value of large numbers. On the home page, select 'Number and Place Value'.

Language support

Encourage students to explain their strategies and use the vocabulary of place value: ten thousand, hundred thousand, million, tenths, hundredths, decimal point. Ask, for example:

- *How many digits does this number have?*
- *What do you know about a five-digit number?*

Draw six boxes on the board. Say to students: *Copy these six boxes onto your whiteboard.*

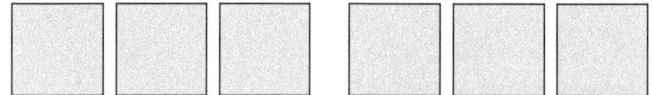

Throw a dice six times. After each throw say to students: *Write the digit in one of your boxes.* Then tell them: *Make the largest number possible with these digits.* Then say: *Make the smallest number possible with these digits.* Repeat this with the following grid to make decimal numbers:

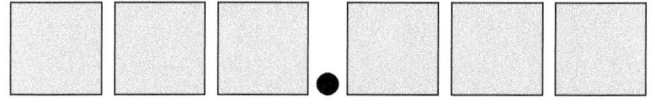

 Main activity

Ask students to work in pairs on the activities on pages 6 and 7 of the Student Book. Tell them to explain to one another what they notice ('When you multiply by …'). Encourage students to explain what they notice very carefully. If any students say to you that 'When you multiply by 10 you add a zero', ask them to multiply 123.4 by 10, as this shows them that this is not always true: 123.4 ´ 10 = 1234 and not 123.40

Differentiation

Supporting: Ask students to describe the patterns they are noticing.

Consolidating: Ask students for a general rule for multiplying and dividing by 10, 100 and 1000.

Extending: Ask students for a general rule for multiplying and dividing by multiples of 10.

Differentiated outcomes	
All students	should carry out the calculations using a calculator and notice the patterns.
Most students	will understand how place value effects the calculations.
Some students	will generalise beyond multiplying and dividing by 10, 100 and 1000.

 Learning review

Select one or two students whom you know have a good explanation. Choose students who explained their ideas well in their pairs. Ask them to share their explanation with the whole class. Ask the class: *Can you give me an example which shows this statement is incorrect?*

'When you multiply by 100, you add two zeros.'

Additional activities

Students can research the salaries of very well paid individuals in the country. Ask students: *How many times the salary of a teacher, or a school cleaner, are these salaries?*

Students can complete Workbook pages 6 and 7.

Answers

Student Book page 6

Answers in the table will vary as students choose the numbers that they will use. Check that their multiplications are correct and that they have written the digits into the correct places in the table.

When you multiply by 10 the digits move 1 place to the left.

When you multiply by 100 the digits move 2 places to the left.

When you multiply by 1000 the digits move 3 places to the left.

Student Book page 7

Answers in the table will vary as students choose the numbers that they will use. Check that their divisions are correct and that they have written the digits into the correct places in the table.

When you divide by 10 the digits move 1 place to the right.

When you divide by 100 the digits move 2 places to the right.

When you divide by 1000 the digits move 3 places to the right.

Workbook pages 6 and 7

	Millions	Hundred thousands	Ten thousands	Thousands	Hundreds	Tens	Ones	.	tenths	hundredths
1.			3	9	7	7	5	.	7	1
2.	1	6	6	5	6	7	1	.	0	0
3.	5	6	2	5	4	2	9	.	0	0
4.	6	2	2	7	6	7	8	.	0	0
5.		4	1	5	1	5	1	.	0	0
6.							9	.	5	8

1C Number properties

Discover

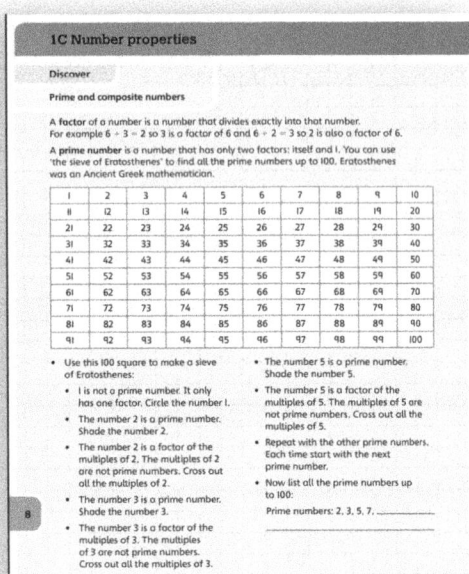
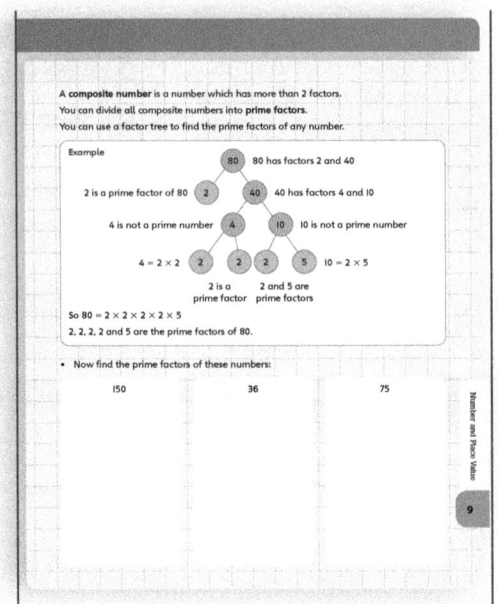

Specific learning foci

- *Recognise prime numbers up to 20 and find all prime numbers less than 100.*
- Find factors of two-digit numbers.

Problem solving focus

- Identify relationships between numbers and make generalised statements using words.

Key vocabulary

Factor, multiple, common multiple, prime number, prime factor, composite number

Resources

- Mini whiteboards and markers

Links to Student Book

See pages 8–9 in Student Book.

Links to Workbook

Workbook page 8

Language support

Ask students to read their answers saying:

- 'A prime number is …'
- 'A composite number is …'
- 'A prime factor is …'

 Introductory activity

Ask one student: *What is your birth date?* (Day only, e.g. 22 if born on the 22nd, 17 if born on the 17th). Write this number on the board. Say to pairs of students: *Write in 2 minutes as many facts as you can about this number.* Ask each student, one by one, to tell you a different fact about the number. Remind students that a **factor** of a number is a number that will divide into it with no remainder.

 Main activity

Ask students in pairs to work through the pages on pages 8 and 9 of the Student Book. Remind students that **multiples** of numbers are 'numbers that appear in the times table of the number' – for example, multiples of 6 are 12, 18, 24, and so on. A factor of a number is a number that divides exactly into it. So the factors of 12 are 1, 2, 3, 4, 6, and 12 as you can divide 12 by each of these numbers without leaving any remainder.

Differentiation

Supporting: Ask students to explain what a factor is; what a multiple is and what a **prime number** is.

Consolidating: Support students in finding **prime factors** by modelling the process.

Extending: Ask students to explore prime factors of the numbers 1–50.

Differentiated outcomes	
All students	should find prime numbers and understand what a factor and a multiple is.
Most students	will find prime factors with support.
Some students	will find prime factors of a wide range of numbers.

 Learning review

Ask students to work in pairs to complete the following sentences:

- *A prime number is …*
- *A composite number is …*
- *A prime factor is …*

Share three or four of these definitions. As a class, choose the class definitions. Write the class definitions and add them to the class Students' Glossary. You can also display the definitions in the classroom for students to refer to.

Additional activities

You can ask students to research the history of prime numbers, and when they were first discovered.

Students can complete Workbook page 8.

Answers

Student Book page 8

Check that students have followed the instructions for analysing the numbers in the 100-square.

Prime numbers: 2, 3, 5, 7, 11, 13, 17, 19, 23, 29, 31, 37, 41, 43, 47, 53, 59, 61, 67, 71, 73, 79, 83, 89, 97

Student Book page 9

Whilst students are working, ask them to explain the method they're using to find the prime factors of the given numbers.

Prime factors:

$150 = 2 \times 3 \times 5 \times 5$

$36 = 2 \times 2 \times 3 \times 3$

$75 = 3 \times 5 \times 5$

Workbook page 8

Whilst students are working, ask them to explain how they can use the factor trees to work out what the factors of the numbers are.

1. $2 \times 2 \times 3 \times 5$
2. $2 \times 2 \times 7$
3. 5×17
4. $2 \times 2 \times 13$
5. $2 \times 2 \times 3 \times 3$
6. $2 \times 2 \times 2 \times 3 \times 3$
7. $2 \times 3 \times 3 \times 5$
8. $2 \times 2 \times 2 \times 2 \times 2 \times 2$
9. 3×29
10. $2 \times 5 \times 5$

Explore

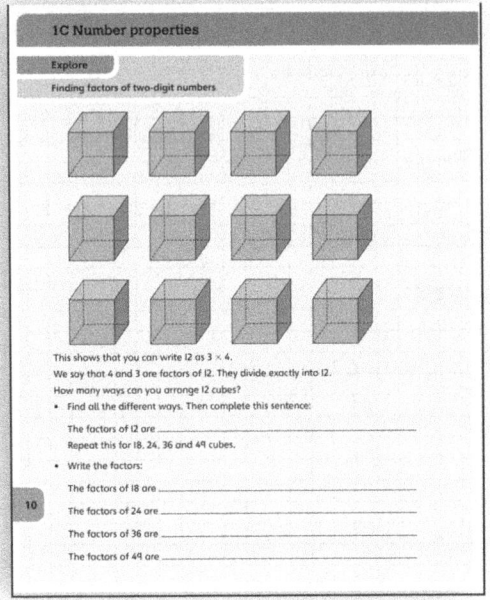

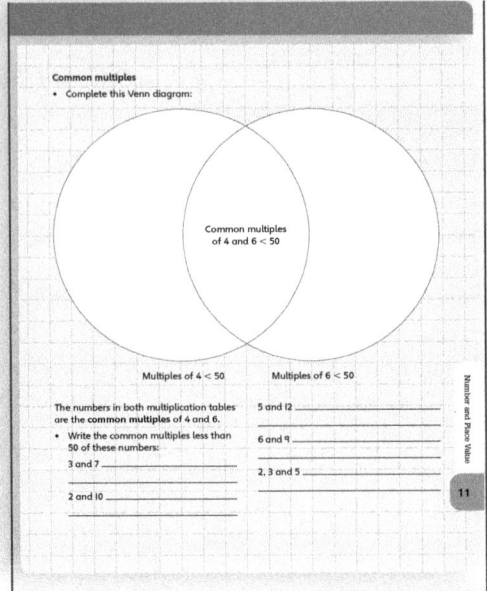

Specific learning foci

- *Recognise prime numbers up to 20 and find all prime numbers less than 100.*
- Find factors of two-digit numbers.

Problem solving focus

- Identify relationships between numbers and make generalised statements using words.

Key vocabulary

Factor, multiple, common multiple, > (greater than), < (less than)

Resources

- Mini whiteboards and markers
- 0–9 digit cards, class set

Links to Student Book

See pages 10–11 in Student Book.

Links to Workbook

Workbook page 9

Language support

Ask students to develop their own definitions of mathematical vocabulary to ensure they develop their own mathematical understanding. Ask, for example:

- *What are the factors of 15?*
- *What are the common multiples of 4 and 10?*
- *Is 7 less than 15?*
- *Is 7 greater than 4?*

 Introductory activity

Take the class outside if possible. Choose twenty-four students. Ask these students to stand in an array (a rectangular grid of rows/columns). They could form a 6 by 4 array, for example. Then ask them to stand in a new array. Repeat until they have found all the possibilities. These are 1×24, 2×12, 3×8, 4×6. Do the same activity with different numbers. Discuss which numbers have the most possibilities and which numbers have the smallest number of possibilities.

 Main activity

Ask students in pairs to complete the activities on pages 10 and 11 of the Student Book so that they can check one another's responses. Check that they understand the meaning of > (**greater than**), < (**less than**) and **common multiple**.

Differentiation

Supporting: Work with students to complete the Venn diagram. Use cut-outs of the numbers to support students so they can move them around on the Venn diagram.

Consolidating: Ask students to explain their reasoning when completing the Venn diagram.

Extending: Ask students to create new Venn diagrams to explore other common multiples.

Differentiated outcomes	
All students	should find **factors** and complete the Venn diagram with support.
Most students	will find all possible factors and complete the Venn diagram.
Some students	will create their own Venn diagrams to explore other common multiples.

 Learning review

Ask students to work in pairs and complete the following sentences:

- *A factor is …*
- *> means …*
- *< means …*

Share three or four of these definitions. As a class, choose the class definitions. Write the class definitions and add them to the class Students' Glossary. You can also display the definitions in the classroom for students to refer to.

Additional activities

You can ask students to write as many facts as they can about the numbers which form their own birth date and the birth dates of other people in their family.

Students can complete Workbook page 9.

Answers

Student Book page 10

Factors of 12 are 1, 2, 3, 4, 6, 12

Factors of 18 are 1, 2, 3, 6, 9, 18

Factors of 24 are 1, 2, 3, 4, 6, 8, 12, 24

Factors of 36 are 1, 2, 3, 4, 6, 9, 12, 18, 36

Factors of 49 are 1, 7, 49

Student Book page 11

Check that students have written numbers in the correct places on the Venn diagram:

Multiples of 4 are: 4, 8, 16, 20, 28, 32, 40, 44

Multiples of 6 are: 6, 18, 30, 42

Common multiples of 4 and 6 are: 12, 24, 36, 48

Common multiples of 3 and 7 are: 21, 42

Common multiples of 2 and 10 are: 10, 20, 30, 40

There are no common multiples of 5 and 12 less than 50.

Common multiples of 6 and 9 are: 18, 36

Common multiple of 2, 3 and 5 is 30.

Workbook page 9
1. 60
2. 48
3. 91
4. 114
5. 14
6. 24
7. $\frac{4}{5}$
8. 153

1D Comparing numbers

Discover

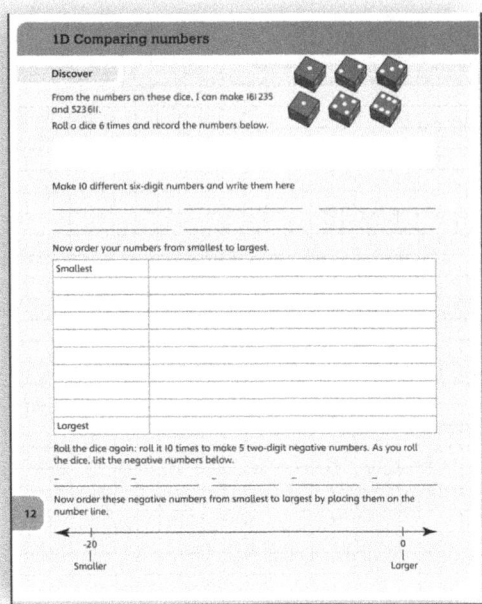

Specific learning focus

- Order and compare positive numbers to one million, and negative integers to an appropriate level.

Problem solving focus

- Use logical reasoning to explore and solve number problems and mathematical puzzles.

Key vocabulary

Ten thousand, hundred thousand, million, negative numbers

Resources

- Set of 9 A4 digit cards with the numerals 1–9 on them
- Set of dice, one dice per student
- Mini whiteboards and markers

Links to Student Book

See page 12 in Student Book.

Links to Workbook

Workbook page 10

Links to Digital Resource Pack

Digital Resource Pack 6 contains two activities which can be used to support students when comparing large numbers. On the home page, select 'Number and Place Value'.

Language support

Ask students to work in pairs to encourage discussion. If you can pair up experienced English speakers with those who are less experienced, this will support language development. Ask students to say the numbers they are forming aloud – model the pronunciation if necessary.

 **Introductory activity**

Ask six students to come to the front of the class. Each should pick a digit card and they should stand in the order in which they came to the front. Ask students to turn to a partner and say the number that the students standing at the front have made. Check that all students can say the number aloud. For example, if the students had picked 7, then 2, then 5, then 3, then 8, then 1, then the number formed would be 725 381 (seven hundred and twenty-five thousand, three hundred and eighty-one).

Ask the students to talk to a partner and decide what the largest number that can be formed with these digits is (875 321 in the case of the digits chosen above). One of the students should rearrange the students at the front so that they form this number. Ask them to explain how they know this is the largest possible number. (You place the largest digit in the largest place value column.) Repeat for the smallest number. If necessary, repeat the whole activity until understanding is secure.

 Main activity

Students in pairs use dice to generate 6-digit numbers and order them. If they need support, remind them of the strategy for finding the largest number that was introduced earlier. Challenge them to find the largest and smallest possible numbers with the digits that they generate. When students generate the **negative numbers**, speak briefly to the whole class to remind them that we say 'negative thirteen' for −13 and not 'minus thirteen'. Also support them in using the number line to compare the negative numbers.

Differentiation

Supporting: Ask students to explain their reasoning when ordering 6-digit numbers.

Consolidating: Ask students to explain their reasoning when ordering 6-digit numbers and support them when ordering negative numbers.

Extending: Ask students to explain their reasoning when ordering 6-digit numbers and negative numbers.

Differentiated outcomes	
All students	should order 6-digit numbers.
Most students	will order 6-digit and negative numbers.
Some students	will support other students in ordering negative numbers.

 **Learning review**

Use a dice to generate five negative numbers of your own and write them on the board at the front of the class. Ask students to order these from smallest to largest on their mini whiteboards. They should work in pairs to support discussion. Draw a 0 to -20 number line on the board at the front of the class. One of the students should mark the numbers you have generated on this number line. Ask students what they notice about ordering negative numbers (the further away from zero the smaller the number – this is the inverse of positive numbers).

Additional activities

Students can find examples of large numbers and negative numbers in everyday life and order them to make comparisons.

Students can complete Workbook page 10.

Answers

Student Book page 12

Answers will vary according to the numbers that students have made using the dice. Check that the numbers have been written correctly in order from smallest to largest.

Workbook page 10

Answers will vary as students make their own numbers. Check that students have written their numbers in appropriate places on the number lines and that they have rounded the numbers correctly.

1D Comparing numbers

Explore

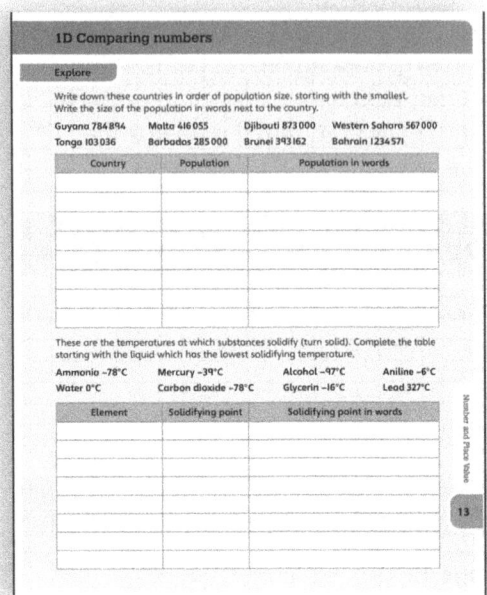

Specific learning focus

- Order and compare positive numbers to one million, and negative integers to an appropriate level.

Problem solving focus

- Use logical reasoning to explore and solve number problems and mathematical puzzles.

Key vocabulary

Ten thousand, hundred thousand, million, negative numbers

Resources

- Set of temperature cards and set of country cards containing the following information:
  - Oymyakon, Russia: −68 °C
  - Vostok Station, Antarctica: −89 °C
  - International Falls, Minnesota: −40 °C
  - Winnipeg, Canada: −62 °C
  - Espoo, Finland: −7 °C
- World map with sticky labels
- Mini whiteboards and markers

Links to Student Book

See page 13 in Student Book.

Links to Workbook

Workbook page 11

Links to Digital Resource Pack

Digital Resource Pack 6 contains two activities which can be used to support students when comparing large numbers. On the home page, select 'Number and Place Value'.

Language support

Work with those learners who are less confident in English and model the pronunciation of the numbers in words. Alternatively, you can help write down the answers for students who can say the numbers but have difficulty in writing them down in English.

Introductory activity

Ask a student to come to the front of the class. They should pick one of the country cards, find the place on the map and stick a label next to it. (You may need to help them in finding the places.) When all five places have been marked, ask the students to stand in order with the coldest place on the left. Ask five more students to come and select a temperature card. They should arrange themselves so that they are standing with the place that they think has recorded that temperature.

Give the students the correct order and ask the students with the temperature cards to move so they are showing the class the correct order. As a class read out the temperatures. Remember to say 'negative seven degrees Celsius' and so on.

Main activity

Students should work individually on the activity on page 13 of the Student Book. However, it will help them to say the numbers aloud to a partner. This helps them speak out their thinking and also allows a partner to check that they are correct.

Differentiation

Supporting: Ask students to explain their reasoning when ordering 6-digit numbers.

Consolidating: Ask students to explain their reasoning when ordering 6-digit numbers and support them when ordering **negative numbers**.

Extending: Ask students to explain their reasoning when ordering 6-digit numbers and negative numbers.

Differentiated outcomes	
All students	should order 6-digit numbers and negative numbers with support.
Most students	will order 6-digit and negative numbers.
Some students	will support other students in ordering negative numbers.

Learning review

Ask students to discuss with a partner other data that uses either very large numbers or negative numbers. If there is time you could research using the internet to find data which the students are interested in.

Additional activities

Students can research other countries populations and temperature data and use this to carry out comparisons

Students can complete Workbook page 11.

Answers

Student Book page 13

Country	Population	Population in words
Tonga	103 036	One hundred and three thousand and thirty-six
Barbados	285 000	Two hundred and eighty-five thousand
Brunei	393 162	Three hundred and ninety-three thousand, one hundred and sixty-two
Malta	416 055	Four hundred and sixteen thousand and fifty-five
Western Sahara	567 000	Five hundred and sixty-seven thousand
Guyana	784 894	Seven hundred and eighty-four thousand, eight hundred and ninety-four
Djibouti	873 000	Eight hundred and seventy-three thousand
Bahrain	1 234 571	One million, two hundred and thirty-four thousand, five hundred and seventy-one

Element	Solidifying point	Solidifying point in words
Lead	327 °C	Three hundred and twenty-seven degrees Celsius
Water	0 °C	Zero degrees Celsius
Aniline	−6 °C	Minus six degrees Celsius
Glycerin	−16 °C	Minus sixteen degrees Celsius
Mercury	−39 °C	Minus thirty-nine degrees Celsius
Ammonia	−78 °C	Minus seventy-eight degrees Celsius
Carbon dioxide	−78 °C	Minus seventy-eight degrees Celsius
Alcohol	−97 °C	Minus ninety-seven degrees Celsius

Workbook page 11

1. 567, 576, 657, 675, 756, 765

2.

Number	Number rounded to the nearest 10	Number rounded to the nearest 100
567	570	600
576	580	600
657	660	700
675	680	700
756	760	800
765	770	800

3. Answers will vary as students can choose any appropriate number from the table in question 2. Check that the answers are correct.

1E Estimation and rounding

Discover

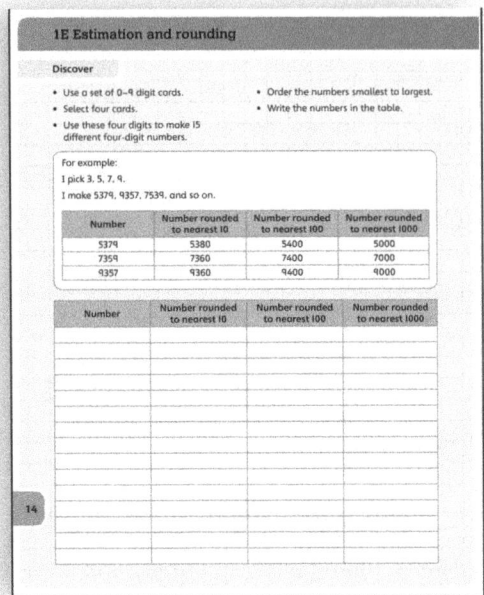

Specific learning focus

- Round whole numbers to the nearest 10, 100 or 1000.

Problem solving focus

- Use ordered lists or tables to help solve problems systematically.

Key vocabulary

> greater than, < less than, ≥ greater than or equal to, ≤ less than or equal to, is approximately equal to, round to the nearest

Resources

- 0–9 digit cards, large set
- 0–9 digit cards class set
- Mini whiteboards and markers

Links to Student Book

See page 14 in Student Book.

Links to Workbook

Workbook page 10

Language support

Model key vocabulary. Ask, for example:

- *What is that number approximately equal to?*
- *What is that number rounded up/down to the nearest 10?*
- *What is that number rounded up/down to the nearest 100?*
- *What is that number rounded up/down to the nearest 1000?*

Ask three or four students to come to the front of the class. Ask each of these students to pick one of the large 0–9 digit cards. Tell them: *Stand in a line facing the class.* Ask the rest of the class to work in pairs to work out: *How many possible arrangements are there?* Then say: *Rearrange the three (or four) students to form each number in order, smallest to largest.* Encourage students to work systematically to check that they have all possible arrangements of the numbers. Each time they form a new number show the class how to **round this to the nearest 10** and the nearest 100, or the nearest 1000.

Use an empty number line to model this. For example: 473 is 470 to the nearest 10.

473 is 500 to the nearest 100.

3585 is 4000 to the nearest 1000.

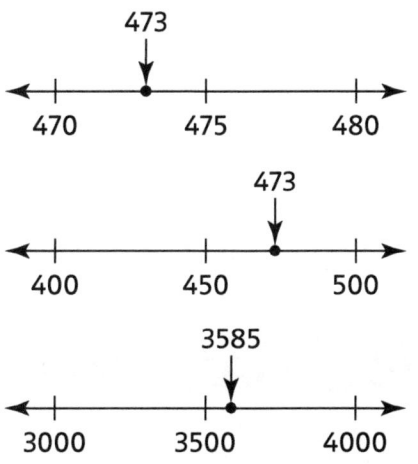

Ask students to work on the activity on page 14 of the Student Book in pairs and to take it in turns to create a number and then to round it. Their partner should check their answers. Ask individual students: *What is the 'rule' for rounding to the nearest 10, 100 and 1000?* Note which students have the clearest descriptions of their rules. These students can support you in the Learning review.

Differentiation

Supporting: Model how to use a number line to support rounding.

Consolidating: Ask students to show you how they use a number line to support them.

Extending: Ask students to explain the rule for rounding.

Differentiated outcomes	
All students	should round numbers with support.
Most students	will round numbers using a number line accurately.
Some students	will explain the rule for rounding clearly.

Ask two students to work together to explain to the rest of the class what the 'rule' is for rounding numbers to the nearest 10, 100 and 1000. Then generate a 4-digit number using the large digit cards. Write this on the whiteboard at the front of the class. Ask students: *Round this to the nearest 10.* They should write their response on the mini whiteboard. Wait five seconds and ask all students to show you at the same time. Repeat, asking students to round to the nearest 100 and then 1000.

Additional activities

You can ask students to find examples of large numbers in newspapers or magazines at home and to round them to the nearest thousand. Alternatively, if the numbers are already rounded, ask: *What is the largest and smallest possible number before it was rounded?*

Students can complete Workbook page 10.

Answers

Student Book page 14

Answers will vary as students use digit cards to make the numbers that they round. Check that the numbers have been rounded correctly to the nearest 10, 100 and 1000. Whilst students are working, ask them to explain the rules they use when rounding numbers.

Workbook page 10

Answers will vary as students make their own numbers. Check that students have written their numbers in appropriate places on the number lines and that they have rounded the numbers correctly.

1E Estimation and rounding

Explore

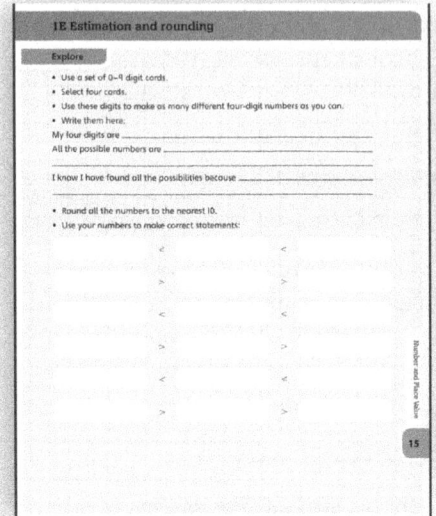
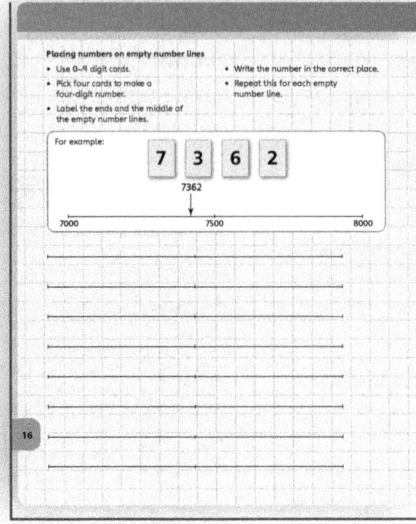
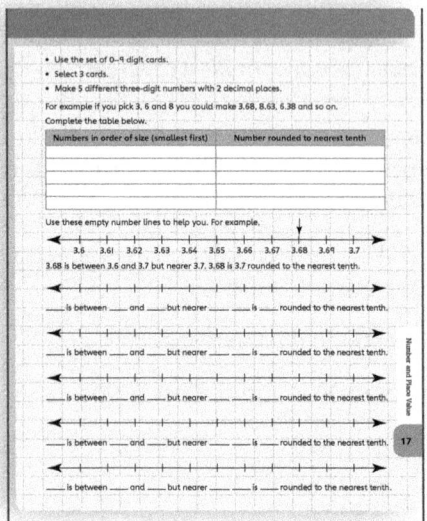

Specific learning foci

- Round whole numbers to the nearest 10.
- *Estimate where 4-digit numbers lie on an empty 0–10 000 line.*
- Round a number with two decimal places to the nearest tenth or to the nearest whole number.

Problem solving focus

- Estimate and approximate when calculating.

Key vocabulary

> greater than, < less than, ≥ greater than or equal to, ≤ less than or equal to, is approximately equal to, round to the nearest

Resources

- 1–20 number cards, large set

Links to Student Book

See pages 15–17 in Student Book.

Links to Workbook

Workbook page 11

Language support

Focus on the language of place value by using the terms thousand, ten thousand and 4-digit number. Ask, for example:

- *What are you rounding to?*
- *What is that number to the nearest 10?*
- *What value is in the middle of the empty number line?*

 Introductory activity

Place a '0' number card on one side at the front of the classroom and a '20' on the other side. Ask four students to come to the front of the class. Tell each student: *Choose a number card.* Then tell them to stand at the front of the classroom in ascending order between the 0 and the 20 so that they are in the correct place on a 'number line'. Now ask these four students to select a digit card each between 0 and 9 and to use these digits to form a 4-digit number. Tell students that they are going to place this 4-digit number on a number line. Ask: *Which thousand is at the lower end? Which thousand is at the upper end?* For example, for the number 5378 the lower limit is 5000 and the upper limit is 6000. Place a label for 5000 at one side at the front of the classroom and a label for 6000 at the other side. Now ask the class to place the 4-digit number as accurately as they can on this 'number line'.

Repeat this as many times as you think necessary.

Main activity

Ask students to complete the activities on pages 15 to 17 of the Student Book. You may choose to group the less confident students together so that you can support them in using empty number lines.

For the first part of the activity on page 15, ask individual students: *What are all the possible numbers with your four digits? How do you know you have found all the possibilities?*

Differentiation

Supporting: Model how to use a number line to support rounding.

Consolidating: Ask students to show you how they use a number line to support them.

Extending: Ask students to explain the rules for rounding.

Differentiated outcomes	
All students	should round numbers with support.
Most students	will round numbers, using a number line accurately.
Some students	will explain the rules for rounding clearly.

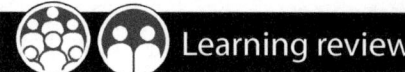 Learning review

Ask the more confident students: *How did you work out where to place the number on the empty number line?* It is important to share a range of methods with the class. Focus on the final question which deals with rounding decimals.

Additional activities

You can create a series of segments of number lines for the classroom wall. You can use these for similar activities.

Students can complete Workbook page 11.

Answers

Student Book pages15 to 17
Answers will vary according to the numbers that students make from their digit cards. Whilst students are working, ask them to explain how they decided how to round their numbers, and place them on the number lines.

Workbook page 11
1. 567, 576, 657, 675, 756, 765

2.

Number	Number rounded to the nearest 10	Number rounded to the nearest 100
567	570	600
576	580	600
657	660	700
675	680	700
756	760	800
765	770	800

3. Answers will vary as students can choose any appropriate number from the table in question 2. Check that the answers are correct.

1F Number sequences

Discover

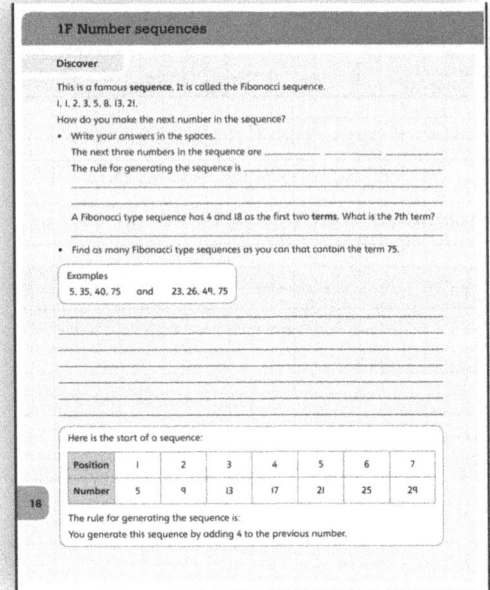

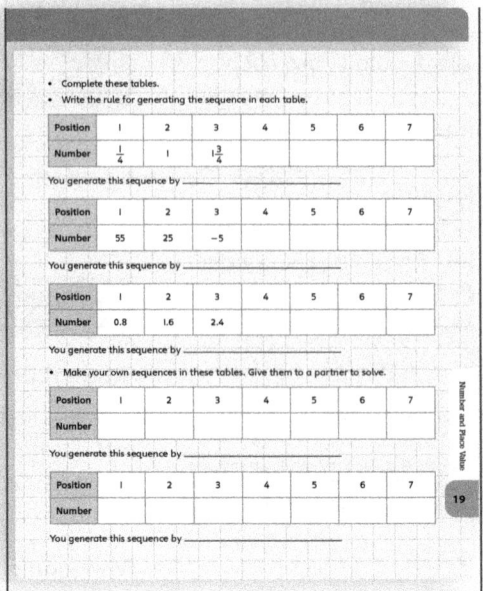

The two images above show pages 18–19 of the Student Book:

Page 18:

1F Number sequences

Discover

This is a famous **sequence**. It is called the Fibonacci sequence.
1, 1, 2, 3, 5, 8, 13, 21.
How do you make the next number in the sequence?
- Write your answers in the spaces.
  The next three numbers in the sequence are _____ _____ _____
  The rule for generating the sequence is _____

A Fibonacci type sequence has 4 and 18 as the first two **terms**. What is the 7th term?

- Find as many Fibonacci type sequences as you can that contain the term 75.

Examples
5, 35, 40, 75 and 23, 26, 49, 75

Here is the start of a sequence:

Position	1	2	3	4	5	6	7
Number	5	9	13	17	21	25	29

The rule for generating the sequence is:
You generate this sequence by adding 4 to the previous number.

Page 19:

- Complete these tables.
- Write the rule for generating the sequence in each table.

Position	1	2	3	4	5	6	7
Number	$\frac{1}{4}$	1	$1\frac{3}{4}$				

You generate this sequence by _____

Position	1	2	3	4	5	6	7
Number	55	25	−5				

You generate this sequence by _____

Position	1	2	3	4	5	6	7
Number	0.8	1.6	2.4				

You generate this sequence by _____

- Make your own sequences in these tables. Give them to a partner to solve.

Position	1	2	3	4	5	6	7
Number							

You generate this sequence by _____

Position	1	2	3	4	5	6	7
Number							

You generate this sequence by _____

Specific learning focus

- Recognise and extend number sequences.

Problem solving focus

- Identify relationships between numbers and make generalised statements using words.

Key vocabulary

Sequence, term, predict, the rule for the pattern

Resources

None needed

Links to Student Book

See pages 18–19 in Student Book.

Links to Workbook

Workbook page 12

Language support

Support students by asking, for example:
- *Can you extend the sequence?*
- *What do you think the next term is?*
- *Can you predict what the tenth term will be?*

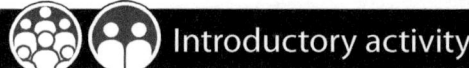

Write the first few terms of a **sequence** on the whiteboard. Ask students to work in pairs.

Ask: *Can you tell me the next number?*

Use the following sequences. Write the first two **terms**, then add the next terms one at a time until students can **predict** the next number in the pattern and explain **the rule for the pattern**.

- 1, 3, 5, 7, 9,
- 3, 6, 9, 12, 15,
- 2, 4, 8, 16, 64,
- 1, 4, 9, 16, 25,

Ask students to write down their own sequences. Ask one student to come to the front of the class and repeat the activity above with their own sequence. Ask the student who gives the correct answer to come to the front of the class and repeat the activity with their sequence.

 **Main activity**

Ask students to work in pairs on the activities on pages 18 and 19 of the Student Book. This is a complex investigation. Students will benefit from working together. Look for good examples made by students, such as long sequences, which can be shared later. Ask students to explain their methods to you. This helps you to check if they will be able to share their ideas with the whole class during the Learning review.

Differentiation

Supporting: Support students in finding the rules for the sequences.

Consolidating: Ask students to speak out their thinking when they are finding the terms in a sequence.

Extending: Encourage students to generate their own sequences.

Differentiated outcomes	
All students	should find the rules for the sequences with support.
Most students	will find the rules for the sequences independently.
Some students	will generate their own sequences.

Select pairs and ask them: *What sequences did you find with 75 in them?*

Additional activities

Students can research the history of the Fibonacci sequence and make presentations to the class. The sequence is attributed to a thirteenth century Italian mathematician but it existed earlier in Indian mathematics texts.

Students can complete Workbook page 12.

Answers

Student Book pages 18–19

The next three numbers in the sequence are 34, 55, 89.

The rule for generating the sequence is add together the two preceding numbers to get the next number in the sequence.

A Fibonacci type sequence has 4 and 18 as the first two terms.

The sequence is 4, 18, 22, 40, 62, 102, 164. So the seventh term is 164.

Check that students have written Fibonacci sequences.

Table 1: $2\frac{1}{2}, 3\frac{1}{4}, 4, 4\frac{3}{4}$

You generate this sequence by adding $\frac{3}{4}$.

Table 2: $-35, -65, -95, -125$

You generate this sequence by subtracting 30.

Table 3: 3.2, 4.0, 4.8, 5.6

You generate this sequence by adding 0.8

Tables 4 and 5: Check that students have created sequences and described the rules correctly.

Workbook page 12

Answers will vary as students create their own number sequences. Check that they have described their sequences correctly.

1F Number sequences

Specific learning focus

- Make general statements about sums, differences and multiples of odd and even numbers.

Problem solving focus

- Make, test and refine hypotheses, explain and justify methods, reasoning, strategies, results or conclusions orally.

Key vocabulary

Odd, even, total, product, general statement

Resources

- Small pieces of card

Links to Student Book

See page 20 in Student Book.

Links to Workbook

Workbook page 13

Language support

Key questions to support language development are, for example:

- *What is the sum?*
- *What is the difference between and …?*
- *What is the rule?*

Use the school hall or an outdoor space for these activities.

Crossing the circle

Arrange a circle of chairs, so that there is one fewer chair than the number of students. Choose one student to stand in the middle of the circle. The other students sit in the chairs. Give all students a small piece of paper each and ask them to write down any two-digit number on the piece of paper. The student in the middle of the circle states a fact about their number. For example, a student with '15' on their piece of paper can say 'My number is divisible by 5', or 'My number is divisible by 3', or 'My number is an **odd** number'. All students who have a number that shares this fact cross the circle to sit in a new chair which is now empty. The student in the middle should quickly sit down on an empty chair. A different student is now in the centre. This student then states a fact about their number. Encourage students to state facts which are common to a lot of numbers. This will result in a lot of students changing places. Also encourage students to state facts which are not common to a lot of numbers. This will result in a small number of students changing places.

Making groups

Ask students to write a single-digit number on the opposite side of their piece of paper. Move the chairs away so that students can move around the space. Every 15 seconds, shout out one of the instructions below – students must try to make the groups with other students. They may need more time to do this. Form groups of 3 so that your **total** is as near to 20 as possible.

- Form groups of 4 so that your total is less than 35.
- Form groups of 5 so that you have an **even** total.
- Form groups of 3 so that you have an odd total.
- Form groups of 2 so that you have an even total.
- Form groups of 2 so that you have an odd total.
- Form groups of 2 so that you have an even **product**.
- Form groups of 3 so that you have an even product.
- Form groups of 2 so that you have an odd product.
- Form groups of 3 so that you have an odd product.

Differentiation

Supporting: Ask students what they are noticing about sums, differences and multiples of odd and even numbers.

Consolidating: Ask students to make **general statements** about sums, differences and multiples of odd and even numbers.

Extending: Ask students to explain why the general statements about sums, differences and multiples of odd and even numbers are true.

Differentiated outcomes	
All students	should play the games and develop their understanding of general statements about sums, differences and multiples of odd and even numbers.
Most students	will make general statements about sums, differences and multiples of odd and even numbers.
Some students	will explain why the general statements about sums, differences and multiples of odd and even numbers are true.

Learning review

Ask students to complete the sentences on page 20 of the Student Book. Ask individual students to read out their additional sentences and justify their conclusions.

Additional activities

Students can draw pictures to try to prove some of the generalisations that they have made.

Students can complete Workbook page 13.

Answers

Student Book page 20

The sum of two even numbers is even.

The sum of two odd numbers is even.

The difference between two even numbers is even.

The difference between two odd numbers is even.

The product of two even numbers is even.

The product of two odd numbers is odd.

Check that students' own general statements explore sums products and differences between three numbers.

Workbook page 13

Answers will include:

$$3 + 4 + 5 + 6 = 18$$
$$3 + 4 + 5 - 6 = 6$$
$$3 + 4 - 5 - 6 = -4$$
$$3 + 4 - 5 + 6 = 8$$
$$3 - 4 - 5 - 6 = -12$$
$$3 - 4 - 5 + 6 = 0$$
$$3 - 4 + 5 + 6 = 10$$
$$3 - 4 + 5 - 6 = -2$$

Answers will include:

$$5 + 6 + 7 + 8 = 26$$
$$5 + 6 + 7 - 8 = 10$$
$$5 + 6 - 7 - 8 = -4$$
$$5 + 6 - 7 + 8 = 12$$
$$5 - 6 - 7 - 8 = -16$$
$$5 - 6 - 7 + 8 = 0$$
$$5 - 6 + 7 + 8 = 14$$
$$5 - 6 + 7 - 8 = -2$$

1 Number and place value

Connect and Review

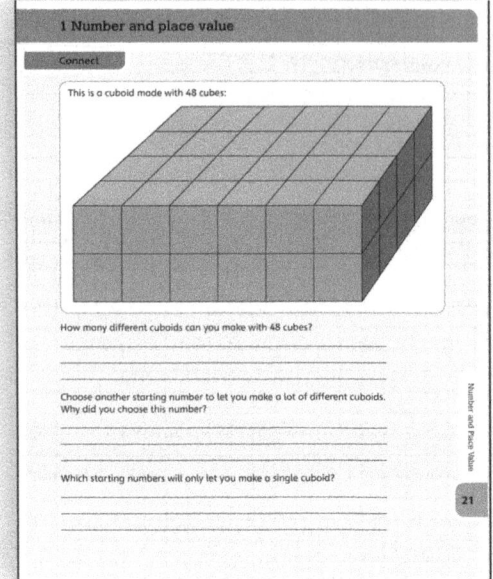

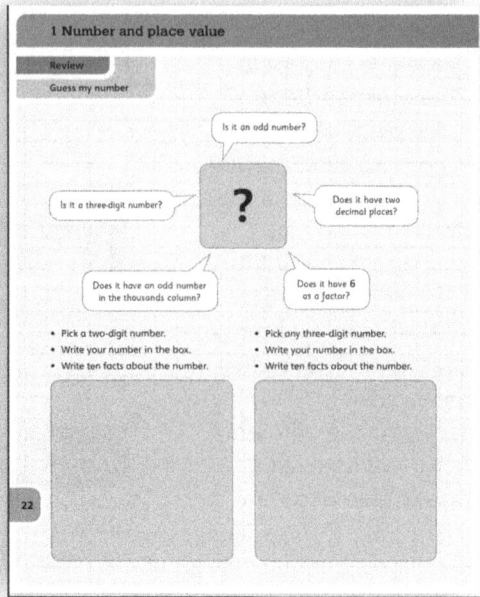

Specific learning foci

- Find factors of two-digit numbers.
- Find some common multiples, e.g. for 4 and 5.
- Recognise prime numbers up to 20 and find all prime numbers less than 100.

Problem solving focus

- Use logical reasoning to explore and solve number problems and mathematical puzzles.

Key vocabulary

Ten thousand, hundred thousand, million, factor, multiple, prime number, prime factor, composite number, common multiple, > greater than, < less than, ≥ greater than or equal to ≤ less than or equal to, is approximately equal to, round to the nearest, sequence, term predict, the rule for the pattern

Resources

- At least 48 cubes for each group.
- Assessment activity 1 for every student (Resource Sheet 1D from www.oxfordprimary.com/OIPMteacher)

Links to Student Book

See page 21 in Student Book.

Links to Workbook

Workbook page 14

Links to Digital Resource Pack

Digital Resource Pack 6 contains two activities which can be used to support students' understanding of the place value of large numbers. On the home page, select 'Number and Place Value'.

Language support

Encourage students to use mathematical terms in their explanations such as factor, multiple and prime number.

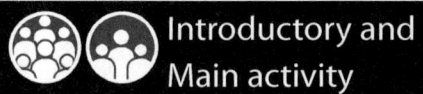 Introductory and Main activity

For Connect activities ask students to work in mixed-attainment groups of four. Encourage them to try to interpret and begin the activity with no teacher input. Organise students into groups and ask them to begin the activity on page 21 of the Student Book.

As students explore the activity, ask questions, for example:

- *Can you show me a cuboid with 48 cubes? How can you record this?*
- *Can you think of a way to record your results in a table?*
- *How will you record your results?*
- *How do you know you have all the possibilities?*

When groups have found all the possibilities with 48 cubes, ask them to explore other starting numbers.

At the end of the Main activity, ask groups to report their results to one another. Students should try to reflect on their learning. Ask individual students: *What have you learnt in the activity?*

Differentiation

All students should work in mixed-attainment groups and so engage with the group task.

Differentiated outcomes
Differentiation will be by outcome and it is expected that all students will engage in the task at their own level.

 Learning review

The Review activity on page 22 of the Student Book is an individual summative assessment and so should be completed by students working on their own.

Additional activities

Students can look at how foodstuffs that come in small cubes, or cuboids, is packaged. Explore the best way to arrange these containers to minimise the surface area of the packaging.

Students can complete Workbook page 14.

Answers

Student Book page 21

The possible cuboids are:

Length	Width	Height
48	1	1
24	2	1
12	2	2
12	4	1
6	4	2
6	8	1
16	3	1
8	3	2
4	4	3

Numbers with a larger number of factors make many cuboids.

Prime numbers only allow you to make a single cuboid.

Student Book page 22

Answers will vary as students choose their own two-digit and three-digit numbers. Check that students' statements about their numbers are correct.

Workbook page 14

Answers will vary as they write their own statements about the given numbers. Check that the statements are correct.

Assessment activity 1

1. c) 87 751
2. c) Seventy thousand
3. c) 56 200
4. b) 2   d) 37
5. b) 42
6. c) 5600
7. 3479 (Smallest), 3497, 3749, 3794, 3947, 3974, 4379, 4397, 4 39, 4793, 4937, 4973, 7 49, 7394, 7439, 7493, 7934, 7943, 9347, 9374, 9437, 9473, 9734, 9743 (Largest)

Overview

Big Idea

The most important idea for students to understand when learning about fractions is the concept of equality. When a shape is divided into fractions (such as quarters) it is divided into equal areas. When calculating fractions of quantities, we divide the quantity into equal parts. It is important that students have a clear understanding of fraction notation. Remind students that a fraction is written as follows:

2 — This is the numerator. It tells you the number of parts in this fraction.

9 — This is the denominator. It tells you how many pieces the whole is divided into.

You will also teach students about equivalent fractions.

These are fractions that may be written differently but which are equal. For example: $\frac{1}{2} = \frac{2}{4} = \frac{3}{6} = \frac{20}{40}$
A fraction such as $\frac{3}{2}$ in which the numerator is larger than the denominator is an improper fraction. These are fractions which are greater than 1. Finally, students will learn about mixed numbers. They are a 'mix' of whole numbers and fractions. For example: we usually write $1\frac{1}{2}$ rather than $\frac{3}{2}$. We usually say 'one and a half' rather than 'three halves'.

Possible misconceptions

Students may be confused when you discuss mixed numbers. They may have the misconception that all fractions must be less than 1. Use real contexts to help students to understand the idea of mixed numbers.

For example: when three people share four pizzas equally each person has $1\frac{1}{3}$ pizzas. Use 3 diagrams to show mixed numbers. Encourage students to use diagrams too. This helps them to have a clear understanding.

You may also notice misconceptions when you ask students to order fractions. For example: students may think $\frac{2}{5}$ is larger than $\frac{2}{3}$ because 5 is larger than 3. The activity on multiple representations of fractions in this unit supports you in dealing with this misconception.

Key vocabulary and language structures

Numerator, denominator (*What is the numerator/denominator?*); equivalent, equivalent fraction (*How can we reduce it to its simplest form?*); is the same as; simplest form; improper fraction, mixed number; half, third, quarter, sixth, eighth, three-quarters, five-eighths, tenths, hundredths, and so on; order in ascending/descending size, ascending/ descending order; greater than, less than, equivalent to; <, >, ≤, ≥; proportion, ratio, in every, for every; decimal, decimal fraction, decimal equivalent percentage, percent, %.

Coverage in lessons

Learning focus	Learning outcomes
Equivalent fractions	Can I recognise equivalence between fractions?
	Can I find equivalent fractions?
	Can I reduce fractions to their simplest form?
Fractions and decimals	Can I recognise equivalence between decimals and fraction forms?
	Can I convert a fraction to a decimal fraction?
Mixed numbers and improper fractions	Can I order mixed numbers and place them between whole numbers on a number line?
	Can I change an improper fraction to a mixed number?
Ratio and proportion	Can I solve simple problems involving ratio and direct proportion?
Percentages	Can I explain what a percentage is?
	Can I find simple percentages of shapes and whole numbers?

Engage

Specific learning foci

- Understand percentage as parts in every 100 and express $\frac{1}{2}, \frac{1}{4}, \frac{1}{3}, \frac{1}{10}, \frac{1}{100}$ as percentages.
- Find simple percentages of shapes and whole numbers.

Problem solving focus

- Solve simple word problems involving percentages.

Key vocabulary

Percentage, %, out of 100

Resources

- Class set of local newspapers or magazines that students read at home

Links to Student Book

See page in 23 Student Book.

Language support

Make a display using the percentages that appear in newspapers and magazines. Include all key vocabulary for reference during the unit.

 Introductory activity

Ask students to work in pairs. Give each pair a newspaper or magazine. Ask them to find as many examples of the **percentage** sign (**%**) as you can in your newspaper or magazine. Then ask each pair to share with the whole class one example from their newspaper. Try to share a wide range of contexts in which the percentage sign is used. You can normally find a % in headlines, adverts and news stories. Each time a student gives an example of a percentage write it on the whiteboard so that at the end of the feedback you have a range of percentages.

Now ask students to talk to their partner about the percentages that they can see on the board. For example: they may know that '50% is equivalent to a half' and that 'you find 10% by dividing by 10'.

 Main activity

Ask each pair to select three examples of percentages used in their newspaper or magazine. Then ask the pairs to use their examples to write a word problem. They must be able to solve this problem themselves. Then ask students to work in groups of six to solve one another's problems. At the end of the session, ask each group to select their group's 'best' problem. Ask each group to justify their choice.

Differentiation

Supporting: Support the students in creating word problems with the percentages they know.

Consolidating: Encourage students to create word problems using a range of percentages.

Extending: Encourage students to create two-step word problems using a range of percentages.

Learning review

Each group should explain their favourite problem and justify why they selected it. Ask one student from each group to model the solution at the front of the class for the whole class.

Additional activities

You can ask students to write percentage problems to explain to their family at home.

2A Equivalent fractions

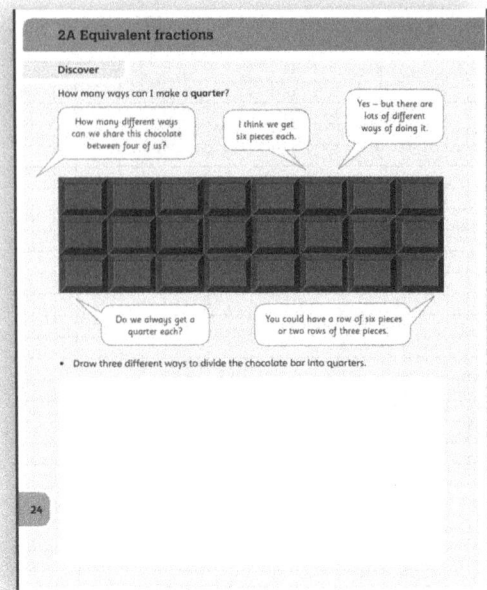
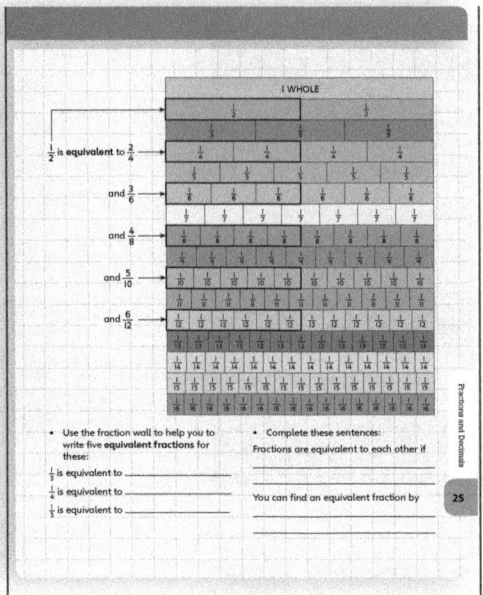

Specific learning foci

- *Recognise equivalence between fractions.*
- Reduce fractions to their simplest form, where this is $\frac{1}{4}$, $\frac{1}{2}$ or $\frac{3}{4}$ or a number of fifths or tenths.

Problem solving focus

- Deduce new information from existing information and realise the effect that one piece of information has on another.

Key vocabulary

Part, whole, equivalent fraction, simplest form, numerator, denominator, half, third, quarter, three-quarters, fifth, sixth, eighth, tenth

Resources

- Small square sheets of paper
- Mini whiteboards and markers

Links to Student Book

See pages 24–25 in Student Book.

Links to Workbook

Workbook page 16

Links to Digital Resource Pack

Digital Resource Pack 6 contains two activities which can be used to support students' understanding of equivalent fractions. On the home page, select 'Fractions and Decimals'.

Language support

As you work with students ask them, for example:

- *What does the numerator/denominator show?*
- *Tell me a fraction which is equivalent to …*
- *How can we reduce that fraction?*

It is important for students to say the fractions out loud, especially halves, quarters and eighths.

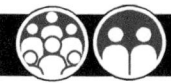 Introductory activity

Give each student a small square of paper. Ask them to fold it in **half**. Then ask them to show you the fold. Ask them to fold the paper in half in a different way. (They may fold horizontally, vertically or along a diagonal.) Then ask the class: *How do you know that you folded the paper exactly in half?* (They should notice equal areas of each half.) Next ask students to fold their square into quarters. Then ask them to think of as many different ways as they can of shading in one **quarter** of the square. Finally, ask students to work in groups of six to produce as many different fractions as they can by folding squares of paper.

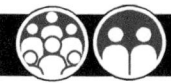 Main activity

Ask students to work on the activity on pages 24 and 25 of the Student Book in pairs. Ask them to write their answers in the text box in their book. Talk to students and introduce the idea of **equivalent fractions**. For

example, students should notice that

$$\frac{1}{4} = \frac{6}{24}$$

$$\frac{1}{8} = \frac{3}{24}$$

$$\frac{1}{2} = \frac{12}{24} \text{ and so on.}$$

Help students to understand that multiplying the

numerator and the **denominator** by the same number produces an equivalent fraction, and that dividing the numerator and denominator by a common factor reduces the fraction to an equivalent (simpler) fraction. Reinforce the importance of equal areas. Discuss the idea of **simplest form**: a fraction that cannot be reduced any more.

Differentiation

Supporting: Ask students to show you a range of equivalent fractions.

Consolidating: Model reducing fractions to their simplest forms.

Extending: Ask students to explain the process for reducing fractions to their simplest forms.

Differentiated outcomes	
All students	should find a range of equivalent fractions.
Most students	will find a range of equivalent fractions and define an equivalent fraction.
Some students	will understand the rule for cancelling fractions to the simplest form.

 Learning review

Ask students to look at the fraction wall diagram on page 25 of the Student Book. Give them 5 minutes to silently write down everything that they notice about the diagram. After 5 minutes, take one fact from each student.

Additional activities

Students can carry out similar activities using other items that can be split into fractions in this way.

Students can complete Workbook page 16.

Answers

Student Book page 24

Answers will vary as students choose their own ways to divide the chocolate bar into quarters. Any answer with 6 squares is acceptable.

Student Book page 25

$\frac{1}{3}$ is equivalent to $\frac{2}{6}, \frac{3}{9}, \frac{4}{12}, \frac{5}{15}$ and any other correct answer.

$\frac{1}{4}$ is equivalent to $\frac{2}{8}, \frac{3}{12}, \frac{4}{16}, \frac{5}{20}$ and any other correct answer.

$\frac{1}{5}$ is equivalent to $\frac{2}{10}, \frac{3}{15}, \frac{4}{20}, \frac{5}{25}$ and any other correct answer.

Fractions are equivalent to each other if they can be reduced to the same fraction.

You can find an equivalent fraction by multiplying the numerator and the denominator by the same number.

Workbook page 16

$\frac{2}{3} : \frac{4}{6}, \frac{8}{12}, \frac{10}{15}$

$\frac{3}{5} : \frac{6}{10}, \frac{12}{15}$

$\frac{5}{6} : \frac{10}{12}$

$\frac{1}{8} : \frac{2}{16}$

$\frac{4}{10} : \frac{2}{5}$

$\frac{2}{12} : \frac{1}{6}$

$\frac{10}{15} : \frac{2}{3}, \frac{4}{6}, \frac{8}{12}$

$\frac{12}{15} : \frac{4}{5}, \frac{8}{10}$

2A Equivalent fractions

Explore

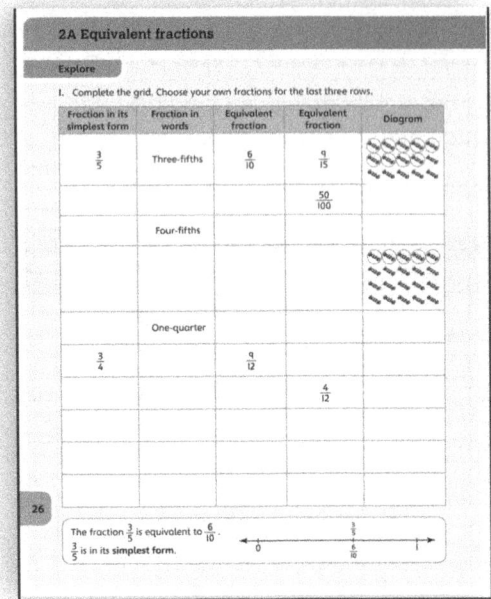

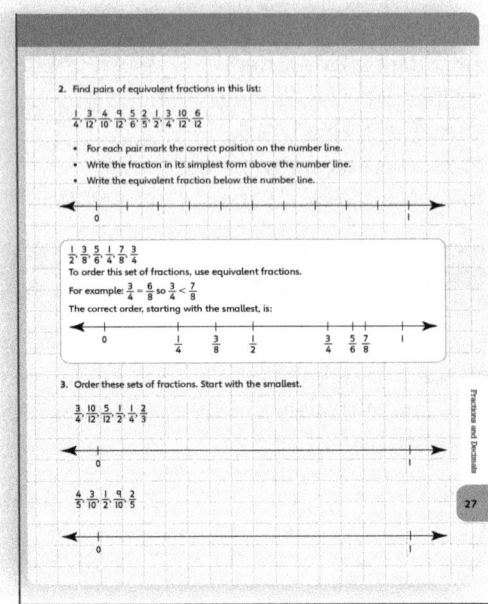

Specific learning foci

- Reduce fractions to their simplest form, where this is $\frac{1}{4}$, $\frac{1}{2}$ or $\frac{3}{4}$ or a number of fifths or tenths.
- *Compare fractions with the same denominator and related denominators.*

Problem solving focus

- Deduce new information from existing information and realise the effect that one piece of information has on another.

Key vocabulary

Part, whole, equivalent fraction, equivalence, simplest form, numerator, denominator, half, third, quarter, three-quarters, fifth, sixth, eighth, tenth

Resources

- Eight sheets of paper with one of the following fractions written on each piece:

$0, \frac{3}{4}, \frac{10}{12}, \frac{5}{12}, \frac{1}{2}, \frac{1}{4}, \frac{2}{3}, 1$

Links to Student Book

See pages 26–27 in Student Book.

Links to Workbook

Workbook page 17

Links to Digital Resource Pack

Digital Resource Pack 6 contains two activities which can be used to support students' understanding of equivalent fractions. On the home page, select 'Fractions and Decimals'.

Language support

As you work with students ask them, for example:

- *What does the numerator/denominator show?*
- *Which fraction is equivalent?*
- *How can we reduce that fraction?*

It is important for students to say the fractions out loud, especially halves, quarters and eighths.

 Introductory activity

Ask students to look at the table on page 26 of the Student Book. Ask students to work in mixed-attainment pairs so that the more confident students can support the less confident students. This also means all students hear the correct vocabulary modelled and use appropriate vocabulary. Ask: *How is the top row filled in?* Then ask individual students to share their discussion with the rest of the class.

 Main activity

Ask students to work in pairs to complete the table on page 26 of the Student Book. They discuss the solutions together. To challenge pairs of students, offer them difficult examples to fill the last three rows in the table. Check individual students' understanding of **equivalence** and **simplest form** as they complete the table. This is to ensure they can answer the questions in the next part of the activity on their own. Students work on their own to identify **equivalent fractions** and place them correctly on the number lines, and then to order sets of fractions.

Differentiation

Supporting: Support students by encouraging them to use drawings of equivalent fractions first.

Consolidating: Ask students to explain how they are deciding where to place fractions on the number line.

Extending: Encourage students to order fractions mentally first, using their knowledge of equivalence.

Differentiated outcomes	
All students	should use number lines to order fractions with support.
Most students	will use number lines to order fractions.
Some students	will order fractions mentally using their knowledge of equivalence.

 Learning review

Ask eight students to come to the front of the class. Give each student one of the pieces of paper on which you wrote fractions. Ask the other students to take it in turns to position the students with fractions so that they form a 'number line' at the front of the class where they are each in the correct place. Ask the class to explain their reasoning as they are placing each student.

Additional activities

You can ask students to look at the fraction wall on the previous page of their book. Ask them to use this fraction wall to make up similar questions to the ones in the Main activity and to ask their friends to solve them. Alternatively, ask students to create a list of 15 fractions in ascending order

Students can complete Workbook page 17.

Answers

Student Book pages 26 and 27

1. Answers will vary as students choose their own equivalent fractions and draw their own diagrams. Check that their equivalent fractions are correct.

2. Draw 0–1 number lines with fractions marked above and below the line.

$\frac{1}{4}$ and $\frac{3}{12}$

$\frac{2}{5}$ and $\frac{4}{10}$

$\frac{1}{2}$ and $\frac{6}{12}$

$\frac{3}{4}$ and $\frac{9}{12}$

$\frac{5}{6}$ and $\frac{10}{12}$

3. 0–1 number lines with fractions marked in the following order:

$\frac{1}{4}, \frac{5}{12}, \frac{1}{2}, \frac{2}{3}, \frac{3}{4}, \frac{10}{12}$

$\frac{3}{10}, \frac{2}{5}, \frac{1}{2}, \frac{4}{5}, \frac{9}{10}$

Workbook page 17

1. $\frac{3}{4} > \frac{3}{8}$

2. $\frac{2}{5} < \frac{5}{10}$

3. $\frac{8}{14} > \frac{3}{7}$

4. $\frac{9}{13} > \frac{4}{9}$

5. $\frac{5}{15} < \frac{3}{6}$

6. $\frac{8}{16} > \frac{3}{8}$

2B Fractions and decimals

Discover

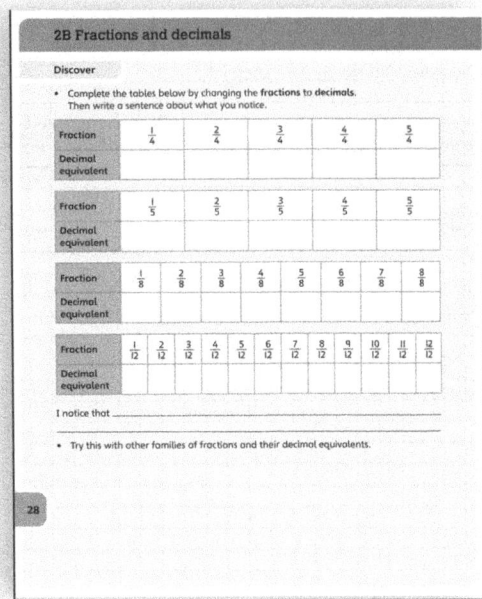

Specific learning focus

- Recognise and use the equivalence between decimal and fraction forms.

Problem solving focus

- Use ordered lists or tables to solve number problems systematically.

Key vocabulary

Part, whole, equivalent fraction, decimal equivalent, numerator, denominator, half, third, quarter, three-quarters, fifth, sixth, eighth, tenth, decimal fraction

Resources

- Counting stick divided into ten sections
- Mini whiteboards and markers
- Calculators

Links to Student Book

See page 28 in Student Book.

Links to Workbook

Workbook page 18

Links to Digital Resource Pack

Digital Resource Pack 6 contains two activities which can be used to support students' understanding of equivalent fractions and decimals. On the home page, select 'Fractions and Decimals'.

Language support

The key phrase in this activity is: *What is the decimal equivalent?*

Use your counting stick – point to the centre and say that this represents zero. Tell the class that each division represents $\frac{1}{2}$. Ask pairs to draw the counting stick on their whiteboards and label the other divisions. Repeat for divisions of 0.1, $\frac{1}{3}$, 0.25 and $\frac{1}{4}$.

Give each student a mini whiteboard. Ask them to write down any fraction and its **decimal equivalent**. They may write simple fractions such as '$\frac{1}{2} = 0.5$', '$\frac{1}{4} = 0.25$' or '$\frac{1}{10} = 0.1$'. Give each student a calculator. Write a selection of the students' fractions and their decimal equivalents on the main board. Ask students to divide 1 by 2 on their calculator. They will see the answer 0.5. Show the class that $\frac{1}{2}$ means 1 divided by 2. Show them that dividing in this way gives the answer 0.5, and that you can use this to find the decimal equivalent of any fraction. Now ask students to work in pairs to explore patterns in the lists of fractions and their decimal equivalents.

 Main activity

Ask students to work in pairs to complete the tables on page 28 of the Student Book and explore the patterns. Explain to the whole class how to write recurring decimals. Do not do this at the beginning of the Main activity. Wait until one of the pairs notices the pattern when they look at the table exploring twelfths. For example:

$$\frac{4}{12} = \frac{1}{3} = 0.333333 \text{ or } 0.\dot{3}$$

Differentiation

Supporting: Ask students to tell you what patterns they are noticing.

Consolidating: Ask students to tell you which **equivalent fractions** they can see.

Extending: Ask students to predict the answers before they carry out the calculations.

Differentiated outcomes	
All students	should complete the equivalence tables and notice patterns.
Most students	will complete the equivalence tables and notice patterns and equivalence.
Some students	will predict the answers before they carry out the calculations.

 Learning review

Ask each student to share something new that they learned with the rest of the class.

Additional activities

You can ask students to look at the completed tables and use the decimal fractions to find equivalent fractions, for example:

$$\frac{1}{3} = \frac{2}{6} = \frac{4}{12}$$
$$\frac{2}{5} = \frac{4}{10}$$

and so on.

Students can complete Workbook page 18.

Answers

Student Book page 28

Quarters: 0.25, 0.5, 0.75, 1, 1.25

Fifths: 0.2, 0.4, 0.6, 0.8, 1

Eighths: 0.125, 0.25, 0.375, 0.5, 0.625, 0.75, 0.875, 1

Twelfths: 0.083$\dot{3}$ 0.16$\dot{6}$, 0.25, 0.$\dot{3}$, 0.41$\dot{6}$, 0.5

0.583$\dot{3}$, 0.$\dot{6}$, 0.75, 0.8$\dot{3}$, 0.91$\dot{6}$, 1

Workbook page 18

1. $\frac{1}{7} = 0.1428571$, $\frac{2}{7} = 0.2857142$, $\frac{3}{7} = 0.4285714$,

   $\frac{4}{7} = 0.5714285$, $\frac{5}{7} = 0.7142857$, $\frac{6}{7} = 0.8571428$, $\frac{7}{7} = 1$

2. $\frac{1}{9} = 0.1111111$, $\frac{2}{9} = 0.2222222$, $\frac{3}{9} = 0.3333333$,

   $\frac{4}{9} = 0.4444444$, $\frac{5}{9} = 0.5555555$, $\frac{6}{9} = 0.6666666$,

   $\frac{7}{9} = 0.7777777$, $\frac{8}{9} = 0.8888888$, $\frac{9}{9} = 1$

3. $\frac{1}{12} = 0.0833$

   $\frac{2}{12} = 0.16\dot{6}$

   $\frac{3}{12} = 0.25$

   $\frac{4}{12} = 0.\dot{3}$

   $\frac{5}{12} = 0.41\dot{6}$

   $\frac{6}{12} = 0.5$

   $\frac{7}{12} = 0.58\dot{3}$

   $\frac{8}{12} = 0.\dot{6}$

   $\frac{9}{12} = 0.75$

   $\frac{10}{12} = 0.8\dot{3}$

   $\frac{11}{12} = 0.91\dot{6}$

   $\frac{12}{12} = 1$

2B Fractions and decimals

Explore

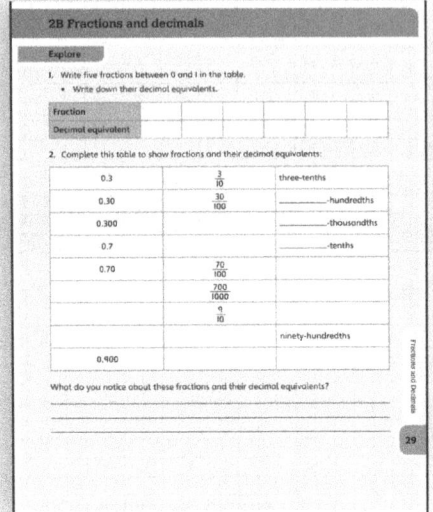 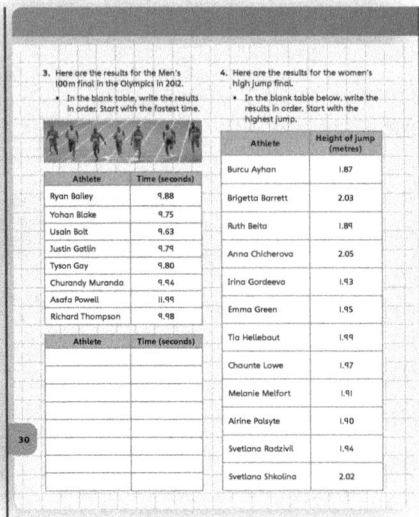 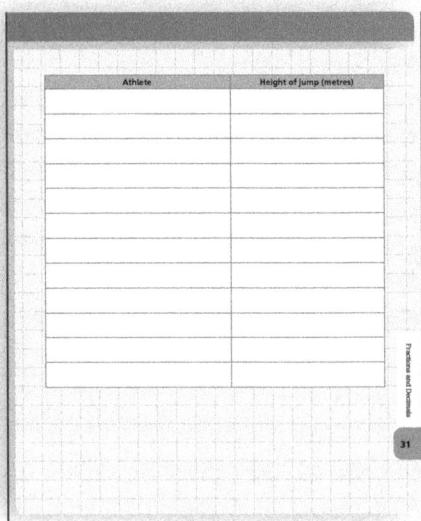

Specific learning foci

- Recognise and use the equivalence between decimal and fraction forms.
- Recognise and use decimals with up to three places in the context of measurement.

Problem solving focus

- Use ordered lists or tables to solve number problems systematically.

Key vocabulary

Part, whole, equivalent fraction, decimal equivalent, numerator, denominator, half, third, quarter, three-quarters, fifth, sixth, eighth, tenth, hundredth, decimal fraction

Resources

- Large cards with the digits 0 and 1 on them
- Mini whiteboards and markers
- Calculators

Links to Student Book

See pages 29–31 in Student Book.

Links to Workbook

Workbook page 19

Links to Digital Resource Pack

Digital Resource Pack 6 contains two activities which can be used to support students' understanding of equivalent fractions and decimals. On the home page, select 'Fractions and Decimals'.

Language support

Writing problems and defining good questions helps to support language development.

Write a word bank on the board to help students to write questions including, for example:

- equivalent (*What is the equivalent decimal?*)
- greater than, less than, in between (*Which fractions are between and …?*)
- decimal, decimal fraction (*Which of these decimal fractions is greater, 0.37 or 0.09?*)

 Introductory activity

Place a large '0' card at one side at the front of the classroom and a '1' on the opposite side. Ask a student to write any fraction between zero and 1 on their mini whiteboard. Then ask the student to come to the front of the class and to stand in the correct place between the '0' and '1'. Ask another student to write down a different fraction between the first fraction and 1. Ask the student to come to the front of the class and to stand in the correct place (between the first student and the '1'). Repeat this until there are five students on the 'number line' at the front of the class. Repeat the activity. This time ask for fractions between '0' and the previous student.

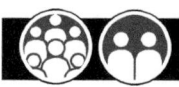 Main activity

Ask students to complete the activities on pages 29 to 31 of the Student Book, working in pairs to compare answers and to share strategies. Pay particular attention to what students notice about the fractions and **decimal equivalents** in terms of **tenths** and **hundredths**. Make a list of all the responses. Write the list on the whiteboard for the whole class.

Differentiation

Supporting: Ask students further questions to assess their understanding of the decimal equivalents for tenths and hundredths. Use a 100-square for support if necessary.

Consolidating: Ask students to explain their strategies for ordering the times and the heights.

Extending: Ask students to tell you a time or a height between two of the given heights.

Differentiated outcomes	
All students	should understand the equivalences between tenths and hundredths and decimal forms.
Most students	will successfully order **decimal numbers** to 3 decimal places.
Some students	will understand the equivalences between tenths, hundredths and thousandths and decimal forms.

Learning review

Ask students to work in pairs to write a finishing time between Ryan Bailey and Yohan Blake. Ask them to show you their answers on their mini whiteboards. Then ask them to write a height which is higher than Ruth Beita's jump but lower than Airine Palsyte's jump. Now ask pairs to write their own questions for the rest of the class. Select five of these questions for the class to answer.

Additional activities

Students can do practical activities which involve measurement and ordering. For example: the time it takes students to write their name five times or the distance to various points in the classroom in metres and centimetres. Alternatively, use other data from athletics or other sporting events.

Students can complete Workbook page 19.

Answers

Student Book pages 29 to 31

1. Answers will vary as students choose their own fractions. Check that students have written the correct decimal equivalent for each of their fractions.

2.

0.3	$\frac{3}{10}$	three-tenths
0.30	$\frac{30}{100}$	thirty-hundredths
0.300	$\frac{300}{1000}$	three-hundred thousandths
0.7	$\frac{7}{10}$	seven-tenths
0.70	$\frac{70}{100}$	seventy-hundredths
0.700	$\frac{700}{1000}$	seven-hundred thousandths
0.9	$\frac{9}{10}$	nine-tenths
0.90	$\frac{90}{100}$	ninety-hundredths
0.900	$\frac{900}{1000}$	nine-hundred thousandths

3. 9.63; 9.75; 9.79; 9.80; 9.88; 9.94; 9.98; 11.99

4. 2.05; 2.03; 2.02; 1.99; 1.97; 1.95; 1.94; 1.93; 1.91; 1.90; 1.89; 1.87

Workbook page 19

A Answers will vary as students make their own numbers. Check that students have put the numbers in order correctly.

B

0.4	0.5	0.6	0.7	0.8	0.9
0.1	0.3	0.5	0.7	0.9	1.1
1	$\frac{3}{4}$	$\frac{1}{2}$	$\frac{1}{4}$	0	$-\frac{1}{4}$
$1\frac{1}{2}$	1	$\frac{1}{2}$	0	$-\frac{1}{2}$	-1
2	2.5	3	3.5	4	4.5

2C Addition pairs

Discover

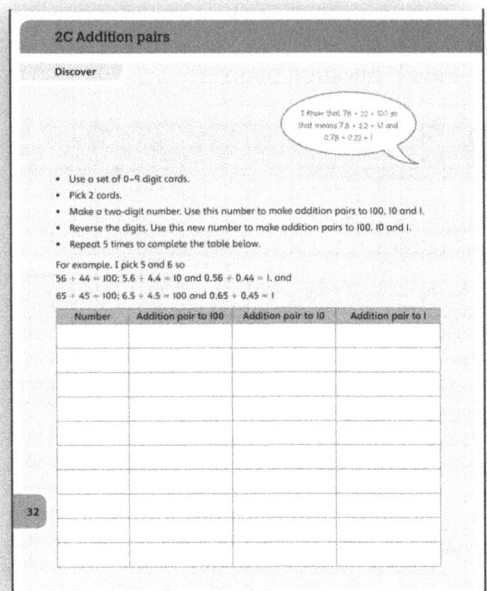

Specific learning focus

- Derive quickly pairs of one-place decimals totalling 10.

Problem solving focus

- Explain why they chose a particular method to perform a calculation and show working.

Key vocabulary

Addition pair, total to 10, total to 1

Resources

- Counting sticks
- 0–9 digit cards, enough for one set for each pair
- Mini whiteboards and markers

Links to Student Book

See page 32 in Student Book.

Links to Workbook

Workbook page 20

Language support

Encourage students to discuss their answers when working in pairs. Model the key language:

- *What is the sum of those two numbers?*
- *What is the addition pair to 100, 10, 1?*

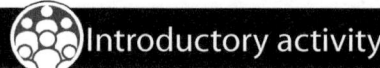

Introductory activity

Use your counting stick to count with the whole class in 100s starting at 0. Point to 200 and ask what would need to be added to make 1000. Repeat with four other numbers. Repeat the activity, this time counting in 10s and repeat again counting in 0.1s.

Ask one student to come to the front and pick two digit cards. Ask them to make a two-digit number with cards and write it on the board. Model the activity on page 32 of the Student Book, referring back to the counting stick if necessary.

 ## Main activity

Students take it in turns to pick two digit cards and make a two-digit number. Working as a pair means that they can check one another's answers and support one another in developing the appropriate vocabulary. As students work on the activity, ask them why they think moving the decimal point results in **totals to 10 and 1**. (We are dividing the numbers we are adding by 10 or by 100, so we will also divide the total by 10 and 100.)

Differentiation

Supporting: Ask students to explain how they are finding pairs to 1 using their knowledge of pairs to 10.

Consolidating: Ask students why their knowledge of pairs to 10 can help.

Extending: Ask students to find pairs to 10 with numbers with 1 decimal place.

Differentiated outcomes	
All students	should find pairs to 1 using their knowledge of pairs to 10.
Most students	will understand the role place value plays in finding pairs to 1 using their knowledge of pairs to 10.
Some students	will find pairs to 1 without needing to refer to pairs to 10.

 ## Learning review

Select two digit cards and write the two-digit number on the board. Working in pairs, students should write the three sums: to 100, to 10 and to 1. You can use this activity to make sure all the students have understood the process. Ask one of the students who explained the reasoning well to you in the Main activity to give the explanation to the whole class.

Additional activities

Develop the idea using three digits, for example:
$132 + 868 = 1000$, $13.2 + 86.8 = 100$, $1.32 + 8.68 = 10$

Students can complete Workbook page 20.

Answers

Student Book page 32

Answers will vary as students make their own numbers. Check that the addition pairs are correct for each number.

Workbook page 20

Number	Addition pair to 100	Addition pair to 10	Addition pair to 1
38	$38 + 62 = 100$	$3.8 + 6.2 = 10$	$0.38 + 0.62 = 1$
85	$85 + 15 = 100$	$8.5 + 1.5 = 10$	$0.85 + 0.15 = 1$
41	$41 + 59 = 100$	$4.1 + 5.9 = 10$	$0.41 + 0.59 = 1$
16	$16 + 84 = 100$	$1.6 + 8.4 = 10$	$0.16 + 0.84 = 1$
73	$73 + 27 = 100$	$7.3 + 2.7 = 10$	$0.73 + 0.27 = 1$
24	$24 + 76 = 100$	$2.4 + 7.6 = 10$	$0.24 + 0.76 = 1$
11	$11 + 89 = 100$	$1.1 + 8.9 = 10$	$0.11 + 0.89 = 1$
89	$89 + 11 = 100$	$8.9 + 1.1 = 10$	$0.89 + 0.11 = 1$
54	$54 + 46 = 100$	$5.4 + 4.6 = 10$	$0.54 + 0.46 = 1$
67	$67 + 33 = 100$	$6.7 + 3.3 = 10$	$0.67 + 0.33 = 1$
14	$14 + 86 = 100$	$1.4 + 8.6 = 10$	$0.14 + 0.86 = 1$
51	$51 + 49 = 100$	$5.1 + 4.9 = 10$	$0.51 + 0.49 = 1$
40	$40 + 60 = 100$	$4.0 + 6.0 = 10$	$0.4 + 0.6 = 1$
5	$5 + 95 = 100$	$0.5 + 9.5 = 10$	$0.05 + 0.95 = 1$
92	$92 + 8 = 100$	$9.2 + 0.8 = 10$	$0.92 + 0.08 = 1$

2C Addition pairs

Explore

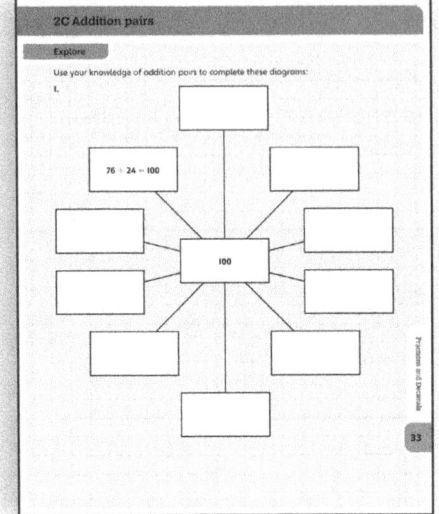
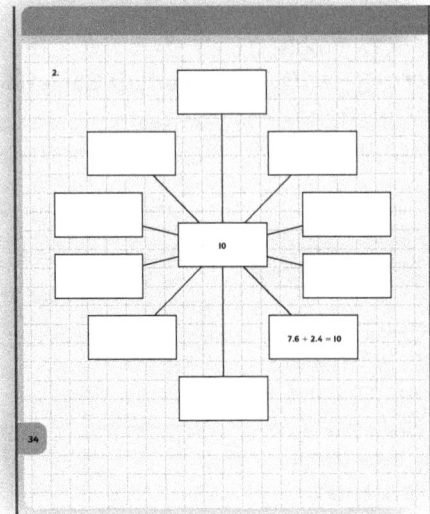
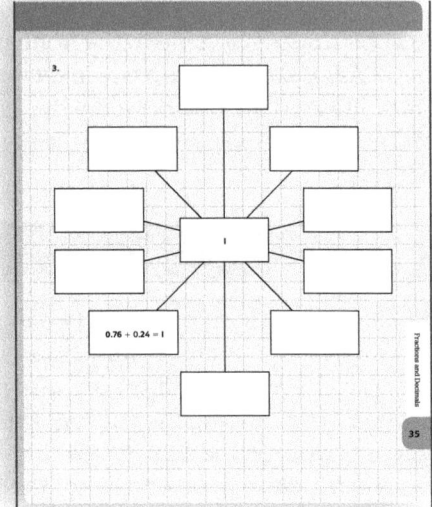

Specific learning focus

- Derive quickly pairs of one-place decimals totalling 10.

Problem solving focus

- Explain why they chose a particular method to perform a calculation and show working.

Key vocabulary

Addition pair, total to 10, total to 1

Resources

- Mini whiteboards and markers

Links to Student Book

See pages 33–35 in Student Book.

Links to Workbook

Workbook page 21

Language support

Encourage students to discuss their answers with you, focusing on the students who you noticed were struggling to explain their thinking in the previous activity. Continue to model the key language:

- *What is the sum of those two numbers?*
- *What is the addition pair to 100, 10, 1?*

 Introductory activity

Write '10' on the board. Give each pair 2 minutes to write as many addition pairs to 10 as they can. The numbers they use must include one decimal place. Choose a pair and take one of their answers. Write it on the board. Ask students to tell you the corresponding **addition pairs** to 100 and to 1. Repeat several times.

 Main activity

The activities on pages 33 to 35 of the Student Book use the ideas from 2C Discover but students work as individuals. Whilst students are working, observe any students you were concerned about in the previous activity so that you can check their understanding and support them if necessary. Encourage students to use their responses to the 100 spider diagram on page 33 to complete the other two diagrams.

Differentiation

Supporting: Ask students to explain how they are finding pairs to 1 using their knowledge of pairs to 10 and 100.

Consolidating: Ask students why their knowledge of pairs to 10 and 100 can help.

Extending: Ask students to find pairs to 1 with numbers with 2 decimal places.

Differentiated outcomes	
All students	should find pairs to 1 using their knowledge of pairs to 10 and 100.
Most students	will understand the role place value plays in finding pairs to 1 using their knowledge of pairs to 10 and 100.
Some students	will find pairs to 1 without needing to refer to pairs to 10 and 100.

 Learning review

As in the previous activity, use the Learning review as an assessment activity. Ask one student for a pair that they used to total 100. Working individually, the students should write the corresponding sums to 10 and to 1.

Additional activities

Complete spider diagrams to 1000, 100, 10 and 1.

Students can complete Workbook page 21.

Answers

Student Book pages 33–35

Answers will vary as students choose their own numbers for the spider diagrams. Check that the number sentences written are correct and that the numbers do total 100, 10 or 1.

Workbook page 21

Answers will vary as students write their own pairs of numbers that total given numbers. Check that the addition pairs are correct.

Discover

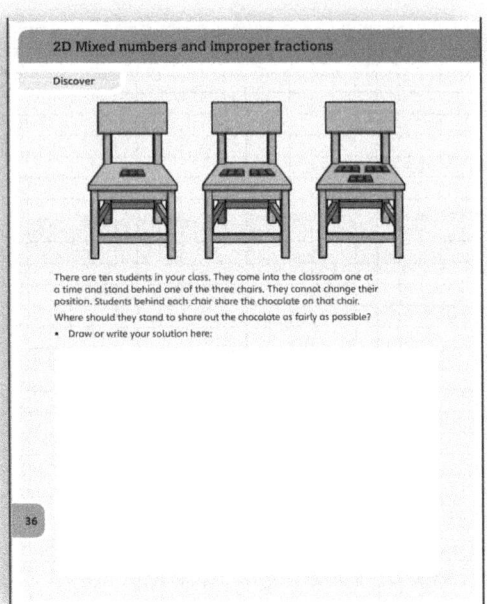

Specific learning foci

- Change an improper fraction to a mixed number.
- *Relate finding fractions to division and use them as operators to find fractions including several tenths and hundredths of quantities.*

Problem solving focus

- Make sense of and solve word problems and represent them.

Key vocabulary

Part, whole, equivalent fraction, simplest form, mixed number, numerator, denominator, half, third, quarter, three-quarters, fifth, sixth, eighth, tenth, decimal fraction, proportion

Resources

- Three chairs
- Six bars of chocolate, each made up of six chunks

Links to Student Book

See page 36 in Student Book.

Links to Workbook

Workbook page 22

Language support

It is important for students to share their solutions with other students and to explain their ideas. This allows them to use their mathematical language. Ask other groups to comment on any differences between the presented solution and their solution. Model key vocabulary in your response, for example:

- improper fraction, mixed number *(What sort of fraction is that?)*
- half, third, sixth
- decimal fraction *(What is the equivalent decimal fraction?)*

 ## Introductory and Main activity

Position three chairs at the front of the classroom. Place one chocolate bar on one chair, two bars on the next chair and three on the final chair. Ask ten students to come to the front of the class. They take it in turns to stand behind a chair. Tell them that they cannot change position after they have chosen a chair.

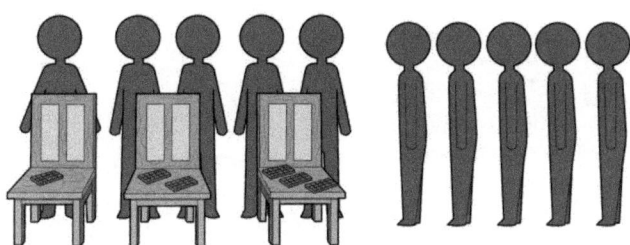

When they are all behind a chair, they will share the chocolate on that chair between them. When you have completed the activity, students should work in groups to work out what the fairest solution to the problem is so that each person has a 'fair share'. Students need to offer a rationale for their solution as different groups will interpret 'fairness' differently.

Differentiation

Students work as a class and in small mixed-attainment groups.

Differentiated outcomes
As this is a game, all students will engage with it at their current level. They will develop new understandings around fractions, mixed numbers and their equivalences through their interactions with other students and the range of diagrams they draw to model the problem.

 ## Learning review

Ask one of the groups to share their solution with the rest of the class. Ask them to include any drawings they did or calculations they made to find the solution.

Additional activities

A similar activity involves placing different numbers of jelly beans on tables in the classroom. Ask students to decide where they want to sit one at a time. Then share out the jelly beans appropriately.

Students can complete Workbook page 22.

Answers

Student Book page 36

Answers will vary. Discuss students' answers with them and ask them to justify their reasoning.

Workbook page 22

1. a) $4\frac{1}{2}$

   b) $4\frac{1}{4}$

   c) $3\frac{1}{5}$

   d) $4\frac{3}{5}$

   e) $2\frac{1}{4}$

   f) $1\frac{5}{6}$

   g) $3\frac{1}{4}$

   h) $3\frac{1}{10}$

2. a) $\frac{13}{14}$

   b) $\frac{33}{8}$

   c) $\frac{35}{8}$

   d) $\frac{47}{9}$

   e) $\frac{19}{10}$

   f) $\frac{81}{8}$

   g) $\frac{34}{5}$

   h) $\frac{42}{11}$

Explore

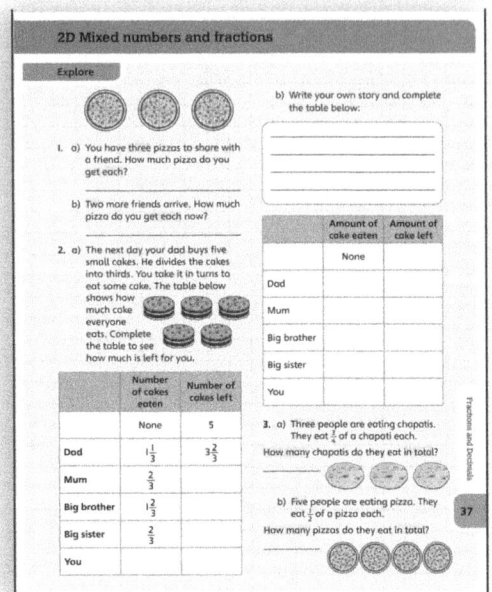
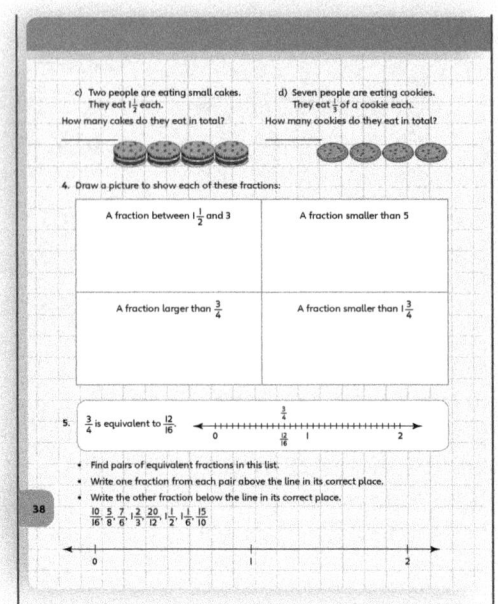

Specific learning foci

- Change an improper fraction to a mixed number.
- *Relate finding fractions to division and use them as operators to find fractions including several tenths and hundredths of quantities.*

Problem solving focus

- Make sense of and solve word problems and represent them.

Key vocabulary

Part, whole, equivalent fraction, simplest form, mixed number, numerator, denominator, half, third, quarter, three-quarters, fifth, sixth, eighth, tenth, decimal fraction, proportion

Resources

- Large circles cut into quarters to represent pizzas
- Mini whiteboards and markers

Links to Student Book

See pages 37–38 in Student Book.

Links to Workbook

Workbook page 23

Language support

Asking students to explain their ideas and share their strategies allows them to practise and use mathematical language. Model key words and phrases in your discussions with students, for example:

- improper number, mixed number
- order in ascending size
- greater than, less than

Introductory activity

Create four 'pizzas' by cutting out four large circles. Sit students in a circle around the 'pizzas'. Ask the following questions. After each question share the pizzas out so that students have a visual image of the fractions. Then put the pizzas in the centre again.

There is one person. How much or how many pizzas do they have? (Answer = 4)

Give all of the pizzas to one student to demonstrate this.

There are two people. How much or how many pizzas do they have each? (Answer = 2)

Give two pizzas to two students to demonstrate this.

There are three people. How much or how many pizzas do they have each? (Answer = $1\frac{1}{3}$ or $\frac{4}{3}$)

Give $\frac{4}{3}$ of a pizza to three different students to demonstrate this.

There are four people. How much or how many pizzas do they have each? (Answer = 1)

Give one pizza to four different students to demonstrate this.

There are five people. How much or how many pizzas do they have each? (Answer = $\frac{4}{5}$)

Give $\frac{4}{5}$ of a pizza to five different students to demonstrate this.

There are six people. How much or how many pizzas do they have each? (Answer = $\frac{2}{3}$)

Give $\frac{2}{3}$ of a pizza to six different students to demonstrate this.

For five and six people, you can ask the class how to cut the pizza.

Main activity

Ask students in pairs to work on the activities on pages 37 and 38 of the Student Book to support one another and to discuss their solutions. Encourage them to draw the solutions before they fill in the tables in the workbook. Ask them to explain their drawings to you. It is important that they represent the first two problems visually. Question 4 on page 38 of the Student Book encourages students to illustrate mixed numbers visually.

Differentiation

Supporting: Work with the students to solve the problems using practical materials.

Consolidating: Ask students to use diagrams to help them solve the problems.

Extending: Ask students to share their strategies for solving the problems.

Learning review

Ask one student to come to the front of the classroom and share their solution to question 5 with the rest of the class. Ask them to explain their working very carefully. Ask the class: *Did anyone do the activity in a different way?*

Additional activities

You can ask students to write different 'fraction stories' about their own families and work on them at home.

Students can complete Workbook page 23.

Answers

Student Book pages 37 and 38

1. a) $1\frac{1}{2}$ **b)** $\frac{3}{4}$

2.

	Number of cakes eaten	Number of cakes left
	None	5
Dad	$1\frac{1}{3}$	$3\frac{2}{3}$
Mum	$\frac{2}{3}$	3
Big Brother	$1\frac{2}{3}$	$1\frac{1}{3}$
Big Sister	$\frac{2}{3}$	$\frac{2}{3}$
You	$\frac{2}{3}$	None

3. a) $2\frac{1}{4}$ **b)** $2\frac{1}{2}$ **c)** 3

d) $27\frac{1}{3}$

4. Check that students' diagrams show the fractions clearly.

5. $\frac{5}{8} = \frac{10}{16}$; $\frac{7}{6} = 1\frac{1}{6}$; $\frac{15}{10} = 1\frac{1}{2}$; $\frac{20}{12} = 1\frac{2}{3}$

(Drawn above and below a 0–2 number line.)

Workbook page 23

Answers will vary as students choose their own improper fractions and equivalent mixed numbers. Check that students' answers match the instructions and show the equivalence of each missed number and improper fraction.

Discover

2E Ratio and proportion

Discover

1. You can buy green paint from two companies.

Paint A is made up from blue and yellow paint in the ratio 1 : 4.

Paint B is made up from blue and yellow paint in the ratio 1 : 7.

You can mix blue and yellow to make different shades of green.

Paint A and Paint B are in the same size tins.

You are making different shades of green. You don't want to use too much paint!

How many tins of paints A and B do you need to make green paint with these ratios of blue to yellow?

1 : 5 _____
1 : 6 _____

2. You want to paint another room orange.

Orange paint is made up from yellow and red paint.

Paint C is made up from red and yellow in the ratio 1 : 4.

Paint D is made up from red and yellow in the ratio 1 : 9.

What is the minimum number of tins of paints C and D you need to make orange made up from red and yellow in the following ratios?

1 : 5 _____
1 : 6 _____
1 : 7 _____
1 : 8 _____

3. Make up a similar question for your partner to solve:

You want to paint another room

_____ paint is made up from _____ and _____ paint.

Paint E is made up from _____ and _____ in the ratio ___:___

Paint F is made up from _____ and _____ in the ratio ___:___

What is the minimum number of tins of paints E and F you need to make _____ made up from _____ and _____ in the following ratios?

_____
_____
_____
_____

Specific learning foci

- *Solve simple problems involving ratio and direct proportion.*
- Reduce fractions to their simplest form, where this is $\frac{1}{4}$, $\frac{1}{2}$, $\frac{3}{4}$ or a number of fifths or tenths.

Problem solving focus

- Solve simple word problems involving ratio and direct proportion.

Key vocabulary

Part, whole, simplest form, third, quarter, three-quarters, fifth, sixth, eighth, tenth, hundredth, ratio, proportion

Resources

- Blue, yellow and red counters or cubes
- Squares of blue, yellow and red paper
- Mini whiteboards and markers

Links to Student Book

See page 39 in Student Book.

Links to Workbook

Workbook pages 24–25

Language support

Asking students to write and present their own problems helps them to develop their language skills. Model key words and phrases in your discussions with students, for example:

- proportion, ratio
- for every, in every (*Three in every four parts are red.*)

 Introductory activity

Stick three blue squares and one yellow square to the whiteboard. Explain that this shows a **ratio** of 1 : 3. Say 'one to three'. Explain that this means that for every one part of yellow there are three parts of blue. Write the ratios 1 : 4, 1 : 5 and 1 : 6 on the whiteboard. Ask students to come to the front and stick up pieces of paper to illustrate these ratios. Ask students to say the ratios ('one to four', 'one to five' and 'one to six').

 Main activity

Ask students to work in pairs on the investigations on page 39 of the Student Book. Give each pair a selection of counters or cubes. They can use these to model the problems. Ask students to use their mini whiteboards and markers to represent the problem. Encourage students to use sketches to illustrate their ideas (and not to try to immediately represent the solution using fractions). You may choose to group less confident students together so that you can model the problem to the whole group.

Differentiation

Supporting: Model the problem for students using cubes and counters.

Consolidating: Ask students to model the problem for you using cubes and counters.

Extending: Ask students to attempt the problem using written methods.

Differentiated outcomes	
All students	should attempt the problems using counters and cubes to support them and solve the problems with support.
Most students	will solve the problems using counters and cubes for support.
Some students	will solve the problems using written methods.

 Learning review

Ask one of the pairs to come to the front and present their made-up problem to the class. Then pick a student to come to the front and to solve the problem. Ask this student to explain their strategy as they solve the problem. Ask the pair who wrote the problem to act as teachers and to support the student as they solve the problem.

Additional activities

Students can explore the characteristics of the class or school using ratios. For example, explore languages spoken, types of travel to school, ways of spending free time, and so on.

Students can complete Workbook pages 24–25.

Answers

Student Book page 39

1. $1 : 5 = 2$ tins of A and 1 tin of B

   $1 : 6 = 1$ tin of A and 2 tins of B

2. $1 : 5 = 4$ tins of C and 1 tin of D

   $1 : 6 = 3$ tins of C and 2 tins of D

   $1 : 7 = 2$ tins of C and 3 tins of D

   $1 : 8 = 1$ tin of C and 4 tins of D

Workbook pages 24–25

1. **a)** Array showing 4 girls in a class of 12

   b) Array showing 6 girls in a class of 24

   c) Array showing 3 girls in a class of 15

   d) Array showing 2 girls in a class of 16

   e) Array showing 15 girls in a class of 20

   f) Array showing 12 girls in a class of 15

2. **a)** $\frac{6}{10} = \frac{3}{5}$; 0.6; 60%

   b) $\frac{9}{10}$; 0.9; 90%

   c) $\frac{1}{10}$; 0.1; 10%

   d) $\frac{5}{10} = \frac{1}{2}$; 0.5; 50%

   e) $\frac{8}{10} = \frac{4}{5}$; 0.8; 80%

3. **a)** 9 tiles should be shaded.

   b) 2 tiles should be shaded.

Explore

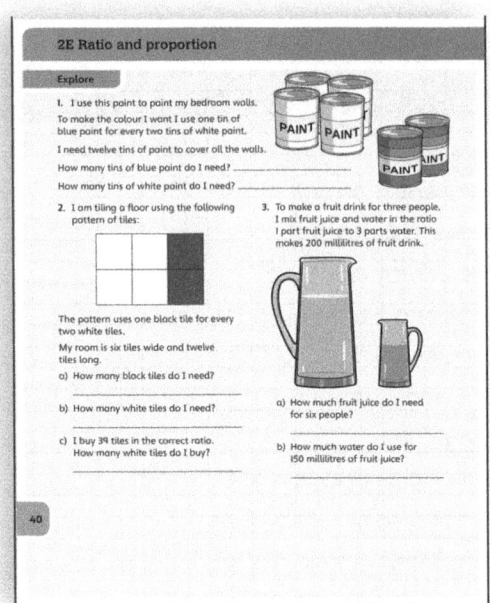

2E Ratio and proportion

Explore

1. I use this paint to paint my bedroom walls.
To make the colour I want I use one tin of blue paint for every two tins of white paint.
I need twelve tins of paint to cover all the walls.
How many tins of blue paint do I need? _____
How many tins of white paint do I need? _____

2. I am tiling a floor using the following pattern of tiles:

The pattern uses one black tile for every two white tiles.
My room is six tiles wide and twelve tiles long.
a) How many black tiles do I need?
_____
b) How many white tiles do I need?
_____
c) I buy 39 tiles in the correct ratio. How many white tiles do I buy?

3. To make a fruit drink for three people, I mix fruit juice and water in the ratio 1 part fruit juice to 3 parts water. This makes 200 millilitres of fruit drink.

a) How much fruit juice do I need for six people?
_____
b) How much water do I use for 150 millilitres of fruit juice?
_____

40

Specific learning foci

- *Solve simple problems involving ratio and direct proportion.*
- Reduce fractions to their simplest form, where this is $\frac{1}{4}$, $\frac{1}{2}$, $\frac{3}{4}$ or a number of fifths or tenths.

Problem solving focus

- Solve simple word problems involving ratio and direct proportion.

Key vocabulary

Part, whole, simplest form, third, quarter, three-quarters, fifth, sixth, eighth, tenth, hundredth, ratio, proportion

Resources

- Blue, yellow and red counters or cubes
- Squares of blue, yellow and red paper
- Mini whiteboards and markers

Links to Student Book

See page 40 in Student Book.

Links to Workbook

Workbook pages 24–25

Language support

Asking students to write their own definitions of key mathematical terms helps you to monitor what students understand by these terms. Support students by giving them model examples (as in the Learning review).

 Introductory activity

Ask students to solve a problem that another pair wrote in 2E Discover. Then ask: *What are the most important things to remember when solving a problem involving **ratio** and **proportion**?* Encourage students to draw pictures. This helps them to understand and solve problems. Share the images that pairs of student used to solve the problem you set them.

 Main activity

Ask students to work on the problems on page 40 of the Student Book in pairs for support and to encourage discussion of strategies. Ask students: *How do you know that your answers are correct?* Ask them to justify that their answers are correct (and not only to give the answers).

Give each pair a selection of counters or cubes. They can use these to model the problems. Ask students to use their mini whiteboards to represent the problem. Encourage students to use sketches to illustrate their ideas (and not to try to immediately represent the solution using fractions). You may choose to group less confident students together so that you can model the problems with the whole group.

Differentiation

Supporting: Model the problems for students using cubes and counters.

Consolidating: Ask students to model the problems for you using cubes and counters.

Extending: Ask students to attempt the problems using written methods.

Differentiated outcomes	
All students	should attempt the problems using counters and cubes to support them and solve the problems with support.
Most students	will solve the problems using counters and cubes for support.
Some students	will solve the problems using written methods.

 Learning review

Ask each pair to write two sentences to answer the questions *'What does ratio mean?'* and *'What is proportion?'*.

Give this example: *25% of the population of a village are students. The ratio of students to adults is 1:3. The proportion of students is $\frac{1}{4}$.* Students should use drawings or sketched to illustrate their sentences.

Additional activities

Students can explore other practical activities that involve ratio. Adapting recipes for larger or smaller groups of people for example.

Students can complete Workbook pages 24–25.

Answers

Student Book page 40
1. 4 tins of blue paint; 8 tins of white paint
2. **a)** 24 black tiles
   b) 48 white tiles
   c) 26 white tiles
3. **a)** 100 millilitres of juice
   b) 450 millilitres water

Workbook pages 24–25
1. **a)** Array showing 4 girls in a class of 12
   b) Array showing 6 girls in a class of 24
   c) Array showing 3 girls in a class of 15
   d) Array showing 2 girls in a class of 16
   e) Array showing 15 girls in a class of 20
   f) Array showing 12 girls in a class of 15

2. **a)** $\frac{6}{10} = \frac{3}{5}$; 0.6; 60%
   b) $\frac{9}{10}$; 0.9; 90%
   c) $\frac{1}{10}$; 0.1; 10%
   d) $\frac{5}{10} = \frac{1}{2}$; 0.5; 50%
   e) $\frac{8}{10} = \frac{4}{5}$; 0.8; 80%

3. **a)** 9 tiles should be shaded.
   b) 2 tiles should be shaded.

2F Percentages

Discover

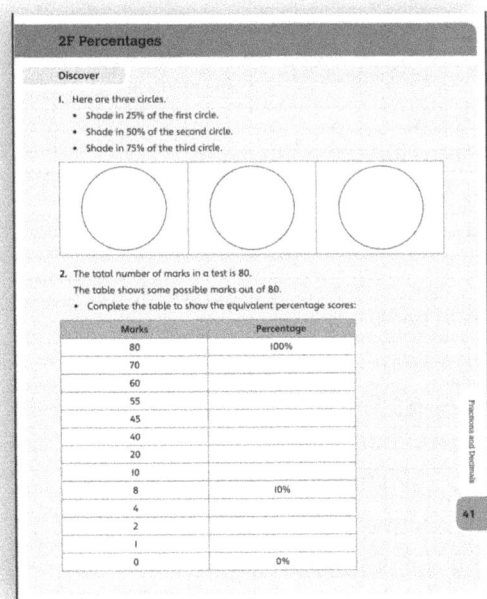

Specific learning foci

- Understand percentage as parts in every 100 and express $\frac{1}{2}, \frac{1}{4}, \frac{1}{5}, \frac{1}{10}, \frac{1}{100}$ as percentages.
- *Find simple percentages of shapes and whole numbers.*

Problem solving focus

- Solve simple word problems involving percentages.

Key vocabulary

25 percent, 50 percent, 75 percent, percentage, out of 100, %

Resources

- Mini whiteboards and markers

Links to Student Book

See page 41 in Student Book.

Links to Workbook

Workbook page 26

Links to Digital Resource Pack

Digital Resource Pack 6 contains two activities which can be used to support students' understanding of percentages. On the home page, select 'Fractions and Decimals'.

Language support

Ask students to explain their ideas. Ask, for example:

How did you work out that a mark of 20 is 25%?

 Introductory activity

Write the number 60 on the whiteboard. Ask students to write down as many fractions and equivalent **percentages** as they can for number 60. (For example: $\frac{1}{2}$ of 60 = 50**%** of 60 = 30; $\frac{1}{10}$ of 60 = 10**%** of 60 = 6.)

Take answers from students, one pair at a time. When a pair has no suggestions, encourage them to use the other facts to create a new fact.

 Main activity

Ask students in pairs to complete the activities on page 41 of the Student Book although they should attempt the questions individually first and then compare the answers. Ask individual students to explain their ideas to you. For example, ask: *How did you work out that a mark of 20 is 25%?*

You can also ask them about marks that do not appear in the table. For example: *My mark is 25. How many **percent** is that?*

Differentiation

Supporting: Ask students for all the equivalent fractions and percentages that they know.

Consolidating: Ask students to explain their thinking as they complete the table.

Extending: Ask students to find as many different percentages as they can for a test marked out of 80.

Differentiated outcomes	
All students	should know equivalences for $\frac{1}{4}$, $\frac{1}{2}$ and $\frac{3}{4}$ and shade circles accurately and complete the table with support.
Most students	will complete the table independently.
Some students	will find percentages which do not appear in the table.

 Learning review

Ask all students to draw a square on their whiteboards. Then ask them to shade in 25%, 33.3%, 80%. Ask them to show you their answers at the same time. Use any errors to clear up misconceptions through teaching.

Additional activities

You can set problems. For example: to work out what 25% of the floor space in the classroom is by drawing a scale drawing; or to work out what the floor space of the classroom is after a 10% reduction.

Students can complete Workbook page 26.

Answers

Student Book page 41

1. Accept any accurate shading that shows shading of 25% of the first circle, 50% of the second circle and 75% of the third circle.

2.

Marks	Percentage
80	100%
70	87.5%
60	75%
55	68.75%
45	56.25%
40	50%
20	25%
10	12.5%
8	10%
4	5%
2	2.5%
1	1.25%
0	0%

Workbook page 26

1. a) $\frac{1}{4}$

   b) $\frac{3}{4}$

   c) $\frac{1}{10}$

   d) $\frac{2}{5}$

   e) $\frac{1}{5}$

   f) $\frac{9}{10}$

   g) $\frac{1}{2}$

   h) $\frac{1}{3}$

   i) $\frac{2}{3}$

   j) $\frac{7}{10}$

2.

Mark (out of 60)	Equivalent %
60	100%
54	90%
45	75%
42	70%
30	50%
24	40%
15	25%
12	20%
6	10%
3	5%

2F Percentages

Explore

2F Percentages

Explore

- Complete this table:

Fraction	Decimal fraction	Percentage	Percentage as an area
$\frac{1}{10}$	0.1	10%	
$\frac{1}{5}$			
$\frac{1}{4}$			
$\frac{3}{10}$			
$\frac{2}{5}$			
$\frac{1}{2}$			
$\frac{3}{5}$			
$\frac{7}{10}$			
$\frac{3}{4}$			
$\frac{4}{5}$			
1 whole			

42

Specific learning foci

- *Understand percentage as parts in every 100 and express $\frac{1}{2}$, $\frac{1}{4}$, $\frac{1}{5}$, $\frac{1}{10}$, $\frac{1}{100}$ as percentages.*
- Find simple percentages of shapes and whole numbers.

Problem solving focus

- Solve simple word problems involving percentages.

Key vocabulary

25 percent, 50 percent, 75 percent, percentage, out of 100

Resources

- Mini whiteboards and markers
- 100-squares for support

Links to Student Book

See page 42 in Student Book.

Links to Workbook

Workbook page 27

Links to Digital Resource Pack

Digital Resource Pack 6 contains two activities which can be used to support students' understanding of percentages. On the home page, select 'Fractions and Decimals'.

Language support

Asking students to explain their reasoning allows them to practise their language skills. It also helps you assess the extent of their understanding of key terms such as half, quarter, third, tenth, hundredth, percentage, percent.

Introductory activity

Write $\frac{1}{4}$, 25% and 50% on the board. Ask the class:

Which is the odd one out? Then ask: *Why?* Some possible answers are '$\frac{1}{4}$ is the odd one out because it is a fraction, and 25% and 50% are **percentages**' or

'50% is the odd one out because $\frac{1}{4}$ and 25% are equivalent'. Encourage students to give a reason for their answer. Repeat for:

- $\frac{1}{10}$, 10% and 0.5
- 80%, 40% and $\frac{2}{5}$

 Main activity

Ask students individually to complete the activities on page 42 of the Student Book. Ask individual students to explain their reasoning to you. For example, ask:

How do you know that $\frac{3}{5}$ is 60%? Set them challenges to find examples that are not in the table. For example: ask them to explore $\frac{1}{8}$, $\frac{2}{8}$, $\frac{3}{8}$ and $\frac{4}{8}$ as percentages.

Differentiation

Supporting: Give students 100-squares to shade in to support them in completing the table.

Consolidating: Encourage students to use their knowledge of equivalences to help them complete the table.

Extending: Ask students to add extra rows to explore eighths as percentages.

Differentiated outcomes	
All students	should complete the table using 100-squares for support.
Most students	will complete the table using their knowledge of equivalence.
Some students	will complete the table using mental recall.

 Learning review

Write the following fractions on separate pieces of paper:

$\frac{3}{4}$; $\frac{3}{8}$; $\frac{1}{4}$; $\frac{3}{5}$; $\frac{3}{10}$; $\frac{1}{10}$; $\frac{16}{20}$

Ask a student to come to the front of the classroom and choose a fraction. Ask them to write the equivalent percentage on the piece of paper. Ask the student: *How do you know this is correct?* Then ask the student to stand in the correct place on an imaginary number line. Repeat with six other students so that when seven students are at the front the fractions are arranged in ascending order on the 'number line'.

Additional activities

You can choose any number as 'number of the week' and display it on the notice board. During the week ask students to write as many facts as they can about the number. Add these facts to the display. Encourage students to include facts about percentages and equivalent fractions.

Students can complete Workbook page 27.

Answers

Student Book page 42

Fraction	Decimal	Percentage	Percentage as an area
$\frac{1}{10}$	0.1	10%	10 squares shaded
$\frac{1}{5}$	0.2	20%	20 squares shaded
$\frac{1}{4}$	0.25	25%	25 squares shaded
$\frac{3}{10}$	0.3	30%	30 squares shaded
$\frac{2}{5}$	0.4	40%	40 squares shaded
$\frac{1}{2}$	0.5	50%	50 squares shaded
$\frac{3}{5}$	0.6	60%	60 squares shaded
$\frac{7}{10}$	0.7	70%	70 squares shaded
$\frac{3}{4}$	0.75	75%	75 squares shaded
$\frac{4}{5}$	0.8	80%	80 squares shaded
1 whole	1	100%	100 squares shaded

Workbook page 27

Answers will vary as students choose their own percentages and amounts. Check that their calculations are correct.

2 Fractions and decimals

Connect and Review

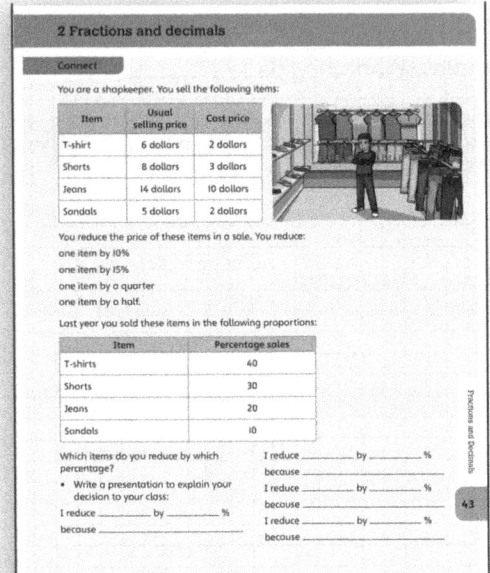

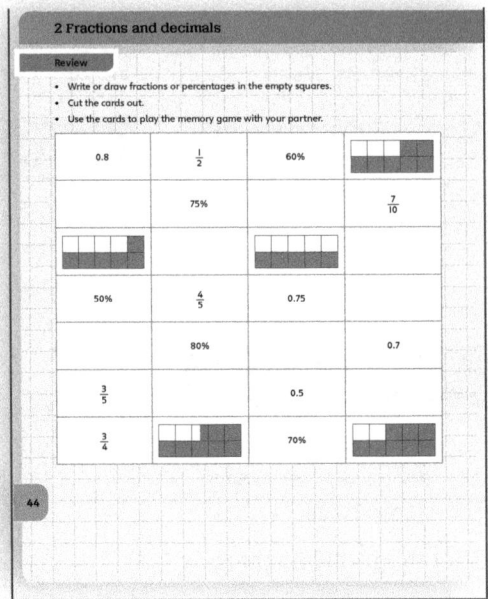

Specific learning foci

- *Find simple percentages of shapes and whole numbers.*
- Understand percentage as parts in every 100 and express $\frac{1}{2}, \frac{1}{4}, \frac{1}{5}, \frac{1}{10}, \frac{1}{100}$ as percentages.

Problem solving focus

- Solve simple word problems involving percentages.

Key vocabulary

Part, whole, equivalent fraction, simplest form, mixed number, improper fraction, numerator, denominator, half, third, quarter, three-quarters, fifth, sixth, eighth, tenth, hundredth, decimal fraction, percentage, ratio, proportion

Resources

- Assessment activity 2 (Resource sheet 2 – see www.oxfordprimary.com/OIPMteacher)

Links to Student Book

See pages 43-44 in Student Book.

Links to Workbook

Workbook page 28

Links to Digital Resource Pack

Digital Resource Pack 6 contains two activities which can be used to support students' understanding of fractions, decimals and percentages. On the home page, select 'Fractions and Decimals'.

Language support

You can use a word and phrase bank to support the presentations, for example:

- percent, percentage, %
- *'The equivalent fraction is ...'*
- *'The decimal equivalent is ...'*

 Introductory and Main activity

Ask students to work in mixed-attainment groups of about four on this activity on page 43 of the Student Book. Encourage them to interpret the problem for themselves. Avoid leading groups too much. Encourage them to reread the problem so that they understand what they need to do. Make sure that you leave plenty of time for students to plan their presentations. It is important that the presentations are well prepared. When the groups have solved the problem and prepared their presentation, ask three groups, in turn, to present their solution to the problem.

At the end of the presentations, ask the class to imagine that they are the shopkeeper and to decide which solution to the problem is the best. Encourage students to give a clear explanation. Ask: *Why do you think this solution is best?*

Differentiation

All students should work in mixed attainment groups and so engage with the group task.

Differentiated outcomes
Differentiation will be by outcome and it is expected that all students will engage in the task at their own level.

 Learning review

The Review activity is an individual summative assessment and so should be completed by students working on their own.

Additional activities

Students can look for real-life problems involving percentages and shopping, in magazines or in publicity leaflets from shops.

Students can complete Workbook page 28.

Answers

Student Book page 43
Answers will vary as students make their own choices about how to reduce the prices. Check that their calculations of percentages are correct.

Workbook page 28
1. T-shirt: $4

Jeans: $12

Trainers: $16

Socks: $1

2. a) 20 cents

b) $9

3. Yes, $24 \div 3 = 8$

4. a) $66

b) $22

c) $44

5. a) $32

b) $3.20

c) $28.80

Assessment activity 2

1. a) $\frac{6}{8}$ **b)** $\frac{30}{40}$

2. b) 0.75

3. c) 1.45, 2.46, 2.5, 2.56

4. a) $1\frac{1}{2}$

5. a) 9

6. b) 40%

7. Answers will vary as students choose their own ways to sort the fractions into two groups. Check that students have grouped the fractions correctly.

Unit 3 Mental Calculation

Overview

Big Idea

Mental calculation has a central place in this scheme. Students develop their sense of number by developing effective and efficient mental methods. This gives them confidence and ability to manipulate numbers and to draw on facts that they already know to develop new facts. Section 3C focuses specifically on techniques you can teach your students to help them derive new facts from known ones.

In order to calculate mentally, students must have clear mental images of the number system. It is important to continue to use images of the number system such as empty number lines and the 100-square. Students have become used to these images in earlier stages of the scheme. Students will also see numbers in terms of arrays (for example, 24 is 2 rows of 12 or 3 rows of 8; this shows that $2 \times 12 = 24$ or $3 \times 8 = 24$). Alternatively, they may use near multiples of 10 or near doubles to simplify a calculation. These strategies are all developed in this unit.

Possible misconceptions

As in Unit 1 you may hear students repeating misconceptions they have developed earlier: for example, that to multiply by 10 'you add a zero'. This 'rule' does not work for decimals, and Section 3A helps students overcome this misconception. Other incorrect statements that you may hear students making are 'You can't take a bigger number from a smaller one' or '6 into 38 doesn't go'. Sections 3A and 3E help you show students that these misconceptions are not true (for example, $15 - 25 = -10$ and 38 divided by 6 is 6 remainder 2, or $6\frac{1}{3}$).

Key vocabulary and language structures

Tens, hundreds, thousands place value represents, stands for; single-, two-, three-, four-digit numbers; a number with one/two decimal places number bonds to 1; near multiples of 10; addition, subtraction, multiplication, division ; sum, product, difference, divisibility (*What is the sum of …?*); divisors, remainder (*Is 15 exactly divisible by 4?*); double, halve, partition, factor, multiple; array, row, column (*How many rows are there in this array?*)

Coverage in lessons

Learning focus	Learning outcomes
Mental strategies for addition and subtraction	Can I remember number facts for numbers to 20?
	Can I use number facts for numbers to 20?
	Can I extend this to working with decimals?
	Can I add two- and three-digit numbers together mentally?
	Can I extend this to near multiples of 100 and 1000?
Mental strategies for multiplication and division	Can I multiply pairs of multiples of 10 mentally?
	Can I explain what happens with near multiples of 10?
	Can I explain the rules for knowing what times tables a number is in?
Using known facts to derive new ones	What new facts can I derive from the multiplication facts that I know already?
	Can I use my number facts up to 20 to help me calculate with numbers with one and two decimal places?
Doubling and halving	Can I quickly double and halve any two-digit number or numbers with decimal places?
	Can I use doubling and halving to help me multiply and divide?
Mental strategies for division of two-digit numbers by single-digit numbers	Can I divide two-digit numbers by a single-digit number mentally?
	Can I explain what happens when there is a remainder?
	Can I use my understanding of place value to help me multiply and divide mentally?

3 Mental Calculation

Engage

Specific learning foci

- Use place value and number facts to add or subtract two-digit whole numbers and to add or subtract three-digit multiples of 10 and pairs of decimals.
- Add/subtract near multiples of one when adding numbers with one decimal place.
- Add/subtract a near multiple of 10, 100 or 1000, or a near whole unit of money, and adjust.

Problem solving focus

- Choose appropriate and efficient mental or written strategies to carry out a calculation, involving addition, subtraction, multiplication or division.

Key vocabulary

Number pairs to 1 near multiples of 10, sum, product, difference, divisibility, divisors, remainder, double, halve, partition factor, multiple, array, row, column

Resources

None needed

Links to Student Book

See page 45 in Student Book.

Language support

Each time a student gives you an answer, whether it is correct or not, remember to ask: *How did you work that out? What strategy did you use?* Explaining their thinking helps students to develop mental calculation strategies and to develop mathematical language. Support the language students need to explain their methods, for example:

- *'The answer is …'*
- *'I worked it out by …'*

 Introductory activity

Write 28 + 17 on the whiteboard. Ask pairs of students to perform this calculation mentally. Then ask students to talk to a partner and explain the strategy they used. To help students with the necessary language you can write 'The answer is …' and 'I worked it out by …' on the board. Take feedback from the class until you have all the different strategies.

Repeat this activity with '4 × 14' and 'What is a half of 78?' On each occasion, spend time sharing the strategies until you have heard each different strategy that was used. Ask students to discuss which they think is the most efficient strategy.

 Main activity

Ask students to work in groups on each of the statements on page 45 of the Student Book in turn. One student in each group should read the question, and then everyone carries out the calculation. Then ask them to share all the strategies that they used. The order in which they do the calculations is not important. After each calculation ask the groups to agree on their most efficient method and write this down.

Differentiation

Supporting: Ask students to explain which strategies they understand so you can assess their current understanding.

Consolidating: Ask students to explain the strategy they are using. Ask if they think another student has a better strategy.

Extending: Ask students to use a range of strategies to carry out calculations and choose the most efficient.

 Learning review

Ask the groups to feedback to the class their most efficient method for each calculation. They may have used different strategies. It is important to value all the different strategies. Focus the discussion on the effectiveness of the strategies. Create a poster for each calculation to show the strategy used. You can refer to the poster throughout the unit.

Additional activities

Students can create their own questions to share with their parents and other adults at home to investigate the strategies that they used.

Discover

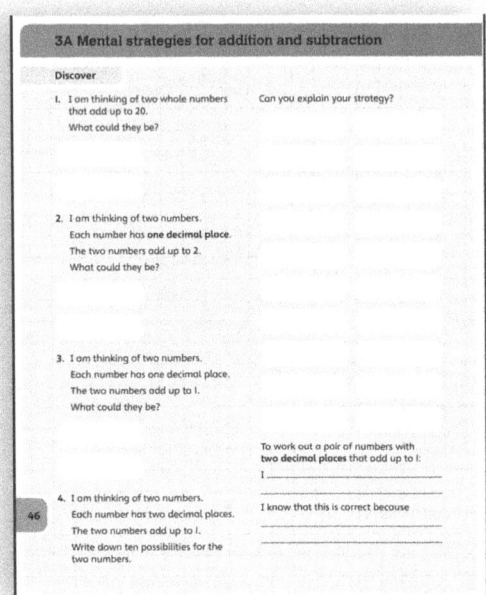

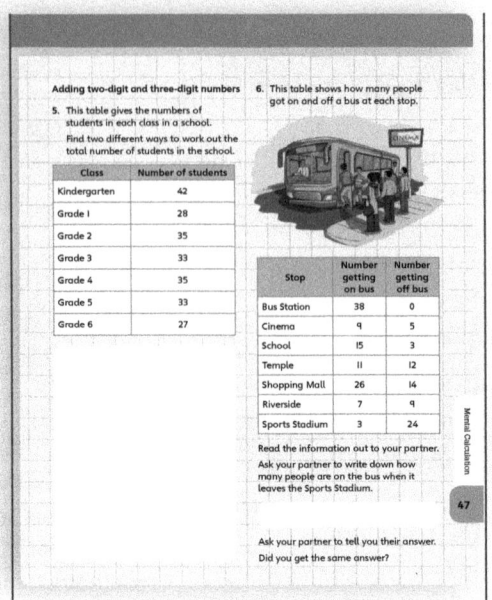

Specific learning foci

- Recall addition and subtraction facts for numbers to 20 and pairs of one-place decimals with a total of 1.
- *Derive quickly pairs of one-place decimals totalling 10.*
- Add/subtract a near multiple of 10, 100 or 1000.

Problem solving focus

- Choose appropriate and efficient mental or written strategies to carry out a calculation involving addition, subtraction, multiplication or division.

Key vocabulary

Number pairs to 1, near multiples of 10, sum, total, difference

Resources

- Mini whiteboards and markers

Links to Student Book

See pages 46–47 in Student Book.

Links to Workbook

Workbook page 30

Links to Digital Resource Pack

Digital Resource Pack 6 contains two activities which can be used to support students' understanding of mental strategies for addition and subtraction. On the home page, select 'Mental Calculation'.

Language support

Support students as they describe the strategies they are using.

Ask: *How did you work that out?* Leave thinking time, and offer prompts such as:

- *What did you do next?*
- *Why did you decide to use that strategy?*

Give each pair of students one whiteboard. Write the number 50 on the board. Give the pairs 2 minutes to write as many questions as they can with the answer 50. They can use any operation. After 2 minutes take one suggestion from each pair and record it. Next ask: *How many ways can I make 15 by adding two whole numbers?* Again, give the pairs 2 minutes to answer. This time ask one pair to report back. Ask: *How do you know you have all the possibilities?*

 Main activity

Ask students in pairs to work on the activities on pages 46 and 47 of the Student Book so they can compare answers and discuss strategies. You may need to give some students support in working with one decimal place. You can use a 0–1 number line divided into tenths to support them and remind them of the number bonds to 1 (0.1 + 0.9; 0.2 + 0.8, and so on).

As students begin to complete the sentences on page 46 of the Student Book, ask the class to share some of their strategies. The class can then move on to the second part of the activities. Ask individual students who successfully complete question 5 (adding the number of students in different classes) to share their strategies with the rest of the group. This helps all students to understand a range of strategies. Note that it is possible to complete question 5 by using mental methods, for example by finding pairs of numbers that combine to make 10.

Differentiation

Supporting: Ask students to complete questions 1–3.

Consolidating: Ask students to complete questions 1–4.

Extending: Ask students to complete questions 5 and 6 and to create their own word problems based on the numbers in question 6.

Differentiated outcomes	
All students	should successfully complete questions 1–3.
Most students	will successfully complete questions 1-4.
Some students	will successfully complete questions 5 and 6.

List the number of students in your school on the board, class by class. Ask students to work in pairs to find the total number of students in the school. Ask one student in each pair to use a calculator and the other student to calculate mentally. Do the calculation yourself in advance so that you have good grouping strategies that you can share. You can also show that you can beat the calculator.

Additional activities

You can ask students to create questions like question 6 about the bus.

Students can complete Workbook page 30.

Answers

Student Book pages 46–47

1.–4. Answers will vary. Check that students' numbers meet the requirements in the questions.

5. The total number of students is 233.

6.

Stop	Number getting on bus	Number getting off bus	Number of people on the bus
Bus Station	38	0	38
Cinema	9	5	42
School	15	3	54
Temple	11	12	53
Shopping Mall	26	14	65
Riverside	7	9	63
Sports Stadium	3	24	**42**

Workbook page 30

Check that students' strategies are appropriate. While students are working, ask them to explain why they chose the methods that they used.

- 83
- 9.5
- 10
- 1013
- 6155
- 12.6
- 3427
- 361
- 4998
- 24.5
- 497
- 84

Explore

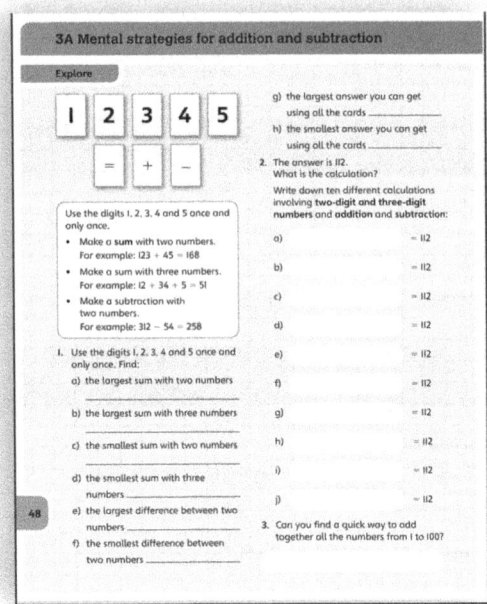

Specific learning focus

- Use place value and number facts to add or subtract two-digit whole numbers.

Problem solving focus

- Choose appropriate and efficient mental or written strategies to carry out a calculation involving addition, subtraction, multiplication or division.

Key vocabulary

Number pairs to 1, near multiples of 10, sum, total, difference

Resources

- Five cards with 1, 2, 3, 4 and + on them
- Mini whiteboards and markers

Links to Student Book

See page 48 in Student Book.

Links to Workbook

Workbook page 31

Links to Digital Resource Pack

Digital Resource Pack 6 contains two activities which can be used to support students' understanding of mental strategies for addition and subtraction. On the home page, select 'Mental Calculation'.

Language support

Support students in describing the strategies they use. Ask: *How did you work that out?*

Leave thinking time and offer prompts such as:

- *What did you do next?*
- *Why did you decide to use that strategy?*

 Introductory activity

Prepare five cards on A4 paper with 1, 2, 3, 4 and a + sign on them. Ask five students to come to the front of the class and to pick one of the cards at random. This will create either an addition of two two-digit numbers or an addition of a single-digit number and a three-digit number. Tell students to work in pairs to calculate the answer mentally, write it on their whiteboards and show you. Ask: *What is the largest possible **total**?*

 Main activity

Ask students to work on the activities on page 48 of the Student Book in pairs so they can compare answers and discuss strategies. As students are working on the first question, ask:

- *How do you know that it is the largest?*
- *Could there be a smaller answer?*

Encourage students to give you extended responses to these questions so that they are able to explain their strategies.

Differentiation

Supporting: Encourage students to find **sums** and **differences** of 2-digit and single-digit numbers and then two 2-digit numbers.

Consolidating: Ask students to describe their mental strategies.

Extending: Ask students how they know that their answers are the largest and smallest possible sums and differences.

Differentiated outcomes	
All students	should find simple totals and differences.
Most students	will find the largest possible totals and differences.
Some students	will generalise to find largest totals and differences.

 Learning review

During the Main activity 'collect' five questions with the answer 112 from the class. Ask students to check these mentally and share their strategies with the whole class.

Additional activities

You can choose a number with one or two decimal places for students to write down questions that have this number as the answer. For example: The answer is 3.5. What is the question?

Students can complete Workbook page 31.

Answers

Student Book page 48

1. a) $5432 + 1 = 5433$

   b) $543 + 2 + 1 = 546$

   c) $125 + 34 = 159$

   d) $15 + 23 + 4 = 42$

   e) $5432 - 1 = 5431$

   f) $123 - 54 = 69$

   g) $543 + 2 - 1 = 544$

   h) $1 + 2 - 543 = -540$

2. Answers will vary as students choose their own calculations with the answer 112.

Workbook page 31

Answers will vary as students make up their own calculations. Check that students' calculations do have the required answers.

Discover

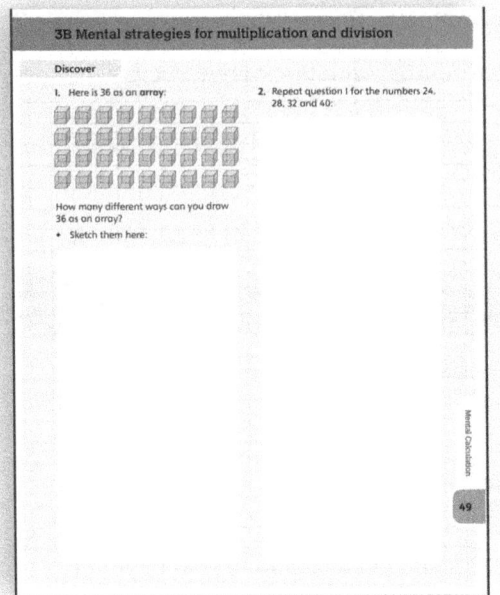

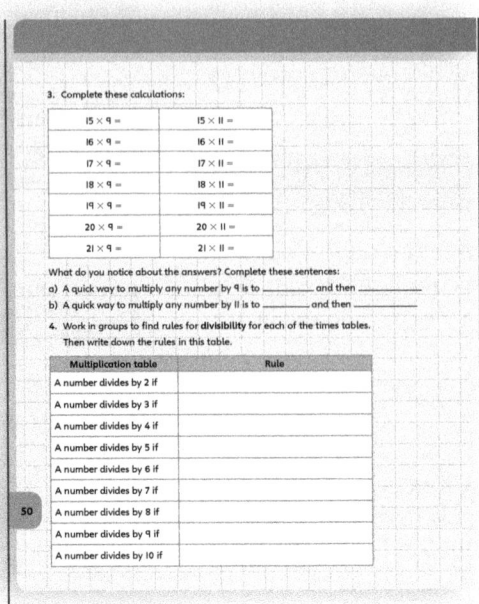

Specific learning foci

- Know and apply tests of divisibility by 2, 4, 5, 10, 25 and 100.
- *Multiply near multiples of 10 by multiplying by the multiple of 10 and adjusting.*
- Multiply pairs of multiples of 10.

Problem solving foci

- *Choose appropriate and efficient mental or written strategies to carry out a calculation involving addition, subtraction, multiplication or division.*
- Explain why they chose a particular method to perform a calculation and show working.

Key vocabulary

Product, divisibility, divisors, factor, multiple, array, row, column

Resources

- Counters
- Prepared cards labelled 25, 50, 75, 80, 100, 150, 175, 200, 210, 225, 250, 290, 300, 550

Links to Student Book

See pages 49–50 in Student Book.

Links to Workbook

Workbook page 32

Links to Digital Resource Pack

Digital Resource Pack 6 contains two activities which can be used to support students' understanding of mental strategies for multiplication and division. On the home page, select 'Mental Calculation'.

Language support

Asking students to write down the divisibility rules allows you to follow their thinking and develops their mathematical vocabulary. Students know the word 'array' from previous years. During the opening activity remind them of the vocabulary by using phrases such as:

- *This is an array.*
- *How many rows/columns?*

Other key vocabulary in this activity is: *21 and 19 are near multiples of 10.*

 Introductory activity

Give pairs of students 36 counters. Ask them to arrange the counters in different **arrays**. They should write down the dimensions of all the arrays that they make. Take feedback from the class and agree on all the possible arrays. Remind the class that the dimensions of the arrays are the **factors** of the number 36. Point out to the students that this is the first activity on page 49 of the Student Book.

 Main activity

Students work in pairs on the first activities in the Student Book. Ask students to discuss their responses to question 3. It asks them to explore strategies for multiplying near multiples of 10. Encourage students to find strategies for themselves. This helps them to see that multiplying by 10 and then adjusting the answer is the quickest strategy. (For example: $15 \times 11 = 15 \times 10 + 15 \times 1 = 165$, $15 \times 9 = 15 \times 10 - 15 \times 1 = 135$)

Ask students to work in groups on question 4. You can prompt the groups looking at 3 and 9 to look at digit sums (for example: $3 \times 6 = 18$ and $1 + 8 = 9$, which is divisible by 3). You could also split the class into small groups and ask each group to explore a different test of **divisibility**.

Language support

Asking students to write down the divisibility rules allows you to follow their thinking and develops their mathematical vocabulary. Students know the word 'array' from previous years. During the opening activity remind them of the vocabulary by using phrases such as:

● *This is an array.*   ● *How many rows/columns?*

Other key vocabulary in this activity is: *21 and 19 are near multiples of 10.*

Differentiated outcomes	
All students	should understand mental methods for multiplying near multiples of 10 with support.
Most students	will find strategies to multiply near multiples of 10.
Some students	will know the strategies to multiply near multiples of 10 and the tests of divisibility.

 Learning review

Ask each group to explain the divisibility rule they found. Tell the other students to write the rules. Draw a three-way Venn diagram on the board, with the circles labelled:

'Multiples of 10'   'Multiples of 100'   'Multiples of 25'

Ask students to come to the front one at a time. Tell each student to choose one of the prepared cards showing two-digit and three-digit numbers. Then ask them to place it in the appropriate place on the Venn diagram. Each time, ask: *Is it a multiple of 10/100/25?*

Ask students to explain their answers.

Additional activities

Students can explore the divisibility rules for numbers such as 30, 50, 75.

Students can complete Workbook page 32.

Answers

Student Book pages 49 and 50

1. 36 can be drawn as 1×36; 2×18; 3×12; 4×9 and 6×6

2. 24 can be drawn as 1×24; 2×12; 3×8 and 4×6
   28 can be drawn as 1×28; 2×14 and 4×7
   32 can be drawn as 1×32; 2×16 and 4×8
   40 can be drawn as 1×40; 2×20; 4×10 and 5×8

3.

$15 \times 9 = 135$	$15 \times 11 = 165$
$16 \times 9 = 144$	$16 \times 11 = 176$
$17 \times 9 = 153$	$17 \times 11 = 187$
$18 \times 9 = 162$	$18 \times 11 = 198$
$19 \times 9 = 171$	$19 \times 11 = 209$
$20 \times 9 = 180$	$20 \times 11 = 220$
$21 \times 9 = 189$	$21 \times 11 = 231$

A quick way to multiply by 9 is to multiply by 10 and then subtract the number you are multiplying.

A quick way to multiply by 11 is to multiply by 10 and then add the number you are multiplying.

4. Accept any answer which describes a sensible rule for divisibility.

Workbook page 32

Answers will vary as students make their own 5-digit numbers. Check that the numbers chosen match the given information and that the answers are correct.

Explore

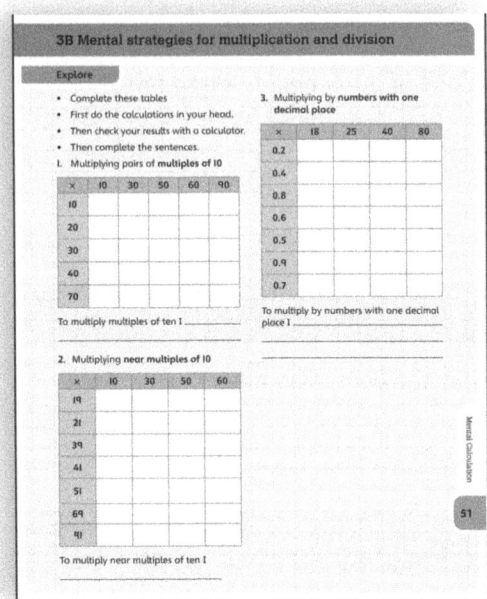

Specific learning foci

- Multiply pairs of multiples of 10.
- Multiply near multiples of 10 by multiplying by the multiple of 10 and adjusting.
- *Use place value and multiplication facts to multiply/ divide mentally, e.g. 0.8 × 7; 4.8 ÷ 6.*

Problem solving foci

- *Choose appropriate and efficient mental or written strategies to carry out a calculation, involving addition, subtraction, multiplication or division.*
- Explain why they chose a particular method to perform a calculation and show working.

Key vocabulary

Product, factor, multiple, near multiples of 10

Resources

- None needed

Links to Student Book

See page 51 in Student Book.

Links to Workbook

Workbook page 33

Links to Digital Resource Pack

Digital Resource Pack 6 contains two activities which can be used to support students' understanding of mental strategies for multiplication and division. On the home page, select 'Mental Calculation'.

Language support

Discussing in pairs helps students to develop their own mathematical vocabulary. Explaining their strategy to the class allows you to assess their understanding.

 Introductory activity

Teach this activity soon after 3B Discover. Ask students to discuss with a partner the following:

- *What strategy can you use to work out 10 × 40 or 20 × 7.2?*
- *How can you work out 31 × 30 mentally?*
- *How can you calculate 0.3 × 40 in your head?*

Group the students in mixed-attainment pairs. The more confident student should explain the strategy to the less confident student who then shares it with the rest of the class. You may need to model how to multiply **near multiples of 10** as a reminder from 3B Discover. Similarly, you may need to point out other strategies such as doubling the answer when multiplying by 30 to get the answer when you multiply by 60.

There are several examples of this sort of strategy in the activities on page 51 of the Student Book.

 Main activity

Ask students to work in pairs on the activities on page 51 of the Student Book so they can discuss the strategies they are using and check answers. You can use this activity as an assessment of prior learning.

Differentiation

Supporting: Model the strategies for multiplying by near multiples of 10 and by numbers with one decimal place.

Consolidating: Ask students to explain their strategies for multiplying by near multiples of 10 and by numbers with one decimal place.

Extending: Ask students to explain their strategies for multiplying by near multiples of 10 and by numbers with one decimal place to other students.

Differentiated outcomes	
All students	should complete the grids with support from other students.
Most students	will complete the grid independently.
Some students	will support other students in understanding the strategies.

 Learning review

During the Main activity, select students or groups who can explain their strategies clearly. Ask these students to present to the whole group as the learning review. Other students should share alternative strategies. Ask students to discuss which strategies they think are the most efficient.

Additional activities

You can ask students to write short revision notes to explain how to multiply **multiples** and near multiples of 10. Tell them to include a range of examples including decimals.

Students can complete Workbook page 33.

Answers

Student Book page 51

1.

×	10	30	50	60	90
10	100	300	500	600	900
20	200	600	1000	1200	1800
30	300	900	1500	1800	2700
40	400	1200	2000	2400	3600
70	700	2100	3500	4200	6300

2.

×	10	30	50	60
19	190	570	950	1140
21	210	630	1050	1260
39	390	1170	1950	2340
41	410	1230	2050	2460
51	510	1530	2550	3060
69	690	2070	3450	4140
91	910	2730	4550	5460

3.

×	18	25	40	80
0.2	3.6	5	8	16
0.4	7.2	10	16	32
0.8	14.4	20	32	64
0.6	10.8	15	24	48
0.5	9	12.5	20	40
0.9	16.2	22.5	36	72
0.7	12.6	17.5	28	56

Workbook page 33

1.

×	20	40	30	60	90
5	100	200	150	300	450
60	1200	2400	1800	3600	5400
70	1400	2800	2100	4200	6300
10	200	400	300	600	900
50	1000	2000	1500	3000	4500

2.

×	20	40	30	60	90
9	180	360	270	540	810
61	1220	2440	1830	3660	5490
69	1380	2760	2070	4140	6210
11	220	440	330	660	990
49	980	1960	1470	2940	4410

3.

×	16	25	50	30	60
0.4	6.4	10	20	12	24
0.8	12.8	20	40	24	48
0.2	3.2	5	10	6	12
0.5	8	12.5	25	15	30
0.3	4.8	7.5	15	9	18

Discover

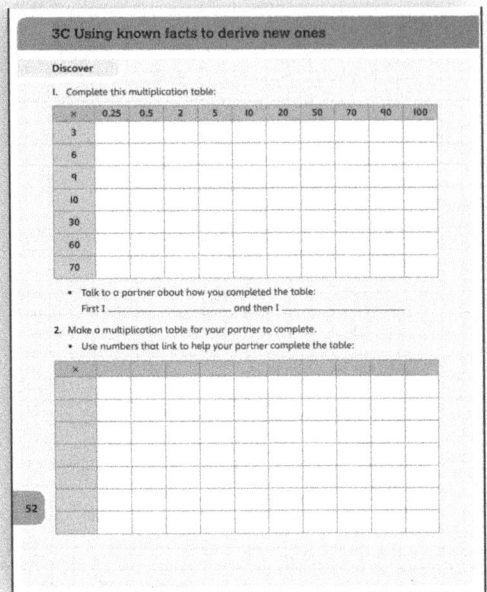
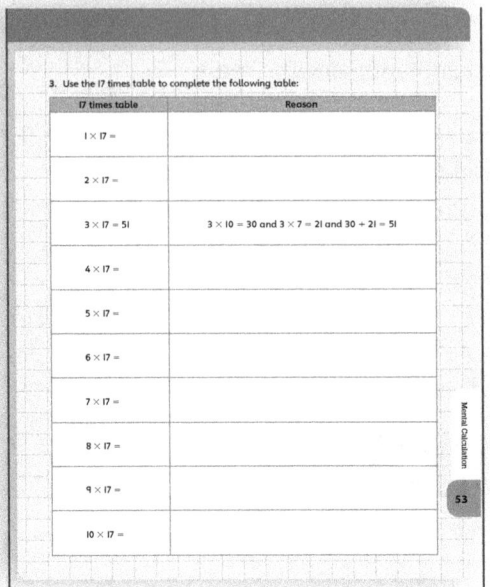

Specific learning focus

- Use place value and multiplication facts to multiply/divide mentally.

Problem solving foci

- Deduce new information from existing information and realise the effect that one piece of information has on another.
- Explain why they chose a particular method to perform a calculation and show working.

Key vocabulary

Product, factor, multiple

Resources

- Video from the internet, showing how to work out the 17 times table

Links to Student Book

See pages 52–53 in Student Book.

Links to Workbook

Workbook page 34

Links to Digital Resource Pack

Digital Resource Pack 6 contains two activities which can be used to support students' understanding of mental strategies for multiplication and division. On the home page, select 'Mental Calculation'.

Language support

Ask questions and model phrases to remind students that the product is the result of multiplication. For example:

- *What is the product of … and …?*
- *The product of … and … is …*

 Introductory activity

Write the following multiplication grid on the whiteboard.

×	7	2	4	3	8
5					
6					
3					
9					
10					

Ask students individually to copy and complete the grid. Then ask:

- *Which row or column did you start with?*
- *Which is the easiest row or column to complete?*
- *How can you use the '3' row to quickly complete the '6' row?* (by doubling)

The aim is to show students how they can use facts that they know to deduce new information.

 Main activity

Ask students to work in pairs on the activities on pages 52 and 53 of the Student Book so they can discuss the strategies they are using and check answers. Tell students to exchange their completed question 2 with a partner. Encourage students to use numbers which they know will challenge their partner but which they will be able to work out.

Differentiation

Supporting: Model the strategies to support students in completing the grids.

Consolidating: Ask students to explain their strategies for completing the grids.

Extending: Ask students to explain their strategies for completing the grids to other students.

Differentiated outcomes	
All students	should complete the grids with support from other students.
Most students	will complete the grid independently.
Some students	will support other students in understanding the strategies for completing the grids.

 Learning review

Ask the pairs to give feedback. Ask, for example: *Was it difficult to complete the multiplication grid? What new facts did you work out?*

As a whole class work on the 17× table. If possible, use a video from the internet to demonstrate this.

Share this feedback as a whole class.

Additional activities

Students can create multiplication grids to try out at home with their families.

Students can complete Workbook page 34.

Answers

Student Book pages 52 and 53

1.

×	0.25	0.5	2	5	10	20	50	70	90	100
3	0.75	1.5	6	15	30	60	150	210	270	300
6	1.5	3	12	30	60	120	300	420	540	600
9	2.25	4.5	18	45	90	180	450	630	810	900
10	2.5	5	20	50	100	200	500	700	900	1000
30	7.5	15	60	150	300	600	1500	2100	2700	3000
60	15	30	120	300	600	1200	3000	4200	5400	6000
70	17.5	35	140	350	700	1400	3500	4900	6300	7000

2. Answers will vary as students choose their own numbers for the multiplication tables. Check that the answers are correct.

3. $1 \times 17 = 17$
$2 \times 17 = 34$
$3 \times 17 = 51$
$4 \times 17 = 68$
$5 \times 17 = 85$
$6 \times 17 = 102$
$7 \times 17 = 119$
$8 \times 17 = 136$
$9 \times 17 = 153$
$10 \times 17 = 170$

Workbook page 34

Check that students' explanations for the 13 times-table are reasonable.

- 13
- 26
- 39
- 52
- 65
- 78
- 91
- 104
- 117
- 130

Check that students' explanations for the 19 times-table are reasonable.

- 19
- 38
- 57
- 76
- 95
- 114
- 133
- 152
- 171
- 190

Explore

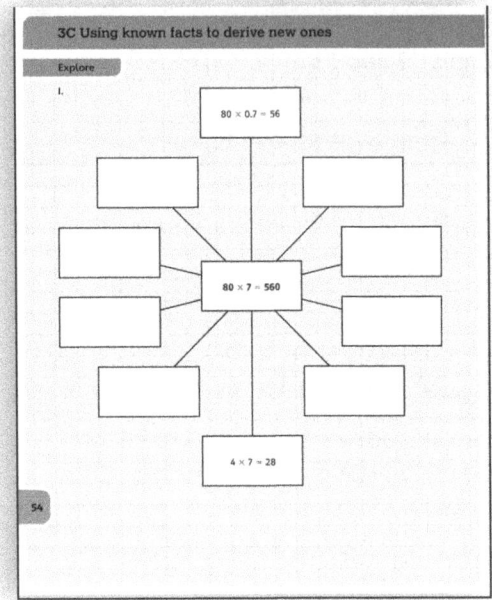
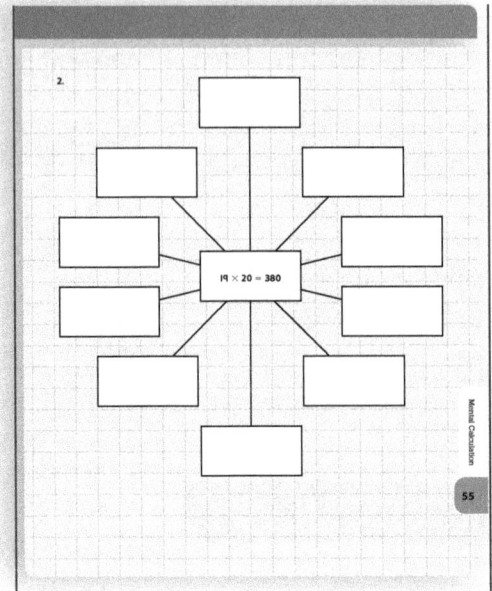

Specific learning focus

● Use place value and multiplication facts to multiply/
divide mentally.

Problem solving focus

● Deduce new information from existing information
and realise the effect that one piece of information
has on another.
● Explain why they chose a particular method to
perform a calculation and show working.

Key vocabulary

Product, factor, multiple

Resources

● None needed

Links to Student Book

See pages 54–55 in Student Book.

Links to Workbook

Workbook page 35

Links to Digital Resource Pack

Digital Resource Pack 6 contains two activities which
can be used to support students' understanding of
mental strategies for multiplication and division. On the
home page, select 'Mental Calculation'.

Language support

Asking students to explain the strategies that they are
using helps them reflect on their learning and apply
this learning in new contexts. Support students to
describe the strategies they are using. Ask: *How did you
work that out?* Leave thinking time and offer prompts,
for example:

● *What did you do next?*
● *Why did you decide to use that strategy?*

Introductory activity

Write $5 \times 8 = 40$ in the centre of the whiteboard. Ask pairs to write down as many related facts as they can in 5 minutes (for example: $5 \times 8 = 40$ so $5 \times 4 = 20$,

$5 \times 0.4 = 2.5$ $0 \times 0.4 = 20$, and so on). After 5 minutes, ask each pair to say one new fact. After each fact, ask: *How did you calculate that?*

Main activity

Ask small groups to make large copies of the spider diagrams on a large sheet of paper. They should take it in turns to add a new fact explaining to the rest of the group why they know this fact is correct. Each student should add three new facts to the diagram. When the large diagram is complete, students can select from the entries to complete the diagrams in their Student Books.

Differentiation

Supporting: Support students in adding new facts to the diagram by prompting.

Consolidating: Ask students to add a range of new facts to the diagrams explaining their thinking.

Extending: Encourage students to challenge themselves in finding new facts.

Differentiated outcomes	
All students	should add new facts to the diagram with support.
Most students	will add a range of new facts to the diagrams, explaining their thinking.
Some students	will add a wide range of new facts to the diagrams, explaining their thinking.

Learning review

Write $19 \times 20 = 380$ at the top left-hand corner of the whiteboard. Say to each student in turn: *Tell me a new fact based on the fact before*. This is to create a chain of facts all around the whiteboard. For example: $19 \times 20 = 380$ so $1.9 \times 20 = 38$ so $1.9 \times 40 = 76$, and so on.

Additional activities

You can start a new chain of facts including decimal places. For example: start with $0.5 \times 0.8 = 0.4$.

Students can complete Workbook page 35.

Answers

Student Book pages 54 and 55

Answers will vary as students derive their own facts from those given. Whilst students are working, ask them to explain how they know each fact. What facts and strategies are they using to help them?

Workbook page 35

Answers will vary as students derive their own facts from those given. Ask students to explain how place value can help them to derive new facts from known facts.

3D Doubling and halving

Discover

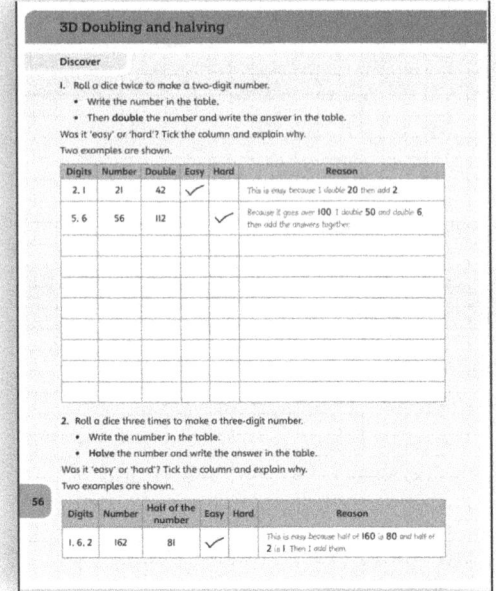
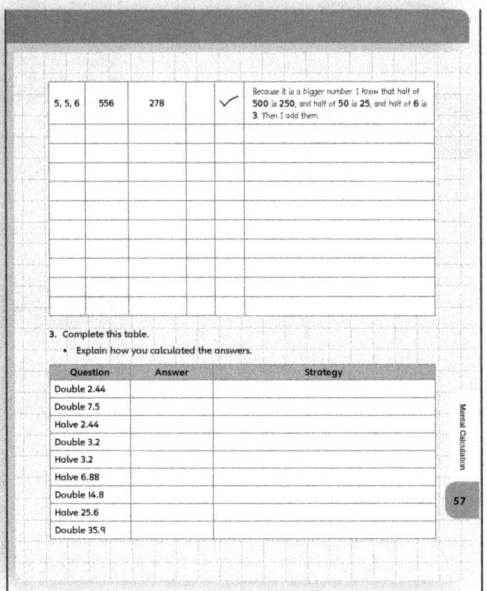

Specific learning focus

- Double quickly any two-digit number, e.g. 78, 7.8, 0.78, and derive the corresponding halves.

Problem solving foci

- Explain why they chose a particular method to perform a calculation and show working.
- *Deduce new information from existing information and realise the effect that one piece of information has on another.*

Key vocabulary

Double, halve, partition

Resources

- Dice
- Mini whiteboards and markers

Links to Student Book

See pages 56–57 in Student Book.

Links to Workbook

Workbook page 36

Language support

Make links between doubling and halving, for example:

- *Double 58 is 116. What is half of 116?*

Continue to ask: *How did you calculate that?*

Introductory activity

Write the following numbers on the board:

28, 32, 15, 39, 62, 50, 20, 78

Read out each number in turn and ask pairs of students to decide: Is it 'easy' to **double** or 'hard' to double? Ask students to justify their choice. They might say 20 is easy because it is a multiple of 10, or 78 is hard because the answer is over 100 so you must **partition** 78 into 70 and 8.

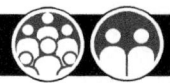 Main activity

Ask students to complete the activities in the Student Book individually, but then encourage students to share their strategies in pairs. Take note of the students who are confident in explaining their strategies. They can help you in the learning review. Questions 2 and 3 are extension material which will support students as they develop methods for adding and subtracting 3-digit numbers.

Differentiation

Supporting: Ask students to complete question 1 and describe their strategy to you. Prompt them to support them.

Consolidating: Ask students to complete question 1 and explain their strategy to you. How do they know the answer is correct?

Extending: Ask students to complete questions 2 and 3.

Differentiated outcomes	
All students	should complete question 1 and describe their strategy with support.
Most students	will complete questions 1 and write down their strategy.
Some students	will complete questions 2 and 3.

 Learning review

Repeat each of the activities on pages 56 and 57 of the Student Book as a whole-class activity using individual whiteboards so that you can assess students' understanding. Roll a dice twice to create a two-digit number. Ask students to write their answer on their whiteboard. Wait 5 seconds and then ask all of the group to show you their answer. Select confident students to explain their strategy. Repeat to create a three-digit number to **halve**, and a three-digit number with one decimal place to double.

Additional activities

You can ask students to explore this problem: *I have one cent on Monday, on Tuesday I have two cents, on Wednesday I have four cents, and so on. How much money do I have after one week? After a month? After how long before I have one million dollars?*

Students can complete Workbook page 36.

Answers

Student Book pages 56 and 57

1. and **2.** Answers will vary as students use dice to make their own two-digit and three-digit numbers. Check that the doubles and halves are correct.

3. Check that the strategies listed are appropriate and efficient.

Question	Answer
Double 2.44	4.88
Double 7.5	15
Halve 2.44	1.22
Double 3.2	6.4
Halve 3.2	1.6
Halve 6.88	3.44
Double 14.8	29.6
Halve 25.6	12.8
Double 35.9	71.8

Workbook page 36

Answers will vary as students use digit cards to make their own 2-digit numbers. Check that the doubles have been calculated correctly.

3D Doubling and halving

Explore

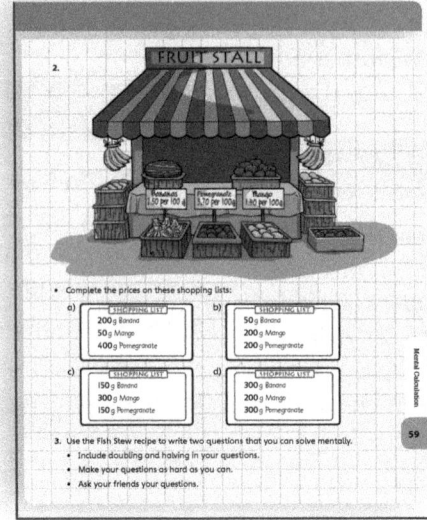

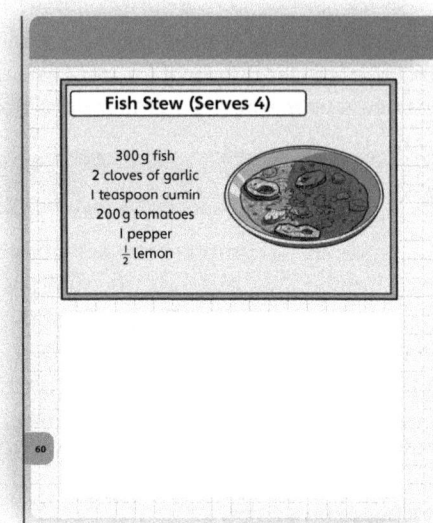

Specific learning focus

- Double quickly any two-digit number, e.g. 78, 7.8, 0.78, and derive the corresponding halves.

Problem solving foci

- Explain why they chose a particular method to perform a calculation and show working.
- Deduce new information from existing information and realise the effect that one piece of information has on another.
- *Solve simple word problems.*

Key vocabulary

Double, halve, partition

Resources

- Dice
- Mini whiteboards and markers

Links to Student Book

See pages 58–60 in Student Book.

Links to Workbook

Workbook page 37

Language support

Continue to make links between doubling and halving, for example:

- *Double 78 is 156. What is half of 156?*
- *How did you calculate that?*

 Introductory and Main activity

Arrange the students in pairs or small groups, and encourage them to explore the word problems on pages 58–60 of the Student Book without any introduction. The more confident students should support the less confident, explaining the strategies they are using. Focus your attention on the less confident students asking them to explain the strategies to you. They can use the strategies from the previous activity immediately. After students complete question 1, bring the class together. Select one pair and write their own question up on the board. Ask the other students to solve the problem in pairs. Ask one pair to explain their strategy. Ask the pair who set the question to check the answer and suggest any alternative strategies.

Students can then complete the rest of the activities in the Student Book.

Differentiation

Supporting: support the students using practical materials.

Consolidating: ask students to explain their strategies to other students so that they understand how to double and halve these numbers.

Extending: Encourage students to create complex word problems of their own.

Differentiated outcomes	
All students	should solve the problems with support.
Most students	will support other students who are less confident.
Some students	will create complex word problems of their own and explain how to calculate the answers.

 Learning review

Ask two different pairs to share the problems they asked using the recipe card (question 3).

Additional activities

Students can use recipes that their family uses at home to invent problems for their friends to solve. Encourage students to invent problems that involve doubling and halving. Students must be able to solve their problems themselves.

Students can complete Workbook page 37.

Answers

Student Book pages 58–60
1. a) $66
   b) $84
   c) $28.50
2. a) 200 g banana = $5; 50 g mango = $0.70; 400 g pomegranate = $14.80
   b) 50 g banana = $1.25; 200 g mango = $2.80; 200 g pomegranate = $7.40
   c) 150 g banana = $3.75; 300 g mango = $4.20; 150 g pomegranate = $5.55
   d) 300 g banana = $7.50; 200 g mango = $2.80; 300 g pomegranate = $11.10
3. Answers will vary as students write their own word questions about the Fish Stew recipe. Check that the answers are correct.

Workbook page 37
1. 8 bananas = $3; 1 mango = $0.40; 3 tomatoes = $1.05; 1 pack of grapes = $0.62
2. 2 bananas = $0.75; 2 mangos = $0.80; 6 tomatoes = $2.10; 4 packs of grapes = $4.48
3. 4 bananas = $1.50; 4 mangos = $1.60; 3 tomatoes = $1.05; 4 packs of grapes = $4.48

Total cost = $9.58

3E Mental strategies for the division of two-digit numbers by single-digit numbers

Discover

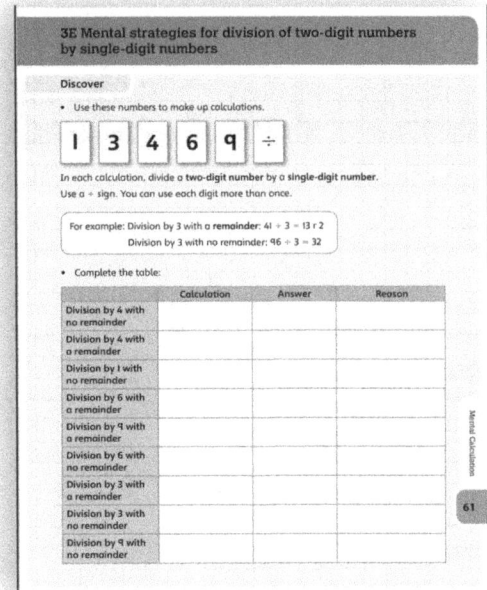

Specific learning focus

- Divide two-digit numbers by single-digit numbers, including leaving a remainder.

Problem solving foci

- Explain why they chose a particular method to perform a calculation and show working.
- *Make, test and refine hypotheses, explain and justify methods, reasoning, strategies, results or conclusions orally.*

Key vocabulary

Divisibility, divisors, divides exactly, remainder, factor, multiple

Resources

- Mini whiteboards and markers

Links to Student Book

See page 61 in Student Book.

Links to Workbook

Workbook page 32

Language support

Ask questions, for example:

- *Does that question leave a remainder?*
- *How do you know?*
- *Does that number divide exactly?*
- Remind students that 36 divides exactly by 12. Say: *12 is a factor of 36.*

 Introductory activity

Ask pairs of students to write the following table on a whiteboard:

36 **divides exactly** by	There is a **remainder** when you divide by

Write the number 36 on the main whiteboard. Ask students to complete the table for 36, with the numbers 1 to 18, for example:

36 Divides exactly by	There is a remainder when you divide by
1, 2, 3, 4, 6, 9, 12, 18	5, 7, 8, 10, 11, 13, 14, 15, 16, 17

Each pair should complete two sentences:

'36 divides by... exactly.' 'There is a remainder of... if you divide 36 by....'

Take feedback from the pairs. Write the corresponding number sentence on the board. For example, if a pair writes *'36 divides by 9 exactly',* then write:

$36 \div 9 = 4$

If they write *'There is a remainder of 3 if you divide 36 by 11',* then write:

$36 \div 11 = 3 \, r \, 3$

 Main activity

Ask students individually to complete the activity on page 61 of the Student Book. As they complete the task encourage them to discuss their reasoning with one another. You may wish to support some students by giving them counters or cubes so that they can divide them into equal groups and equal groups with 'left-overs' or remainders. Encourage other students to draw images to help them.

Differentiation

Supporting: Give student practical materials and model how to use them.

Consolidating: Encourage students to use sketches to illustrate some answers.

Extending: Encourage students to complete the table using their knowledge of division facts and factors.

Differentiated outcomes	
All students	should complete table with teacher support and practical materials.
Most students	will complete table practical materials or sketches.
Some students	will complete the table, using their knowledge of division facts and factors.

 Learning review

Ask students to discuss with a partner:

- *'What did you learn in the activity today?'*
- *'Today I learnt that ...'*

Then take feedback from pairs to the whole class. Note the most important points. Students can use these in the next lesson.

Additional activities

You can ask students to create division tables for all the numbers from 1 to 50 as in the Introductory activity.

Students can complete Workbook page 32.

Answers

Student Book page 61

Answers will vary as students use the given digits to two-digit and one-digit numbers. Check that the calculations are correct and match the information in the table.

Workbook page 32

Answers will vary as students make their own 5-digit numbers. Check that the numbers chosen match the given information and that the answers are correct.

Explore

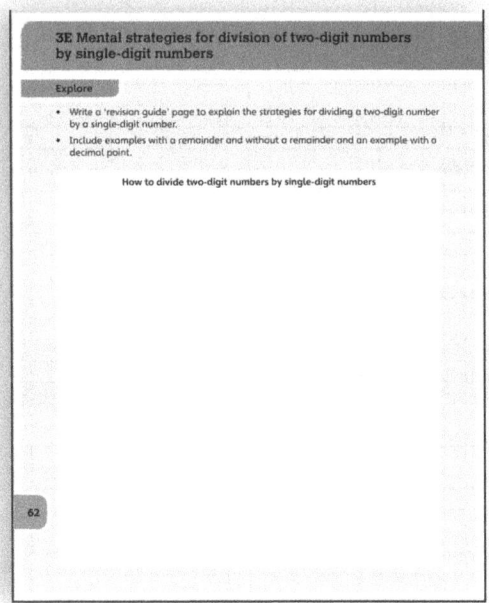

Specific learning focus

- Divide two-digit numbers by single-digit numbers, including leaving a remainder.

Problem solving foci

- Explain why they chose a particular method to perform a calculation and show working.
- *Make, test and refine hypotheses, explain and justify methods, reasoning, strategies, results or conclusions orally.*

Key vocabulary

Divisibility, divisors, divides exactly, remainder, factor, multiple

Resources

- Mini whiteboards and markers

Links to Student Book

See page 62 in Student Book.

Links to Workbook

Workbook page 30

Language support

The small group discussion will support language learners as they will hear the key vocabulary modelled by more confident English speakers. You may wish to support them in writing their own guide. Encourage them to read the guide aloud to you.

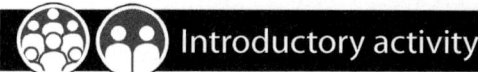 Introductory activity

Ask students to discuss in pairs: *What features does a 'good revision guide' have?* Ask them to write a list of features in pairs. Use examples of revision guides you use in the class to help them. Features may include:

- Important vocabulary with definitions
- Worked examples
- Examples for us to try with answers and so on.

List the features on the whiteboard. This gives students a framework to use in the following activities.

 Main activity

Ask students to work in small mixed-attainment groups to write notes and develop a draft of a revision guide. Then ask students to create their own revision guide from these notes.

Differentiation

Students work in mixed-attainment groups. Differentiation will be through the discussion process and in the individual outcomes.

Differentiated outcomes
All students will contribute to the discussion about developing a revision guide and will have input into the draft revision guide. More confident students will model for less confident students how to put the guide together. All students will benefit from this discussion and will develop their understanding through writing their own guide.

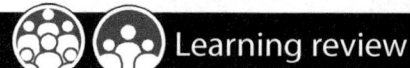 Learning review

Ask groups to exchange their revision guides. They can assess other groups' revision guides. Encourage students to use the criteria that you listed in the Introductory activity. Ask each group to write down two positive points and one area that needs to be developed.

Additional activities

Students can take the revision guide home and use it with their parents.

Students can complete Workbook page 33.

Answers

Student Book page 62

Answers will vary as students write their own revision guides. Check that the statements that students write are correct.

Workbook page 33

1.

×	20	40	30	60	90
5	100	200	150	300	450
60	1200	2400	1800	3600	5400
70	1400	2800	2100	4200	6300
10	200	400	300	600	900
50	1000	2000	1500	3000	4500

2.

×	20	40	30	60	90
9	180	360	270	540	810
61	1220	2440	1830	3660	5490
69	1380	2760	2070	4140	6210
11	220	440	330	660	990
49	980	1960	1470	2940	4410

3.

×	16	25	50	30	60
0.4	6.4	10	20	12	24
0.8	12.8	20	40	24	48
0.2	3.2	5	10	6	12
0.5	8	12.5	25	15	30
0.3	4.8	7.5	15	9	18

3F Adding and subtracting near multiples

Discover

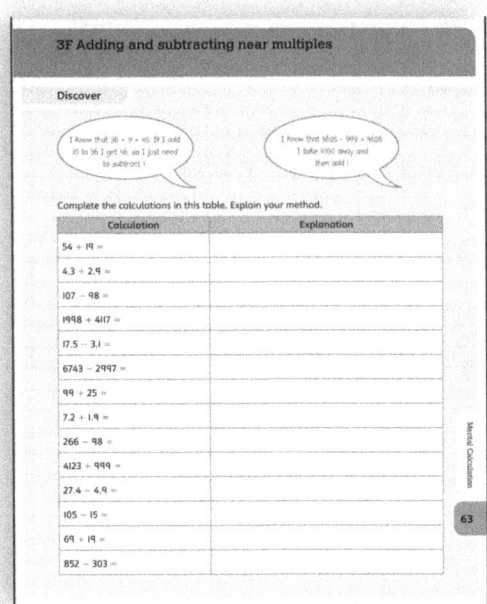

Specific learning foci

- Add/subtract a near multiple of 10, 100 or 1000, or a near whole unit of money, and adjust.
- Add/subtract near multiples of 1 when adding numbers with 1 decimal place.

Problem solving focus

- Explain why they chose a particular method to perform a calculation and show working.

Key vocabulary

Near multiples of $\dfrac{10}{1}$, sum, difference

Resources

- Mini whiteboards and markers

Links to Student Book

See page 62 in Student Book.

Links to Workbook

Workbook page 30

Links to Digital Resource Pack

Digital Resource Pack 6 contains two activities which can be used to support students. On the home page, select 'Mental Calculation'.

Language support

It is important that students get used to describing their strategies. Sometimes students will find it easier to do this in their first language. If they find it difficult to describe the strategy in English, ask them to use their first language and support them in translating this into English.

 Introductory activity

Write 199 + 345 = on the board. The students should work in pairs. One of the pair should give the answer to their partner and explain how they know that this is the answer. They can use mini whiteboards if necessary. Take feedback from one of the pairs. Listen for individuals who can describe their strategy well. Repeat for 3723 − 1998 and 7.2 + 5.9. Students should alternate roles.

 Main activity

The students work in the same pairs to complete the activity on page 63 of the Student Book. One student carries out the calculation – the other one checks it. They then each describe their strategy before they write it in the table. The best strategy for some of the examples may be counting on. You should also accept any effective mental method. Discuss the most efficient methods with pairs of students. It may be appropriate to introduce to model the calculations with a number line or to show students how to adjust the answer of you round to the nearest 10, 100 or 1000 before calculating.

For example: 54 + 19 is the same as (54 + 20) − 1

Differentiation

Supporting: You may choose to work with a small group to model the strategy of rounding and adjusting.

Consolidating: Ask students to carry out the calculations and explain their strategies.

Extending: Ask students why they think their strategy is the most efficient.

Differentiated outcomes	
All students	should carry out the calculations with support.
Most students	will carry out the calculations and explain their strategies.
Some students	will carry out the calculations and use the most efficient strategy.

 Learning review

One of each pair should set a calculation for their partner to carry out. This should be a calculation similar to those on page 63 of the Student Book. Repeat this four times. Select two examples for the whole class to carry out. For each calculation make sure the students explain their strategy carefully.

Additional activities

Students can write word problems involving near multiples that can be solved by the strategies used in the Main activity. They should use real-life contexts such as money or measurements.

Students can complete Workbook page 30.

Answers

Student Book page 63

Students provide their own explanations for the calculations.

Calculation
54 + 19 = 73
4.3 + 2.9 = 7.2
107 − 98 = 9
1998 + 4117 = 6115
17.5 − 3.1 = 14.4
6743 − 2997 = 3746
99 + 25 = 124
7.2 + 1.9 = 9.1
266 − 98 = 168
4123 + 999 = 5122
27.4 − 4.9 = 22.5
105 − 15 = 90
69 + 19 = 88
852 − 303 = 549

Workbook page 30

Check that students' strategies are appropriate. While students are working, ask them to explain why they chose the methods that they used.

- 83
- 9.5
- 10
- 1013
- 6155
- 12.6
- 3427
- 361
- 4998
- 24.5
- 497
- 84

Explore

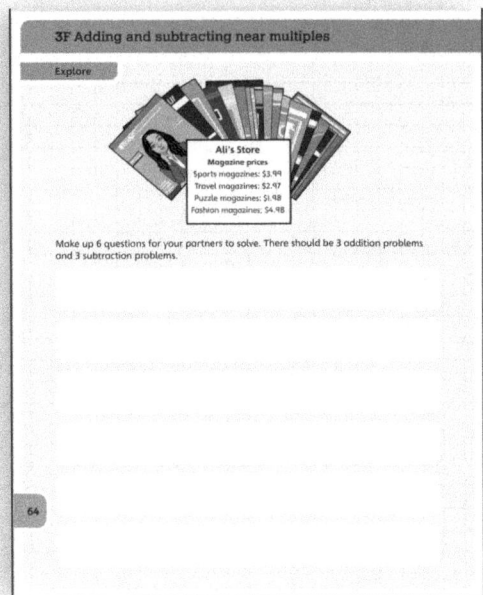

Specific learning foci

- Add/subtract a near multiple of 10, 100 or 1000, or a near whole unit of money, and adjust.
- Add/subtract near multiples of 1 when adding numbers with one decimal place.

Problem solving focus

- Explain why they chose a particular method to perform a calculation and show working.

Key vocabulary

Near multiples of $\frac{10}{1}$, sum, difference

Resources

- Mini whiteboards and markers

Links to Student Book

See page 64 in Student Book.

Links to Workbook

Workbook page 31

Language support

As with the previous activity, it is important that students get used to describing the strategies they are using. It may be more effective for them to do this in their first language. If they find it difficult to describe the strategy in English, ask them to use their first language and support them in translating this into English.

 Introductory activity

Ask students to open the Student Book at page 64. Give out the mini whiteboards so that the students have one each. Ask the question: *I buy a sports magazine and a puzzle magazine. How much do I spend?*

Give the students time to carry out the calculation in a pair. Ask pairs to hold up their mini whiteboards so you can see the answer. Select one of the students to describe the strategy that they used. If any of the students have made an error ask them to talk through their calculation so that they can find their mistake. Repeat with the question:

I go to the shops with $23.55 and buy a fashion magazine. How much do I have left?

 Main activity

The students should work in pairs and take it in turns to set one another word problems to solve. They only write the problem down when they have both carried out the calculation and can describe the strategy that they have used. As the students work on the activity, visit the pairs and collect a range of examples to use for the Learning review.

Differentiation

Supporting: Ask students to create questions to you so you can model how to solve them.

Consolidating: Encourage students to challenge themselves with the problems they create.

Extending: Encourage students to create two- and three-step problems.

Differentiated outcomes	
All students	should create simple problems.
Most students	will create more complex problems.
Some students	will create two- and three-step problems.

 Learning review

Ask one of the students to come to the front and set the class one of their problems. (Draw on someone that you have chosen during the main activity.) The students should solve this in pairs and tell the student who set the problem how they carried out the calculation. Repeat with a range of problems that you have seen.

Additional activities

Students should visit shops and set word problems using real prices from the shops. They can set these for one another to solve or use them with family members.

Students can complete Workbook page 31.

Answers

Student Book page 64

Answers will vary as students make up their own addition and subtraction problems. Check that the students' answers are correct.

Workbook page 31

Answers will vary as students make up their own calculations. Check that students' calculations do have the required answers.

3 Mental calculation

Connect and Review

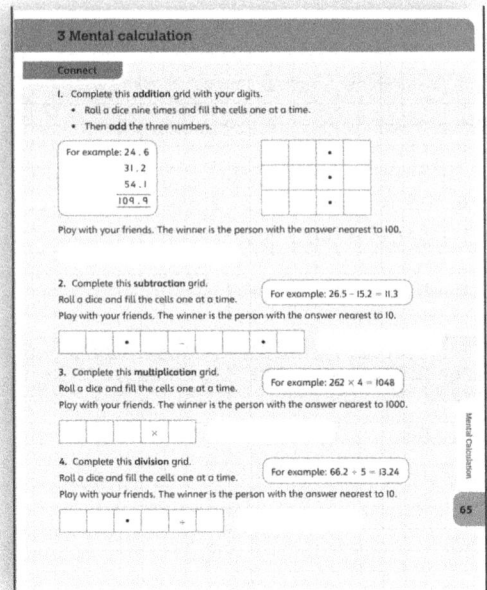

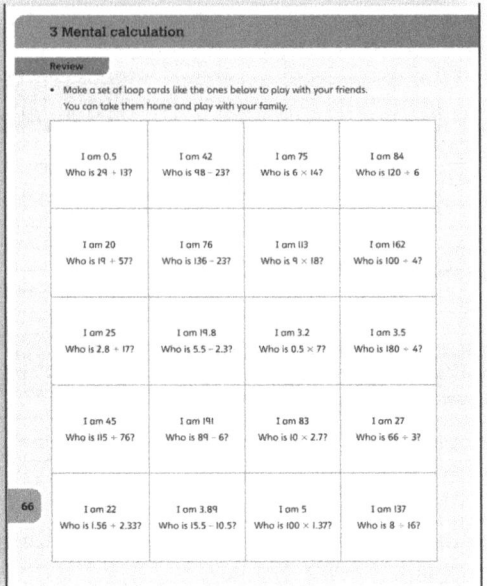

Specific learning foci

- Use place value and number facts to add or subtract two-digit whole numbers and to add or subtract three-digit multiples of 10 and pairs of decimals.
- Use place value and multiplication facts to multiply/ divide mentally.

Problem solving focus

- Choose appropriate and efficient mental or written strategies to carry out a calculation, involving addition, subtraction, multiplication or division.

Key vocabulary

Number pairs to 1 near multiples of 10, sum, product, difference, divisibility, divisors, remainder, double, halve, partition factor, multiple, array, row, column

Resources

- Mini whiteboards and markers
- Assessment activity 3 (Resource sheet 3 – see www. oxfordprimary.com/OIPMteacher)

Links to Student Book

See pages 65–66 in Student Book.

Links to Workbook

Workbook page 38

Links to Digital Resource Pack

Digital Resource Pack 6 contains two activities which can be used to support students' understanding of mental strategies for the four operations. On the home page, select 'Mental Calculation'.

Language support

Use the vocabulary of place value, for example:

- *What is the value of that digit?*
- *What does that digit represent?*
- *Tens, hundreds, thousands, tenths*

Ask, for example: *Why did you place that digit there?*

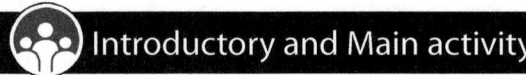
Introductory and Main activity

Copy the grid for question 1 on page 65 of the Student Book onto the whiteboard. Divide the class into mixed-attainment groups of four or five students. Ask the class to play this game against one another. Roll the dice. Ask the groups to decide where to place the digit. They must place a digit after each roll of the dice. After a digit is placed they cannot move it. After nine rolls of the dice the groups add up their totals. The winner is the group with the answer nearest to 100. Ask the class: *What strategy did you use?* Play this game and the other games on page 65 of the Student Book as many times as you think useful.

Ask the class to play against one another in groups of four or five students taking it in turns to roll the dice. Play one of the games with each group. Note the strategies that students use both to place the digits and to carry out the calculations.

Copy the grid for question 2 on page 65 of the Student Book onto the board. Roll a dice six times. Write down the result each time. Ask the groups to work out where to place the digits to give (a) the best possible result, (b) the worst possible result.

Differentiation

Students should work in mixed attainment groups to support one another in playing the game.

Differentiated outcomes
This is an activity designed to offer differentiation by outcome.

Learning review

Students should complete the Review activity as individuals as it is a summative assessment. You may want to help write the answers for those less confident with writing or in speaking English.

Additional activities

Students can play these games with their family at home.

Students can complete Workbook page 38.

Answers

Student Book page 65

Answers will vary as students use digit cards to make the numbers for the calculations. Check that students' answers are correct.

Workbook page 38

Answers will vary as students choose their own calculations to match given statements. Check that the calculations are correct and do meet the requirements of the questions.

Assessment activity 3

1. **c)** 700 000
2. **b)** $117
3. **c)** $7.50
4. **a)** $22.53
5. **b)** 16 700
6. **a)** 2871
7. **b)** $8.50
8. **c)** 64
9. and **10.** Accept any accurate methods.

Unit 4 Addition and Subtraction

Overview

Big Idea

The Big Idea in this unit is moving from informal written methods to a formal written method. It is also important that students can make decisions about when to use a formal algorithm and when to use mental methods. Students should use mental methods as a first option. They should only rely on formal written methods when mental methods are inappropriate. The 'number sense' that they have developed through using these materials will support them. Students should be able to estimate the answer to a calculation before applying an algorithm. This helps them to know that the answer they get is 'sensible'.

Students should be able to partition to support them in understanding 'column addition and subtraction'.

For example, they should know that:

$$
\begin{array}{rcl}
39 &=& 30 + 9 \\
+52 &=& 50 + 2 \\
\hline
\mathbf{91} &=& \mathbf{80 + 11}
\end{array}
$$

Possible misconceptions

You may see students using algorithms incorrectly because they don't remember rules.

For example, a student may write:

$$
\begin{array}{r}
85 \\
-48 \\
\hline
\mathbf{43}
\end{array}
$$
   This is not correct.

They remember a teacher saying 'you can't take a bigger number from a smaller number' or 'you always take the smaller number from the bigger number' so they subtract 5 from 8. It is important that you ask students: *What method did you use?* This helps you to correct misconceptions such as this.

Key vocabulary and language structures

Place value: units, tens, hundreds, thousands, tenths, hundredths, decimal point; stands for, represents; number bonds, partition; positive, negative, directed numbers, above/ below zero; addition, subtraction, operation; tens boundary, hundreds boundary

Coverage in lessons

Learning focus	Learning outcomes
Adding and subtracting three-digit numbers	Can I add two- and three-digit numbers with the same or different numbers of digits/decimal places?
Adding and subtracting money	Can I add two- and three-digit numbers with the same or different numbers of digits/decimal places involving money?
Using negative numbers	Can I find the difference between a positive and a negative integer and between two integers in a context?

4 Addition and Subtraction

Engage

Specific learning focus

- Add two- and three-digit numbers with the same or different numbers of digits.

Problem solving focus

- Choose appropriate and efficient mental or written strategies to carry out a calculation involving addition, subtraction.

Key vocabulary

Place value: ones, tens, hundreds, thousands, tens boundary, ones boundary

Resources

- None needed

Links to Student Book

See page 67 in Student Book.

Language support

Support students with the language:

- Ask questions, for example: *Does that move across the 'tens boundary' / 'hundreds boundary'?*
- Use the language of place value accurately: *'carry tens'* or *'carry hundreds'* as appropriate.
- Do not always refer to *'carry 1'*.

Introductory and Main activity

Ask students initially to work in mixed-attainment groups of about four with no help on the problem on page 67 of the Student Book. After 5 minutes ask: *What method are you using to solve the problem?* Make sure students understand that:

- each letter stands for a different digit – so O, N and E are all different digits
- a letter always represents the same digit – so 'O' is the same digit in each row of the addition.

Ask questions to ensure that students understand the principle of 'carrying' over the **tens boundary** and **hundreds boundary**. Encourage the use of mental methods for the simple number bonds. When they have completed this activity, ask the pairs to create a similar

problem for other pairs to solve. Encourage them to use repeated letters in the words that they are adding. They can also include decimals. Encourage them to develop their problems to include examples that are subtractions. It is easier to set a calculation using numbers and change it to letters rather than the other way around.

Differentiation

All students are expected to engage in the activity and will draw on their current understanding of addition and subtraction as well as place value to contribute to the discussion.

This is an introductory activity to the unit, so use it to carry out assessments of students' current understanding to inform your teaching throughout the rest of the unit.

Learning review

Ask a group who successfully solved the problem to share their strategy with the rest of the class. Then choose one of the problems which has been set by a pair of students for the whole class to solve.

Additional activities

Students can create more complex problems of this type: for example, adding 4-digit and three-digit numbers, or working with two places of decimals.

Answers

Student Book page 67

One possible answer is

$$
\begin{array}{r}
382 \\
+\ 974 \\
\hline
1356
\end{array}
$$

Discover

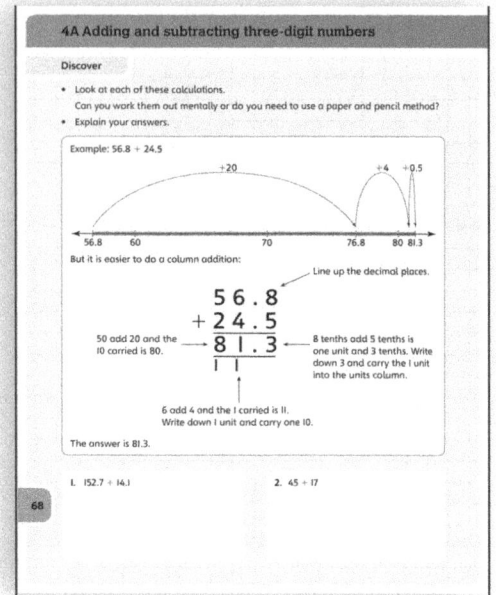

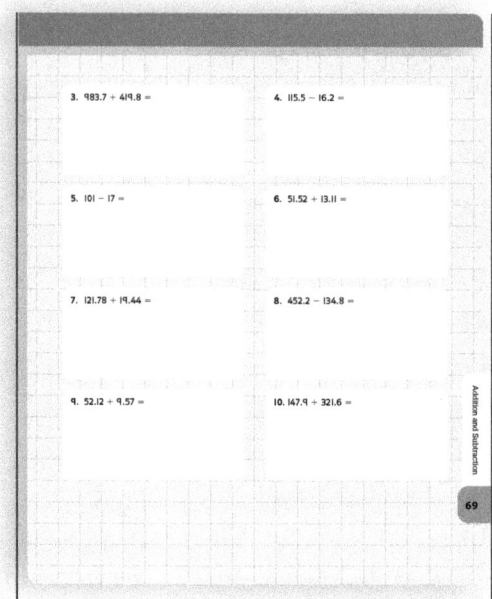

Specific learning foci

- Add two- and three-digit numbers with the same or different numbers of digits.
- *Add or subtract numbers with the same and different numbers of decimal places.*

Problem solving focus

- Choose appropriate and efficient mental or written strategies to carry out a calculation involving addition, subtraction.

Key vocabulary

Place value: ones, tens, hundreds, thousands, tenths, hundredths, decimal point

Resources

- Mini whiteboards and markers

Links to Student Book

See pages 68–69 in Student Book.

Links to Workbook

Workbook page 40

Links to Digital Resource Pack

Digital Resource Pack 6 contains two activities which can be used to support students' use of column addition and subtraction when calculating. On the home page, select 'Addition and Subtraction'.

Language support

Listen to students as they explain the strategies they used for deciding if to calculate mentally or using a written method. This allows you to understand if they are making effective choices. Use the language of place value accurately: '*carry*' tens or *carry hundreds* as appropriate. Do not always refer to 'carry one'. This is modelled in the example on page 68 of the Student Book.

Write '86.7 + 35.4' on the whiteboard. Ask pairs to calculate the addition mentally and write the answer down. Ask:

- *What mental strategy did you use?*
- *Which digits did you add first?*
- *How did you partition the numbers?*

Ask students to calculate the addition using an empty number line on their whiteboards. Ask a student to illustrate this method to the rest of the class.

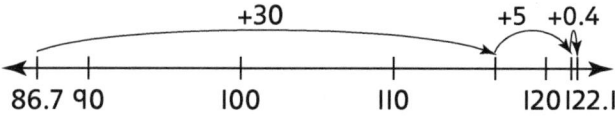

Now illustrate the calculation using a column method. Model the key vocabulary as shown on page 68 of the Student Book.

 Main activity

Ask students to work individually on the questions on pages 68 and 69 of the Student Book. Then ask them to check their answers with those of a partner to check that they agree on the correct answers. Ask students to work in pairs to find the errors in any incorrect answers. Notice any common errors so that you can use these as teaching points in the review.

Differentiation

Supporting: You may choose to group less confident learners together so you can model the written method.

Consolidating: Encourage students to look back at calculations to correct any errors.

Extending: Encourage students to estimate before carrying out the calculations.

Differentiated outcomes	
All students	should carry out calculations with support.
Most students	will carry out the calculations spotting and correcting errors.
Some students	will estimate first so they can check the reasonableness of their answers.

Use the first part of the Learning review to deal with any common errors. Write an incorrect calculation that you noticed during the Main activity on the board. Ask students to find the error in the calculation and explain how to correct it.

Then ask students to discuss in pairs: *Which questions did you calculate mentally? Which questions did you use a written method for?* Encourage students to explain carefully how they made their choices.

Additional activities

Students can write calculations for one another. They can then challenge one another to see if they can calculate more quickly using a mental method or a written method.

Students can complete Workbook page 40.

Answers

Student Book pages 68 and 69

1. $152.7 + 14.1 = 166.8$
2. $45 + 17 = 62$
3. $983.7 + 419.8 = 1403.5$
4. $115.5 - 16.2 = 99.3$
5. $101 - 17 = 84$
6. $51.52 + 13.11 = 64.63$
7. $121.78 + 19.44 = 141.22$
8. $452.2 - 134.8 = 317.4$
9. $52.12 + 9.57 = 61.69$
10. $147.9 + 321.6 = 469.5$

Workbook page 40

203.9	444
101.3	1391
908	338.8
1155	54.1
9.7	155.63

4A Adding and subtracting three-digit numbers

Explore

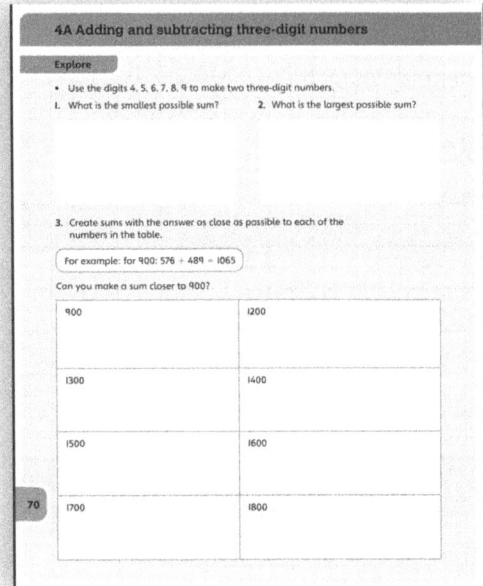

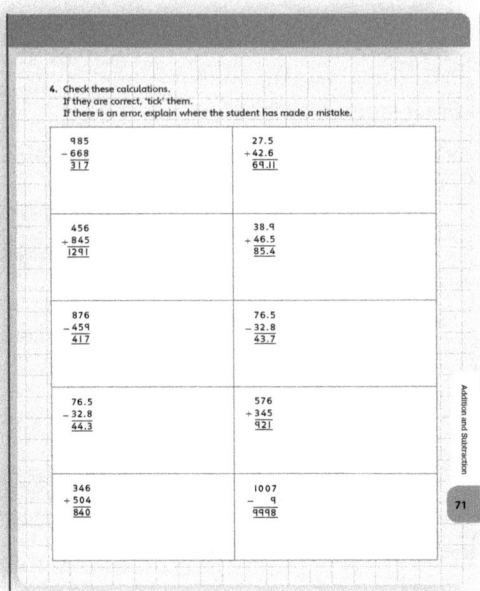

Specific learning foci

- Add two- and three-digit numbers with the same or different numbers of digits.
- *Add or subtract numbers with the same and different numbers of decimal places.*

Problem solving foci

- Choose appropriate and efficient mental or written strategies to carry out a calculation involving addition, subtraction.
- *Explain why they chose a particular method to perform a calculation and show working.*

Key vocabulary

Place value: ones, tens, hundreds, thousands, tenths, hundredths, decimal point

Resources

- Mini whiteboards and markers
- Large A4 cards with the digits 3, 5, 7, 9 and a '+' sign on

Links to Student Book

See pages 70–71 in Student Book.

Links to Workbook

Workbook page 41

Links to Digital Resource Pack

Digital Resource Pack 6 contains two activities which can be used to support students' use of column addition and subtraction when calculating. On the home page, select 'Addition and Subtraction'.

Language support

Use the language of place value accurately: *'carry' tens* or *carry hundreds* as appropriate. Do not always refer to 'carry 1'. This is modelled on page 68 of the Student Book.

 ## Introductory activity

Ask four students to come to the front and choose one of the four number cards 3, 5, 7, 9. Direct them to stand in a line. Hold the '+' sign so that you make an addition of two two-digit numbers (for example: 53 + 79). Ask students (working in pairs): Calculate the answer mentally. Write the answer on your whiteboard. Ask students:

Which method did you use to calculate the answer mentally?

Ask students to move one student in the line to a different position, to make the answer bigger. (For example: 53 + 97.) Again, ask the pairs to calculate this mentally. Discuss the difference between the two answers. Ask: *Did you know this before*? Ask students to move a different person in the line, this time to make a smaller answer. Ask students to calculate the answer mentally. Discuss the difference between the two answers.

 ## Main activity

Ask students to work individually to complete the activities on pages 70 and 71 of the Student Book. Encourage pairs and groups to share their answers to the questions on page 70. It is important for students to check and correct the errors in the questions on page 71. This helps them spot their own errors in the future.

Differentiation

Supporting: Focus on adding two three-digit numbers. You may wish to group students together who would benefit from focusing on questions 1–3.

Consolidating: Encourage students to estimate to spot errors and then to explain what the errors are.

Extending: Encourage students to create their own sets of calculations containing common errors for partners to work on.

Differentiated outcomes	
All students	should add two three-digit numbers accurately and spot errors with support.
Most students	will spot errors and explain how to correct them.
Some students	will use estimation to spot errors as well as other methods.

 ## Learning review

There are five errors in the calculations in question 4. Ask a different student to come to the front and explain each of the errors. Then ask them to calculate the answer correctly and to model the method to the rest of the class.

Additional activities

You can ask students to create 'incorrect' questions for their parents to 'correct' at home.

Students can complete Workbook page 41.

Answers

Student Book pages 70–71
1. Smallest possible sum: 468 + 579
2. Largest possible sum: Largest possible 864 + 975
3. Answers will vary as students create their own additions. Accept any answer where there is evidence that students have thought about where to place the digits in the 100s column.

4.

Correct	Error – Have added 0.6 and 0.5 to make 0.11 and not 1.1
Error – Have not 'carried' the ten when adding 6 + 5 to make 11.	Correct
Correct	Correct
Error – have found difference between 5 and 8 rather than subtract 8 from 5	Correct
Error – Have not 'carried' the ten when adding 6 + 4 to make 10.	Error – should be 998. Error in partitioning 1007.

Workbook page 41

Answers will vary as students choose their own numbers to make additions and subtractions with answers that fit the challenges. Check that students' answers to their calculations are correct.

4B Adding and subtracting money

Discover

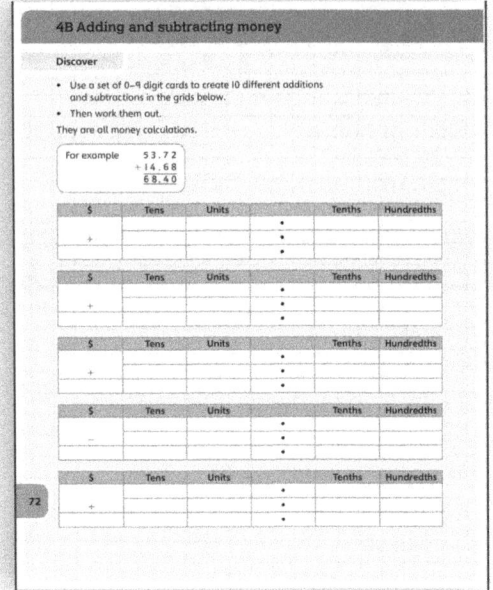

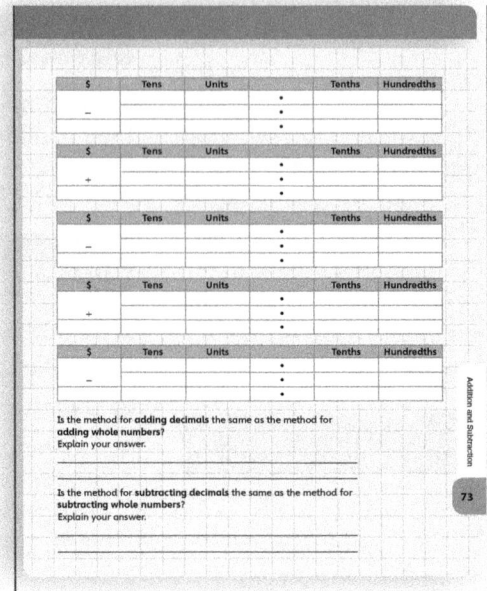

Specific learning focus

- Add or subtract numbers with the same and different numbers of decimal places, including amounts of money.

Problem solving foci

- Choose appropriate and efficient mental or written strategies to carry out a calculation involving addition, subtraction.
- *Explain why they chose a particular method to perform a calculation and show working.*

Key vocabulary

Place value: ones, tens, hundreds, thousands, tenths, hundredths, decimal point, dollars, cents (or national equivalents)

Resources

- Mini whiteboards and markers
- Dice
- 0–9 digit cards, set for each student

Links to Student Book

See pages 72–73 in Student Book.

Links to Workbook

Workbook pages 42 and 43

Links to Digital Resource Pack

Digital Resource Pack 6 contains two activities which can be used to support students' use of column addition and subtraction when calculating. On the home page, select 'Addition and Subtraction'.

Language support

For support, students can refer to their class poster in future lessons. During the Main activity, make links between money and the vocabulary of decimals. Use tenths and hundredths to describe cents or the equivalent.

Draw this place value grid on the whiteboard.

$	Tens	Ones	Decimal point	Tenths	Hundredths
			.		
			.		
+			.		

Ask students to come to the front of the class one at a time. Each time ask the student to roll a dice. Then ask them to place the digit from the dice throw in one of the empty cells to create an addition calculation. Ask students to try to create an addition with the largest possible sum. As each student places their digit, ask them: *What does this digit represent?* For example: *'a 6 in the **tens** column represents 60 dollars'*, or *'a 3 in the **hundredths** column represents 3 cents'.* When the last student has placed their digit, ask students to calculate the answer using a written method. Ask them to explain their strategy as they do the calculation. Repeat this activity to create a subtraction calculation.

 Main activity

Ask students to work individually on the activity in pairs on the activities on pages 72 and 73 of the Student Book. They should take it in turns to create a problem and to solve the problem that their partners has set them. The person setting the problem should check the answer and correct the calculation if any errors have been made. Before completing the final questions, ask pairs to discuss the similarities and differences between:

- the algorithms for adding and subtracting whole numbers
- the algorithms for adding and subtracting decimals.

Differentiation

Supporting: You may wish to group students together who would benefit from further modelling of the column addition method.

Consolidating: Encourage students to estimate to spot errors and then to explain what the errors are.

Extending: Encourage students to set word problems using one of the calculations they have carried out.

Differentiated outcomes	
All students	should carry out the calculations accurately and spot errors with support.
Most students	will spot errors and explain how to correct them.
Some students	will explain the methods clearly.

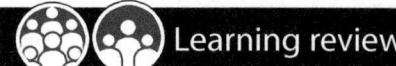

Ask students to work in small groups and share their responses to the final questions. They should create a poster to describe the similarities and differences between the algorithms for adding and subtracting whole numbers and adding and subtracting decimals. Share these posters and display them on the classroom wall for the rest of the unit.

Additional activities

You can ask students to list all the real-life contexts in which they find decimals. They can create a poster using extracts from magazines and newspapers.

Students can complete Workbook pages 42 and 43.

Answers

Student Book pages 72 and 73

Answers will vary as students use digit cards to make different additions and subtractions. Check that their answers are correct.

Workbook pages 42 and 43

1. $48.34
2. Yes, there will be $1.45
3. $28.81
4. No change, because the items in question 3 cost $1.45 more than $25.
5. $20.55
6. $11.26

Explore

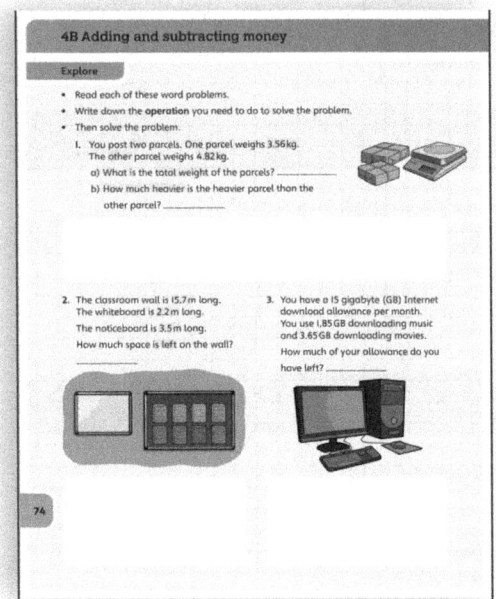

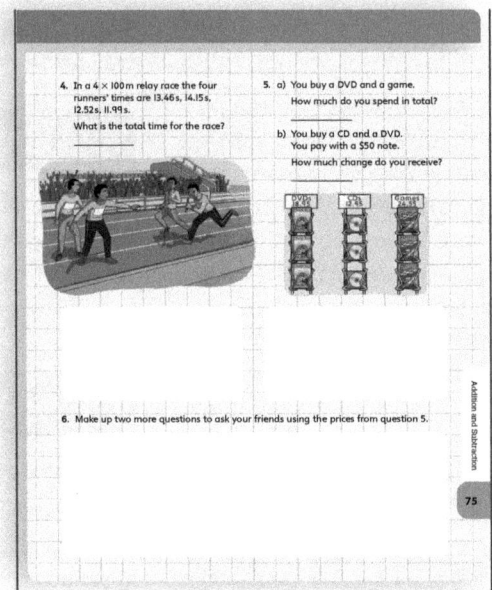

Specific learning focus

- Add or subtract numbers with the same and different numbers of decimal places, including amounts of money.

Problem solving foci

- Choose appropriate and efficient mental or written strategies to carry out a calculation involving addition, subtraction.
- Explain why they chose a particular method to perform a calculation and show working.
- *Make sense of and solve word problems, single and multi-step.*

Key vocabulary

Place value: ones, tens, hundreds, thousands, tenths, hundredths, decimal point, dollars, cents (or national equivalents)

Resources

- Mini whiteboards and markers
- Dice
- Metre rules or measuring tapes

Links to Student Book

See pages 74–75 in Student Book.

Links to Workbook

Workbook page 43

Links to Digital Resource Pack

Digital Resource Pack 6 contains two activities which can be used to support students' use of column addition and subtraction when calculating. On the home page, select 'Addition and Subtraction'.

Language support

Make links between money, other real-life contexts and the vocabulary of decimals. Use 'tenths' and 'hundredths'.

 Introductory activity

Ask pairs to write down as many examples as they can of the use of decimals in real life (for example: money, measurement, volume, weight, and so on). Ask a student to measure your height. Ask another student to measure the height of the door. Ask pairs of students to calculate the difference between my height and the height of the door. Then ask pairs to measure objects in the classroom. Ask them: *Make a list of objects with a total length as near to 2 metres as possible.*

 Main activity

Encourage students to complete the word problems on pages 74 and 75 of the Student Book in pairs. For question 6, tell students to create their problems to one another. Select a 'good' problem to share with the class as the Learning review.

Differentiation

Supporting: You may wish to group students together who would benefit from support.

Consolidating: Encourage students to create challenging word problems of their own.

Extending: Encourage students to create two-step word problems.

Differentiated outcomes	
All students	should solve the word problems with support.
Most students	will solve the word problems and set simple word problems.
Some students	will explain their methods clearly and set two step problems of their own.

 Learning review

Ask one pair to ask their problem for question 6 to the rest of the class. Ask another pair to come to the front of the class to solve the problem on the board. Encourage the rest of the class to support them.

Additional activities

Students can use real-life data from magazines or newspapers to ask problems to one another and their families.

Students can complete Workbook pages 42 and 43.

Answers

Student Book pages 74 and 75
1. **a)** 8.38 kg
   b) 1.26 kg
2. 10 m
3. 9.5 GB
4. 52.12 seconds
5. **a)** $43.50
   b) $18.10

Workbook pages 42 and 43
1. $48.34
2. Yes, there will be $1.45
3. $28.81
4. No change, because the items in question 3 cost $1.45 more than $25.
5. $20.55
6. $11.26

4C Using negative numbers

Discover

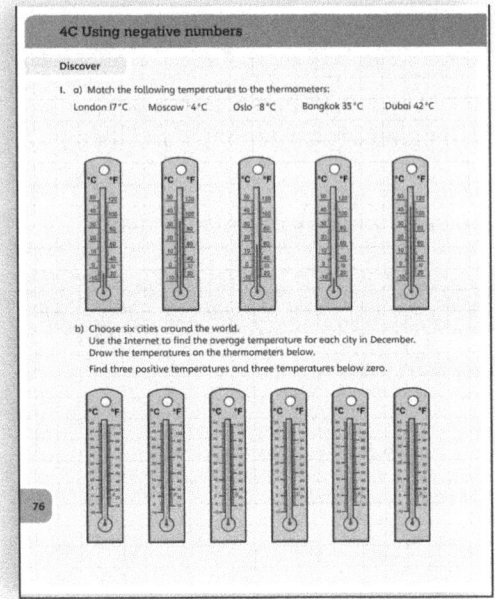

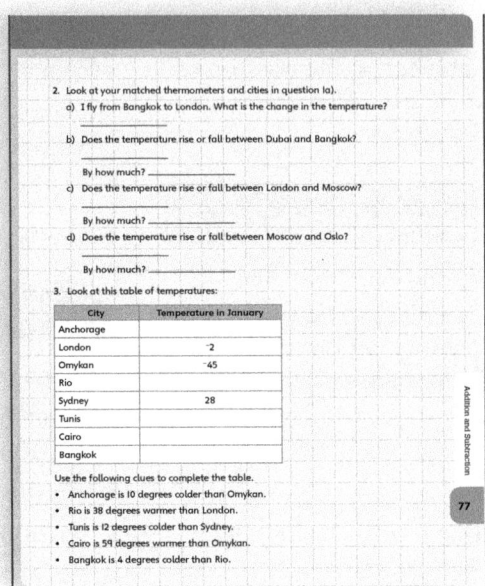

Specific learning focus

- Find the difference between a positive and negative integer, and between two negative integers in a context such as temperature or on a number line.

Problem solving foci

- Choose appropriate and efficient mental or written strategies to carry out a calculation involving addition, subtraction.
- *Identify relationships between numbers and make generalised statements.*

Key vocabulary

Positive, negative, directed numbers, above/below zero

Resources

- A4 cards labelled −5, −6, 0, +9, +14
- Mini whiteboards and markers

Links to Student Book

See pages 76–77 in Student Book.

Links to Workbook

Workbook page 44

Links to Digital Resource Pack

Digital Resource Pack 6 contains two activities which can be used to support students' addition and subtraction of negative numbers. On the home page, select 'Addition and Subtraction'.

Language support

Use the vocabulary 'positive 9', 'negative 15'. Ask questions, for example: *Is it greater or less than zero?*

Link this to vocabulary such as 'above/below zero (freezing)' for temperature.

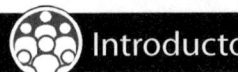 Introductory activity

Ask five students to come to the front of the class. Tell them to pick one card each. Ask students to stand in a line so that they create a reasonably accurate number line. Then ask four other students to come to the front one at a time. Ask each student to write a number on their whiteboard and to stand in the correct position on the number line between two of the students already in the line.

 Main activity

Ask students to complete the activity on pages 76 and 77 of the Student Book in pairs so that they can discuss and check one another's answers. If there is access to the Internet, students can research temperatures in cities around the world. If this is not possible, bring in information sheets which you have prepared previously, or use atlases which contain this information.

Differentiation

Supporting: Ask students to focus on questions 1. Use the thermometers to support students in calculating differences by counting on or counting back.

Consolidating: Encourage students to explain their methods for finding differences.

Extending: Encourage students to create more complex problems based on temperatures.

Differentiated outcomes	
All students	should read **positive** and **negative** temperatures accurately with support.
Most students	will support other students in reading positive and negative temperatures
Some students	will find differences between positive and negative temperatures.

 Learning review

Complete the table in question 3 on the whiteboard. Ask students to work in pairs to write down three facts from the table. For example: 'It is 43 degrees warmer in London than Omykan.'

Additional activities

Students can use the information sheets or information from the Internet to create their own table. They can then write clues and problems like those in question 3.

Students can complete Workbook pages 44 and 45.

Answers

Student Book pages 76 and 77

1. a)

London 17 °C → thermometer 3

Moscow –4 °C → thermometer 1

Oslo –8 °C → thermometer 4

Bangkok 35 °C → thermometer 2

Dubai 42 °C → thermometer 5

2. a) It is 18 degrees colder

    b) Falls by 7 degrees

    c) falls by 21 degrees

    d) Falls by 4 degrees

3.

City	Temperature in January
Anchorage	–55
London	–2
Omykan	–45
Rio	36
Sydney	28
Tunis	16
Cairo	14
Bangkok	32

Workbook pages 44 and 45

1. Check that students have marked the correct temperature on each thermometer.

Bangkok: warmest = 27 °C, coldest = 20 °C

Moscow: warmest = 21 °C, coldest = –8 °C

Reykjavik: warmest = 9 °C, coldest = –5 °C

North Pole: warmest = 13 °C, coldest = –28 °C

2. a) 7 °C

    b) 29 °C

    c) 14 °C

    d) 41 °C

    e) 35 °C

    f) 49 °C

    g) 11 °C

    h) 28 °C

Explore

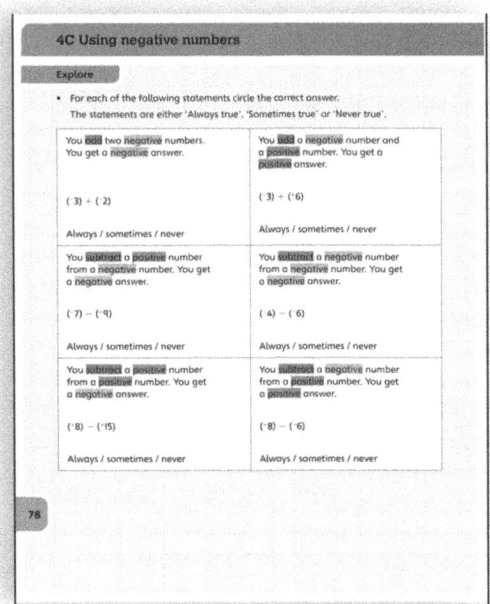

Specific learning focus

- Find the difference between a positive and negative integer, and between two negative integers in a context such as temperature or on a number line.

Problem solving foci

- Choose appropriate and efficient mental or written strategies to carry out a calculation involving addition, subtraction.
- *Identify relationships between numbers and make generalised statements.*

Key vocabulary

Positive, negative, directed numbers, above/below zero

Resources

- Large A4 cards labelled −10, −4, 0, +3, +8
- Mini whiteboards and markers

Links to Student Book

See pages 78 in Student Book.

Links to Workbook

Workbook page 45

Links to Digital Resource Pack

Digital Resource Pack 6 contains two activities which can be used to support students' addition and subtraction of negative numbers. On the home page, select 'Addition and Subtraction'.

Language support

Use the vocabulary *'positive 9', 'negative 15'*. Ask: *Is it greater or less than zero?*

Introduce the phrase *'directed numbers'*. Link this to directions on the number line, for example: *Movement to the right is positive and to the left is negative.*

Introductory activity

Draw a number line from −10 to +10 on the whiteboard. Ask five students to come to the front of the class. Tell them to pick one card each. Ask each student to place their number on the number line on the board.

Ask: *What is five more than* **negative** *four?*

Write $-4 + (+5) =$

What is seven less than **positive** three?

Write $+3 - (+7) =$

Remind students: *Move to the right on the number line to add and move to the left on the number line to subtract.*

Write $-4 - (-5) =$

Say: *Subtracting moves to the left but the negative sign reverses the direction so $-4 - (-5) = +1$ and we move to the right.*

Write $+4 - (-7) =$

Say: *Subtracting moves to the left but the negative sign reverses the direction so $+4 - (-7) = +11$ and we move to the right.*

 Main activity

Tell students to work in mixed-attainment groups of between 4–6 students on the activities on page 78 of the Student Book. Ask the groups to make a poster for each statement. Tell them to include examples to show that their conclusion is correct. Then ask students to copy the answers into page 78 of the Student Book individually.

Differentiation

All students should engage in the discussion to make general statements. You may want to help write the answers for some of the less confident students.

Differentiated outcomes
The differentiation is by outcome for this activity as each student will interpret the statements in slightly different ways to complete their own posters.

 Learning review

Ask a group to present one of the statements that they know is always true.

Ask a group to present one of the statements that they know is sometimes true.

Ask a group to present one of the statements that they know is never true.

Encourage group discussion about why the general statements are true.

Additional activities

Students can draw number lines to show the range of numbers for which the statements are true.

Students can complete Workbook pages 44 and 45.

Answers

Student Book page 78

Always	Sometimes
Always	Sometimes
Sometimes	Always

Workbook pages 44 and 45
1. Check that students have marked the correct temperature on each thermometer.
   Bangkok: warmest = 27 °C, coldest = 20 °C
   Moscow: warmest = 21 °C, coldest = −8 °C
   Reykjavik: warmest = 9 °C, coldest = −5 °C
   North Pole: warmest = 13 °C, coldest = −28 °C

2. **a)** 7 °C
   b) 29 °C
   c) 14 °C
   d) 41 °C
   e) 35 °C
   f) 49 °C
   g) 11 °C
   h) 28 °C

4 Addition and subtraction

Connect and Review

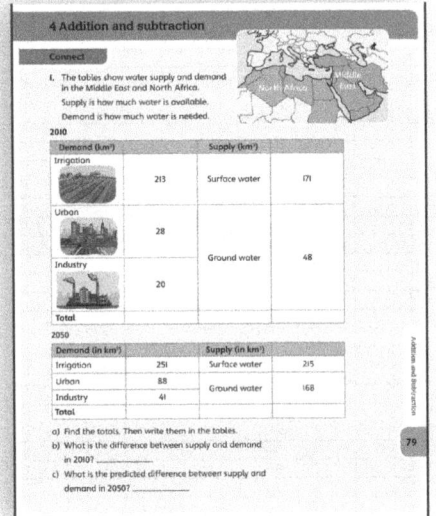

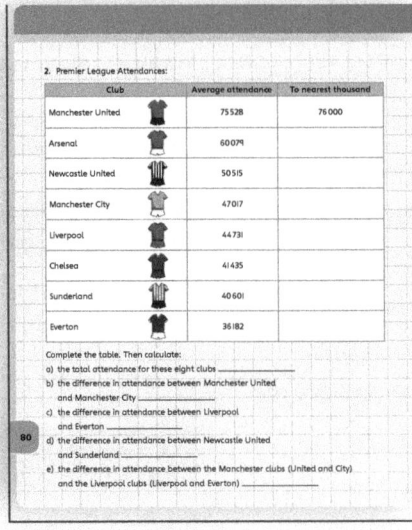

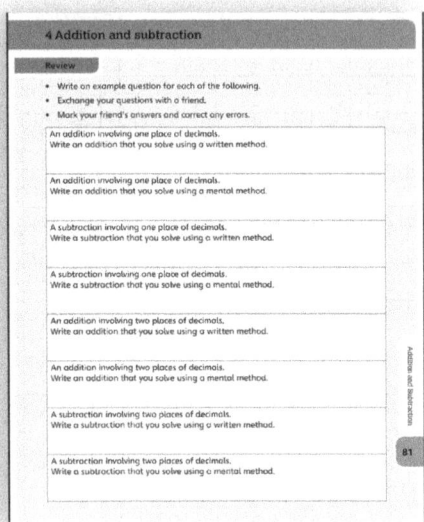

See pages 79–81 in Student Book.

Specific learning focus

- Add or subtract numbers with the same and different numbers of decimal places, including amounts of money.

Problem solving foci

- Choose appropriate and efficient mental or written strategies to carry out a calculation involving addition, subtraction.
- Explain why they chose a particular method to perform a calculation and show working.
- *Make sense of and solve word problems, single and multi-step.*

Key vocabulary

Place value: ones, tens, hundreds, thousands, tenths, hundredths, decimal point

Resources

- Mini whiteboards and markers
- Assessment activity 4 – one per student (Resource sheet 4 – see www.oxfordprimary.com/OIPMteacher)

Links to Student Book

See pages 79–81 in Student Book.

Links to Workbook

Workbook page 46

Links to Digital Resource Pack

Digital Resource Pack 6 contains two activities which can be used to support students' addition and subtraction of different numbers. On the home page, select 'Addition and Subtraction'.

Language support

Ask: *What operation do you need to use to solve this problem.* Monitor students as they interpret the tables. This allows you to support their language development.

Introductory and Main activity

Ask students to work in mixed-attainment groups of four. Encourage them to try to interpret and begin the activity without any teacher input. Organise students into groups and ask them to begin the activity on pages 79 and 80 of the Student Book.

Explain the data table on page 79 of the Student Book. Ask the following questions. Ask students to work in pairs to write the answer to each question on their whiteboard. Ask them to explain their strategy when they give the answer.

- *How much water was needed for urban and industry use in 2010?*
- *How much more water was needed for irrigation than was available from surface water in 2010?*
- *How much more surface water will be available in 2050 than was available in 2010?*

The group should then explore the rest of the questions together.

Ask groups to write down two facts about the UK Premier Football League attendances based on the table on page 80 of the Student Book. Share these facts as a whole class.

Differentiation

Students should work in mixed-attainment groups to support one another in playing the game.

Differentiated outcomes
This is an activity designed to offer differentiation by outcome.

 Learning review

Students should complete the Review activity on page 81 of the Student Book as individuals as it is a summative assessment. You may want to help write the answers for those less confident with writing or in speaking English.

Additional activities

Students can write questions for one another based on the water supply and demand data table. They can also make comparisons between the attendances at the premier league grounds and their own national league.

Students can complete Workbook page 46.

Answers

Student Book pages 79 and 80

1. a)

	Demand	Supply
Total 2010	261	219
Total 2050	380	383

b) Difference 2010 = 42

c) Difference 2015 = 3

2. Premier League Attendances

Club	Average attendance	To nearest thousand
Manchester United	75 528	76 000
Arsenal	60 079	60 000
Newcastle United	50 515	51 000
Manchester City	47 017	47 000
Liverpool	44 731	45 000
Chelsea	41 435	41 000
Sunderland	40 601	41 000
Everton	36 182	36 000

a) Total attendance

b) 28 511

c) 8549

d) 9914

e) 41 632

Student Book page 81

Answers will vary as students write their own example questions to match the statements. Check that students' answers to their calculations are correct.

Workbook page 46

1. 2.04 m

2. 1.49 m

3. 5.31 m

4. 2.19 m

5. Answers will vary as students choose the prices of the items to make the total of $10.55. Check that the students' calculations are correct.

6. −22 and 8

7. −5 and 17

8. −3 °C

Assessment activity 4

1. a) they did not carry into the tens column

2. a) 647

3. c) −10 and +2

4. b) 31 degrees

5. a) You are 14 cm taller.

6. d) $8.61

7. Answers will vary as students write their own calculations with the required answers. Accept any accurate calculations.

Unit 5 Multiplication and Division

Overview

Big Idea

This unit develops students' mental and informal methods of multiplication. This helps them to understand and apply a formal column method of multiplication. There are two Big Ideas to focus on.

Make sure that students use their knowledge of place value to estimate answers before they calculate. Also make sure they check the sense of their answers. This is particularly important with large answers.

It is important that students understand the meaning of the algorithms that you teach. It is easier for students to remember an algorithm when they understand why it works. It also means that they don't simply follow rules which they do not understand.

Possible misconceptions

A common misconception is students misapplying algorithms. They may not apply their understanding of place value. For example, they may calculate:

$$\begin{array}{r} 356 \\ \times\ \ 34 \\ \hline 1068 \\ 1424 \\ \hline 2492 \\ \hline \end{array}$$

1068 (Multiplying by 3 rather than 30)

2492 (Now check by estimating: $30 \times 350 = 10500$ so 2492 is not a sensible answer.)

Key vocabulary and language structures

Place value; multiple, product; partition; estimate; double, halve; share, share equally; divide, division, divisor, dividend, remainder factor, quotient

Coverage in lessons

Learning focus	Learning outcomes
Multiplying by two-, three- and four-digit numbers	Can I choose an efficient method when I multiply?
	Can I say what the digits of a number represent?
Dividing three-digit numbers by two-digit numbers	Can I choose an efficient method when I divide?
	Can I use division to solve problems involving money?
Divisions with remainders	Can I explain what a mixed number is?
	Can I divide with fractions?
	Can I write answers involving fractions and decimals?
	Can I divide by a single-digit number?
	Can I represent the remainder of a division in different ways?
Using the arithmetical laws for multiplication and division	Can I use the commutative, associative and distributive laws for multiplication?

5 Multiplication and Division

Engage

Specific learning foci

- *Multiply two- or three-digit numbers by two-digit numbers.*
- Multiply pairs of multiples of 10.

Problem solving foci

- Estimate and approximate when calculating, e.g. use rounding and check working.
- *Explain why they chose a particular method to perform a calculation and show working.*

Key vocabulary

Place value, multiple, product, partition, estimate, double, halve, share, share equally, divide, division, divisor, dividend, remainder, factor, quotient

Resources

- Mini whiteboards and markers

Links to Student Book

See page 83 in Student Book.

Language support

Use the language of place value as you explain the calculation strategies. For example: for the column method below, say:

6 multiplied by 20 is 120 so I write down 20 and carry 100.

Do **not** say: *Put a zero down and multiply by 2.*

```
    286
×    29
  5720
  2574
  8294
```

 Introductory activity

Group the students in pairs and try to group a more confident student with a less confident student. Write the calculation 229 × 29 on the board. Ask pairs to estimate the answer.

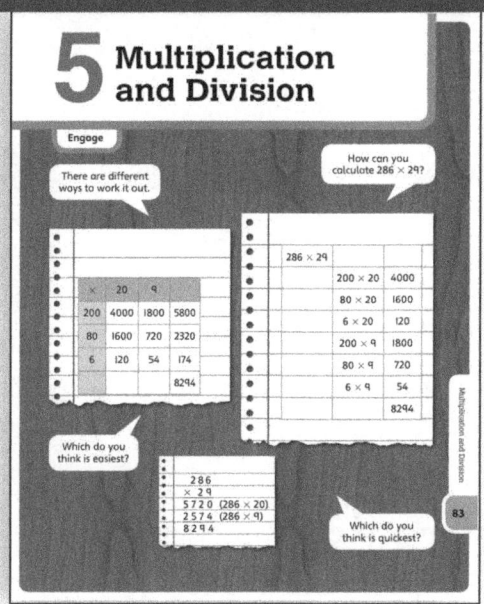

Ask one pair for their estimate. Check the estimate with the other pairs. Agree on the estimate. Ask the pairs to calculate the answer. Select two or three pairs to present their solutions. The less confident member of the pair should present the solution which the more confident partner should have explained to them. Choose pairs that used different methods to calculate the answer, including using multiples of 10.

 Main activity

Put together groups of 4 by doubling up the pairs. Ask groups to explore the discussion on page 83 of the Student Book. Students in each group take it in turns to explain each different strategy.

Differentiation

Supporting: Group students with more confident others who can explain the methods.

Consolidating: Encourage students to share their methods with other students.

Extending: Ask students which methods they prefer. Ask them to justify their response.

 Learning review

Ask one of the groups to come to the front. Ask each student to explain one of the methods from page 83 of the Student Book. As a class, decide on the advantages and disadvantages of each of the methods.

Additional activities

Students can ask their parents and other adults at home: 'How do you calculate a three-digit number multiplied by a two-digit number?' They can share the strategies at the beginning of the next lesson.

5A Multiplying by two-, three- and four-digit numbers

Discover

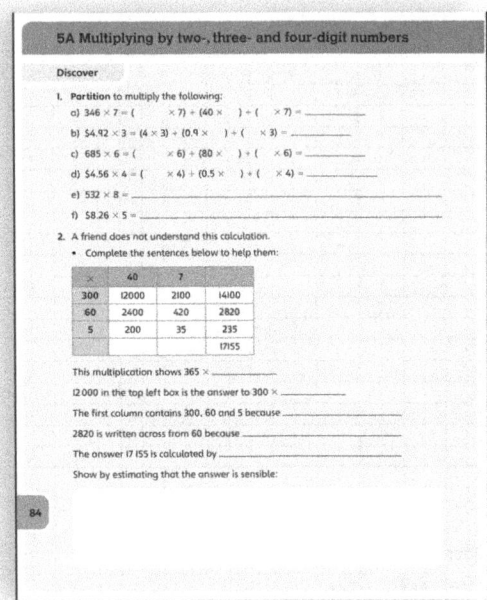
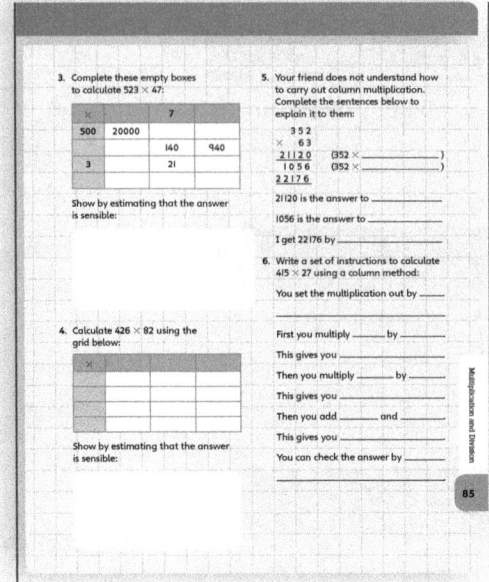

Specific learning foci

- *Multiply two- or three-digit numbers by two-digit numbers.*
- Multiply pairs of multiples of 10.

Problem solving foci

- Estimate and approximate when calculating, e.g. use rounding and check working.
- *Explain why they chose a particular method to perform a calculation and show working.*

Key vocabulary

Place value, partition, partitioning, estimate, grid method

Resources

- Mini whiteboards and markers; dice

Links to Student Book

See pages 84–85 in Student Book.

Links to Workbook

Workbook pages 48 and 49

Links to Digital Resource Pack

Digital Resource Pack 6 contains two activities which can be used to support students' multiplication of different numbers. On the home page, select 'Multiplication and Division'.

Language support

Model and use the language of place value while explaining the calculation strategies. Correct students if they forget to do this.

Introductory activity

Ask four students to come to the front. Roll a dice three times to make a three-digit number. Write the number on the board. Ask the students at the front of the class to **partition** the number on their whiteboards. They then stand in order at the front of the class to show the result on their whiteboards. For example: 216 is shown as 200 + 10 + 6. Repeat with a three-digit number with two decimal places. For example: $2.65 is shown as 2 + 0.6 + 0.05

Model the **grid method** as follows. Remind the class that they have seen this method in Stage 5. We are going to calculate 216 × 52. So, we draw the following grid.

×	50	2	
200			
10			
6			

Work through the multiplication step-by-step, reminding students that the grid represents the **partitioning** of the numbers until the grid is complete. So the grid represents:

(200 × 50) + (200 × 2) + (10 × 50) + (10 × 2) + (6 × 50) + (6 × 2)

First estimate the answer: 50 × 200 is larger than 10 000. Next, carry out the multiplications to fill each cell. Then total up all the cells to find the answer by adding across the cells, and finally by adding the final column.

 Main activity

Ask students to work on the activities on pages 84 and 85 of the Student Book in pairs. Tell them to check each other's answers for questions 2 to 5. You may choose to group the less confident students together so that you can model the grid method for them.

Differentiation

Supporting: Work with less confident students to support them in using the grid method.

Consolidating: Ask students how the compact method relates to the grid method.

Extending: Ask students to explain the compact method step-by-step.

Differentiated outcomes	
All students	should use the grid method with support.
Most students	will use the grid method to carry out calculations.
Some students	will model the method in questions 5 and 6.

 Learning review

Write 415 × 27 on the whiteboard. Ask a confident student to explain how to carry out the calculation. Follow the explanation on the board. Make sure that you follow the instructions correctly.

Additional activities

Roll a dice to create another similar calculation. Ask students to work on the calculation in pairs using a mini whiteboard. One student explains the method. The other student follows their instructions.

Students can complete Workbook pages 48 and 49.

5A Multiplying by two-, three- and four-digit numbers

Explore

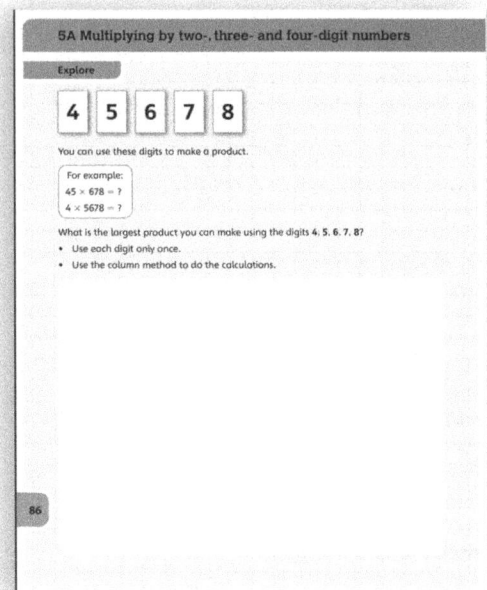

Specific learning foci

- *Multiply two- or three-digit numbers by two-digit numbers.*
- Multiply pairs of multiples of 10.

Problem solving foci

- Estimate and approximate when calculating, e.g. use rounding and check working.
- *Explain why they chose a particular method to perform a calculation and show working.*

Key vocabulary

Place value, multiple, product, partition, partitioning, estimate, grid method

Resources

- Mini whiteboards and markers

Links to Student Book

See page 86 in Student Book.

Links to Workbook

Workbook page 49

Links to Digital Resource Pack

Digital Resource Pack 6 contains two activities which can be used to support students' multiplication of different numbers. On the home page, select 'Multiplication and Division'.

Language support

As students work on the activity ask them to estimate the product. Ask them to predict answers. Prompt with questions, for example:

- *What do you think the product will be?*
- *Will this answer be larger or smaller than that answer?*

 Introductory activity

Group the students in pairs and try to group a more confident student with a less confident student. Write these calculations on the board.

$45 \times 768 =$ $54 \times 768 =$

Ask pairs to discuss and decide which multiplication has the larger answer. Take feedback and ask students to explain their answer.

Then write: $64 \times 587 =$ $58 \times 764 =$

Ask: *Which multiplication has the larger answer?* This time ask students to estimate an answer to each calculation first. Ask students to explain their answer.

 Main activity

Put together groups of four by doubling up the pairs. Ask students to work in groups of four on the activity on page 86 of the Student Book. They can try different calculations. Emphasise that they do not need to find all the possible products. Tell them to use their knowledge of place value to try to decide which calculations are most likely to give large products.

Differentiation

All students should engage in the investigation together.

Differentiated outcomes
Students will offer different suggestions based on their current understandings and will develop their understanding of place value and multiplication methods through discussion.

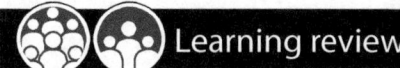 Learning review

Ask one group to present their result to the rest of the class. Ask other students to comment on any differences in their solutions.

Additional activities

Students can find the highest product and the next highest product. They can find the difference between the two answers and explain the reason for this.

Students can complete Workbook page 50.

Answers

Student Book page 86

$864 \times 75 = 64\,800$ is the largest product.

Workbook pages 48 and 49
1. a) 1944
   b) 3192
   c) 2445
   d) 2412
   e) 1905
   f) 4613
2. a) 9984
   b) 13 886
   c) 23 328
   d) 10 536
3. a) 13 708
   b) 8505
   c) 22 854
   d) 15 466

Discover

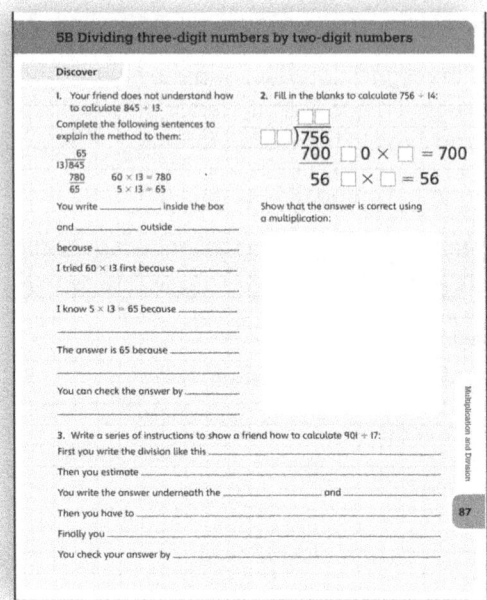

Specific learning focus

- Divide three-digit numbers by single-digit numbers including those leaving a remainder and divide three-digit numbers by two-digit numbers (no remainder) including sums of money.

Problem solving foci

- Estimate and approximate when calculating.
- *Explain why they chose a particular method to perform a calculation and show working.*

Key vocabulary

Place value, estimate, divide, division, divisor, dividend, remainder, factor, quotient

Resources

- Mini whiteboards and markers

Links to Student Book

See page 87 in Student Book.

Links to Workbook

Workbook page 50

Links to Digital Resource Pack

Digital Resource Pack 6 contains two activities which can be used to support students' division of different numbers. On the home page, select 'Multiplication and Division'.

Language support

Students may need support in their explanations for this activity. Encourage by asking questions, for example:

- *Why is that the first step?*
- *What is your estimate for the answer?*
- *What number facts do you know about that number?*
- *You know 10 times a number. How can you work out 15 times that number?*

 **Introductory activity**

Group the students in pairs and try to group a more confident student with a less confident student. Write '912 ÷ 16' on the board. Ask pairs to **estimate** the answer. Give them 2 minutes to do this. Ask pairs to show you their answers. Pick three different answers. Ask the pairs: *How did you decide your estimate?* Then ask the pairs to calculate the answer in any way they can. Again, share the responses. Then write the calculation on the board. Remind students that **division** is a process of sharing. A division with no **remainder** means that the amount can be shared equally with nothing 'leftover'. Model this method. Say the phrases:

16 .912   (*Write the **divisor** outside. Write the dividend inside.*)

$$\begin{array}{r} 5 \\ \hline 16 \cdot 912 \\ 800 \end{array}$$

(*First estimate 910 ÷ 16. 50 × 16 = 800. Write down 800.*)

$$\begin{array}{r} 57 \\ \hline 16 \cdot 912 \\ 800 \\ \hline 112 \end{array}$$

(*912 − 800 = 112. Now estimate 112 ÷ 16. 7 × 16 = 112 exactly.*)

(*50 + 7 gives the answer 57.*)

 **Main activity**

Ask students to work in the same pairs for the activity on page 87 the Student Book. Encourage them to explain the calculations to one another. This gives them support with the calculations and the language.

Differentiation

Supporting: Work with less confident students to support them in using the written method.

Consolidating: Ask students to explain the written method to you as they use it.

Extending: Ask students to explain the written method step-by-step.

Differentiated outcomes	
All students	should use the written method with support.
Most students	will use the written method to carry out calculations.
Some students	will model the written method in questions 3.

 Learning review

Write '901 ÷ 17' on the board. Ask one, more confident, student to explain how to carry out the calculation. Write down each step as they describe it. Ask questions to make sure that students are clear about each step, for example:

- *Why do you write that digit in that column?*
- *What is the value of that digit?*

Additional activities

Students can explain their method to their parents or other adults at home. They can also set them some practice calculations.

Students can complete Workbook page 50.

Answers

Student Book page 87

1. Answers will vary as students write their own instructions. Accept any correct instructions. For example:

You write 845 inside the box and 13 outside the box because you are dividing 845 by 13.

I tried 60 × 13 first because I know that 60 × 12 is 720.

I know 5 × 13 = 65 because 5 × 12 is 60.

The answer is 65 because 60 + 5 is 65.

You can check the answer by multiplying 65 and 13.

2.
$$\begin{array}{r} \boxed{5}\boxed{4} \\ \boxed{1}\boxed{4})\overline{756} \\ 700 \quad \boxed{5}\,0 \times \boxed{1}4 = 700 \\ 56 \quad \boxed{4} \times \boxed{1}4 = 56 \end{array}$$

3. Answers will vary as students write their own instructions. Accept any correct instructions.

Workbook page 50

1. 32

2. 63

3. 58

4. 38

Explore

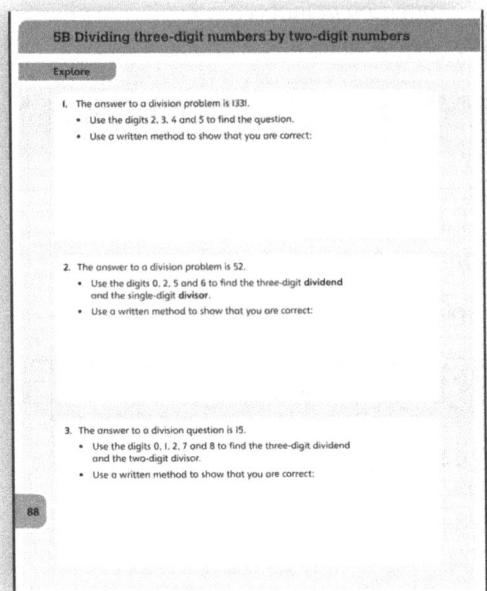

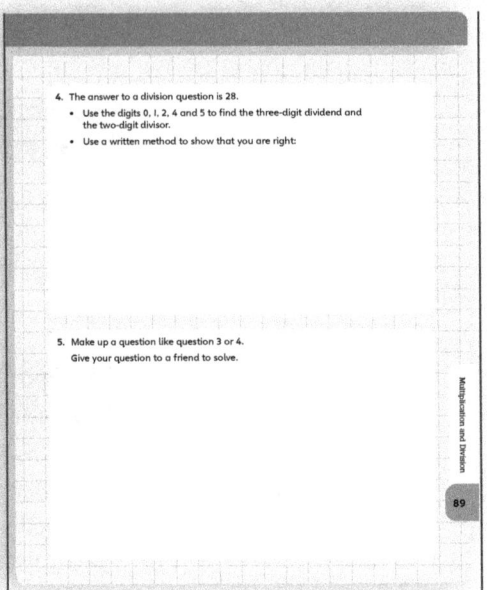

Specific learning focus

- Divide three-digit numbers by single-digit numbers including those leaving a remainder and divide three-digit numbers by two-digit numbers (no remainder) including sums of money.

Problem solving foci

- Estimate and approximate when calculating.
- *Explain why they chose a particular method to perform a calculation and show working.*

Key vocabulary

Place value, estimate, double, divide, division, divisor, dividend, remainder, quotient

Resources

- Mini whiteboards and markers

Links to Student Book

See pages 88–89 in Student Book.

Links to Workbook

Workbook page 51

Links to Digital Resource Pack

Digital Resource Pack 6 contains two activities which can be used to support students' division of different numbers. On the home page, select 'Multiplication and Division'.

Language support

A good way to organise the group work to support language development is to ask one of the group to describe the process and the rest who write down the solution. Tell the students who are writing not to write down anything they don't understand until the explanation is clarified. This ensures the explanation is clear.

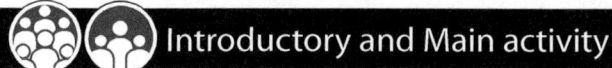 Introductory and Main activity

Put together mixed-attainment groups of four students to work in groups of four on the activity on pages 88 and 89 of the Student Book. They will need to try different calculations. Emphasise that they do not need to find all the possible calculations just those that meet the requirements of the question. Tell them to use their knowledge of place value to try to decide which calculations are most likely to give the correct answer and then to carry out the calculation.

Differentiation

All students should engage in the investigation together.

Differentiated outcomes
Students will offer different suggestions based on their current understandings and will develop their understanding of place value and division methods through discussion.

 Learning review

Ask one group to present their result to the rest of the class. Ask other students to comment on any differences in their solutions. At each step ask students to try to speak out their thinking.

Select one or two of the problems that groups have created for question 5 to share with the whole class.

Additional activities

Students can take their problems home to share with their parents and other adults at home.

Students can complete Workbook page 51.

Answers

Student Book pages 88 and 89

Answers will vary as students make up their own calculations with the required answers. Check that students' calculations are correct and that their methods are appropriate.

Workbook page 51

Answers will vary as students make up their own calculations with the required answers. Check that students' calculations are correct.

5C Division with remainders

Discover

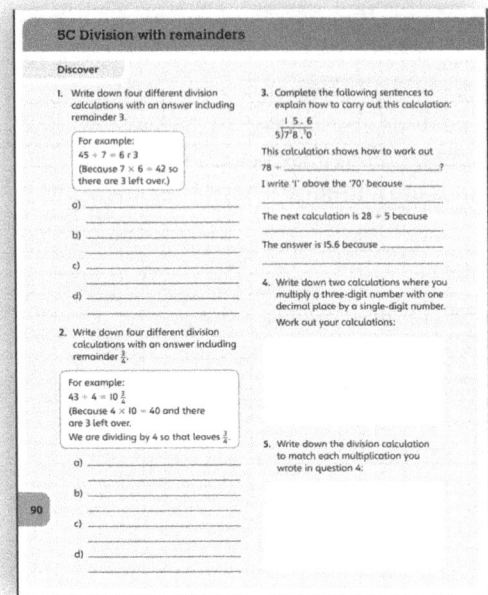

Specific learning focus

- Give an answer to division as a mixed number, and a decimal.

Problem solving focus

- Explain why they chose a particular method to perform a calculation and show working.

Key vocabulary

Place value, estimate, share, share equally, divide, division, divisor, dividend, remainder, factor, quotient

Resources

- Mini whiteboards and markers
- Dice

Links to Student Book

See page 90 in Student Book.

Links to Workbook

Workbook page 52

Links to Digital Resource Pack

Digital Resource Pack 6 contains two activities which can be used to support students' division of different numbers. On the home page, select 'Multiplication and Division'.

Language support

Model the correct use of the language of place value as discussed in the introduction.

For example:

- *I am dividing by …*
- *The remainder is …*
- *This is the same as …*

 **Introductory activity**

Roll the dice. Write the number on the board. Ask pairs: *Write a **division** calculation with an answer that has this number as a remainder.* For example: if you roll a 2, students write a division calculation with a remainder of 2. Give students two minutes to write down their answer. Ask pairs for their answers. Ask them: *How did you work it out?* Select one of the calculations. Model how to leave the **remainder** as a fraction. For example:

$17 \div 3 = 5 \text{ r } 2$

I am dividing by 3 so this is the same as $5\frac{2}{3}$ or

$32 \div 5 = 6 \text{ r } 2$

I am dividing by 5 so this is the same as $6\frac{2}{5}$

Repeat, this time modelling an answer as a decimal, for example:

$$5\,\overline{\smash{)}32.^20}^{\displaystyle 6.4}$$

Say: 32 divided by 5 is 6 remainder 2. 20 tenths divided by 5 is four tenths. The answer is 6.4.

 **Main activity**

Ask students to work in pairs on the activities on page 90 of the Student Book. They can support one another and check answers. They should write down two calculations each for questions 1 and 2 then check answers before writing down all four examples on page 90 of the Student Book. Only ask the most confident students to complete questions 3–5.

You may choose to group the least confident students together so that you can model the idea of remainders using practical materials.

Differentiation

Supporting: Model division with remainders using practical materials.

Consolidating: Focus on questions 1 and 2 to consolidate understanding.

Extending: Focus on questions 3–5 and ask students to create word problems based on division.

Differentiated outcomes	
All students	should carry out calculations with support.
Most students	will create calculations leaving remainders, using their knowledge of factors.
Some students	will explain the written division methods.

 Learning review

Ask one pair to give you their multiplication calculations from question 4. Ask the other students to write down the answer to the multiplication and the division that matches it.

Additional activities

Students can repeat question 4 to create multiplications of three-digit numbers by two-digit numbers. They can then find the matching division calculations.

Students can complete Workbook page 52.

Answers

Student Book page 90

Answers will vary as students write their own calculations with the required remainders and instructions. Check that students' calculations and instructions are correct.

Workbook page 52

1. $7\frac{3}{5}$, 7.6

2. $78\frac{1}{2}$, 78.5

3. $14\frac{1}{3}$, 14.333

4. $10\frac{3}{8}$, 10.375

5. $11\frac{1}{2}$, 11.5

6. $25\frac{3}{5}$, 25.6

7. $5\frac{3}{5}$, 5.6

8. $65\frac{2}{5}$, 65.4

9. $12\frac{3}{8}$, 12.375

10. $29\frac{1}{4}$, 29.25

Explore

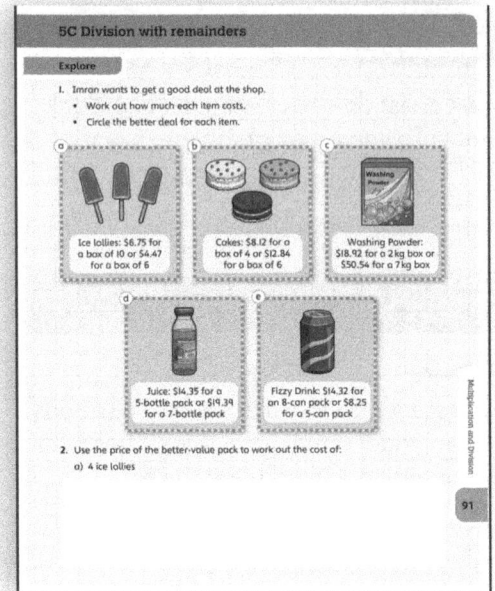
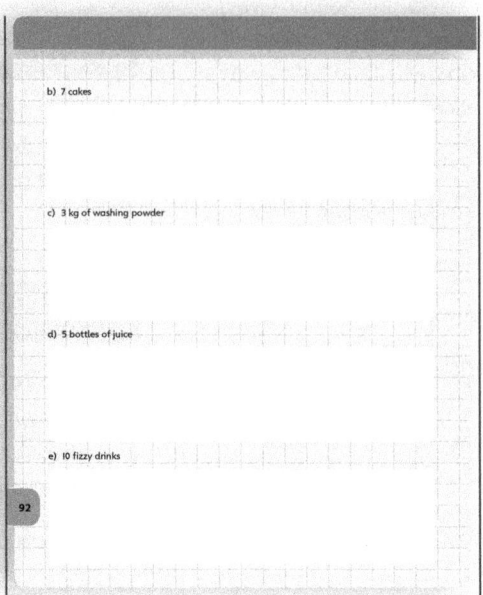

Specific learning foci

- Give an answer to division as a mixed number, and a decimal.
- Multiply two-, three- or four-digit numbers (including sums of money) by a single-digit number.
- *Divide three-digit numbers by single-digit numbers including those leaving a remainder and divide three-digit numbers by two-digit numbers (no remainder) including sums of money.*

Problem solving foci

- Choose and use appropriate mental and written strategies to carry out a calculation involving multiplication or division.
- *Make sense of and solve word problems, single and multi-step.*

Key vocabulary

Place value, estimate, share, share equally, divide, division, divisor, dividend, remainder, factor, quotient

Resources

- Real-life supermarket products (e.g. breakfast cereal) in different-sized packets, with their prices

Links to Student Book

See pages 91–92 in Student Book.

Links to Workbook

Workbook page 53

Links to Digital Resource Pack

Digital Resource Pack 6 contains two activities which can be used to support students' division of different numbers. On the home page, select 'Multiplication and Division'.

Language support

Use the language of problem solving throughout the activity. Ask, for example:

- *How do you know which calculation to use?*
- *How did you work that out?*
- *Is that answer reasonable?*

 Introductory activity

Group students in mixed-attainment groups of 4 to 6. If possible, use an example from a local supermarket, for example: breakfast cereal sold in different-sized packets. Ask students: *Which packet of cereal is the best value?* Groups may give different answers depending on the size of their family or issues of storage. A useful strategy is to find a price per 100 g to make comparisons. Select a group to share their solution and then ask other groups to comment.

 Main activity

Groups should continue to work together on the activity on pages 91 and 92 of the Student Book, which builds on the ideas in the introduction. Make sure that the more confident students share their thinking carefully with other students who are less confident. Students can check they have the same answers for question 1 as other groups before continuing with question 2. If their answers are different, encourage students to find their errors and correct them before they continue.

Differentiation

All students should engage in the investigation together.

Differentiated outcomes
Students will offer different suggestions based on their current understandings and will develop their understanding of place value and multiplication and division methods through discussion.

 Learning review

Ask groups to explain to the rest of the class how they calculated the answers to questions 2a and 2c.

Additional activities

Students can visit local supermarkets to find other examples. They can bring their examples in for the class to solve in future lessons.

Students can complete Workbook page 53.

Answers

Student Book pages 91 and 92
1. **a)** Box of 10
   b) Box of 4
   c) 7 kg box
   d) 7-bottle pack
   e) 5-can pack
2. **a)** $2.70
   b) $14.21
   c) $21.66
   d) $13.85
   e) $16.50

Workbook page 53
1. 90 cents
2. 90 cents
3. about 5 cents
4. $1.17
5. $1.27

Discover

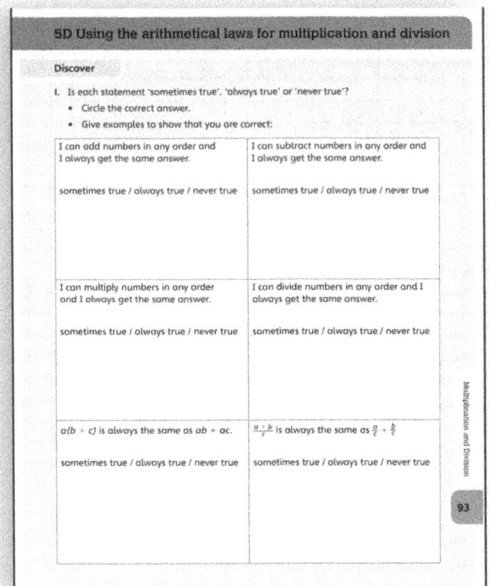

Specific learning focus

- Know and apply the arithmetic laws as they apply to multiplication (without necessarily using the terms commutative, associative or distributive).

Problem solving focus

- Make, test and refine hypotheses, explain and justify methods, reasoning, strategies, results or conclusions orally.

Key vocabulary

Multiple, product, divide, division, divisor, dividend, factor, quotient, associative law, commutative law, distributive law

Resources

- Dice
- Calculators
- Paper for notes
- Mathematical dictionaries

Links to Student Book

See pages 93–94 in Student Book.

Links to Workbook

Workbook page 54

Links to Digital Resource Pack

Digital Resource Pack 6 contains two activities which can be used to support students' multiplication and division of different numbers. On the home page, select 'Multiplication and Division'.

Language support

Writing their own definitions for the mathematical laws supports students in understanding the meanings of 'commutative', 'distributive' and 'associative'. Ask students questions as they work. For example:

- *Is it true for negative numbers?*
- *Is it true for fractions?*
- *Is it true when there is a zero?*

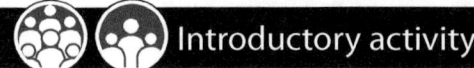 Introductory activity

Write '*a* (*b* + *c*)' on the board. Roll a dice three times. Replace '*a*' with the first number you roll. Replace '*b*' with the second number you roll. Replace '*c*' with the third number you roll. For example: You roll 3, 5 and another 3. You write: '3(5 + 3)'

Tell the class: *This is the same as 3 × 8, which is 24.*

Tell the class:

You can also write this as (3 × 5) + (3 × 3) = 15 + 9 = 24.

Ask: *Is this always true? Or is it only true sometimes?* Students should work in mixed-attainment groups of 4 to 6 to try different numbers in order to test the statement out.

The activities in this unit look at similar questions. Remind students to try with fractions and negative numbers to 'test' if the statements are always true.

 Main activity

Ask students to work on the activities on page 93 of the Student Book in small groups. They can each test out the statements with different numbers. Tell the groups to use mathematics dictionaries to support them in developing their definitions of the **associative law**, the **commutative law** and the **distributive law**. Remind them to use examples with numbers to illustrate their definitions.

Differentiation

All students should engage in the investigation together.

Differentiated outcomes
Students will offer different suggestions based on their current understandings and will develop their understanding of arithmetical laws and multiplication and division methods through the discussions that they have. Join in the discussions so that you can make assessments of individual students' current understanding.

 Learning review

Ask the groups to share their definitions. As a class, agree on a single definition for each law. Create a class poster to display. You can refer to this poster in future lessons.

Additional activities

You can ask students to explore the rules of associativity, commutativity and distributivity for addition and subtraction.

Students can complete Workbook page 50.

Answers

Student Book pages 93 and 94

1.

Always true	Sometimes true
Always true	Sometimes true
Always true	Always true

2. Check that students' definitions of the associative, commutative and distributive laws are correct and that their examples are appropriate.

Workbook page 54

1. 1700

2. 2600

3. 1260

4. 900

5. 1600

6. 380

7. 22 400

8. 1900

9. 240

10. 2900

11. 3800

12. 840

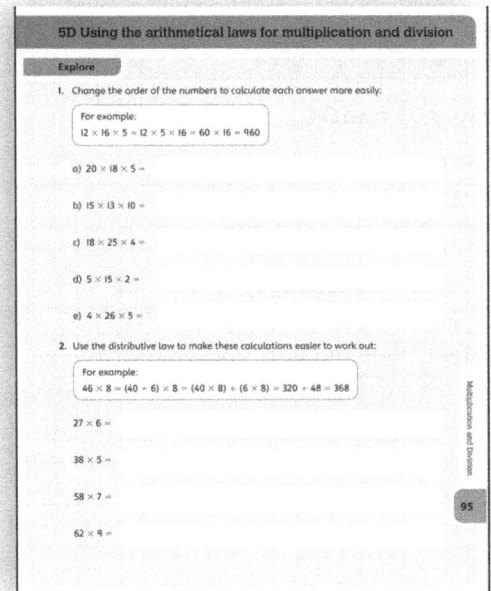

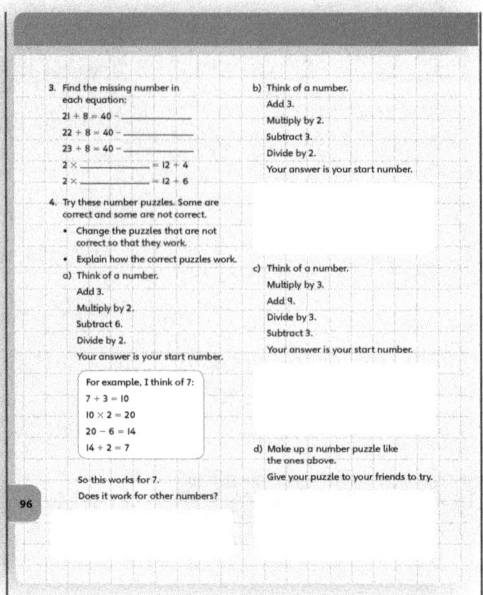

Specific learning focus

● Know and apply the arithmetic laws as they apply to multiplication (without necessarily using the terms commutative, associative or distributive).

Problem solving focus

● Make, test and refine hypotheses, explain and justify methods, reasoning, strategies, results or conclusions orally.

Key vocabulary

Multiple, multiplication, product, divide, division, divisor, dividend, double, halve, factor, quotient, associative law, commutative law

Resources

● None needed

Links to Student Book

See pages 95–96 in Student Book.

Links to Workbook

Workbook page 55

Links to Digital Resource Pack

Digital Resource Pack 6 contains two activities which can be used to support students' multiplication and division of different numbers. On the home page, select 'Multiplication and Division'.

Language support

Ask students to explain how they devised their own number puzzles. Make sure that they are clear in their understanding at each step. Ask, for example:

● Why did you choose to divide at this step?
● Why did you choose that digit?
● How do you know that this puzzle works?

Introductory activity

Group the students in pairs so that one of the pair is confident in using mental methods for **multiplication**. Ask students to start the activities on pages 95 and 96 of the Student Book immediately, sharing strategies with one another or modelling strategies for less confident students. As they work, ask individual students to explain their strategies to you. After 5 minutes, bring the class together. Select three students with slightly different strategies to explain their method. Ask the class to agree which strategy they prefer.

 Main activity

Ask students to complete questions 1 to 4c in pairs. When they have completed question 4d tell, them to test out their question on a friend. Select some of the most challenging number puzzles to use in the Learning Review. Remind students that multiplying by 2 is referred to as 'doubling' and dividing by 2 is the same as 'halving'.

Differentiation

Supporting: Arrange groups for support together.

Consolidating: Ask students to explain their strategies to you and to other students.

Extending: Ask students to devise more complex number puzzles.

Differentiated outcomes	
All students	should carry out calculations with support from other students.
Most students	will carry out calculations and support other students.
Some students	will confidently explain a range of strategies.

 Learning review

Share three or four of the best number puzzles as a whole class. Ask the student who devised the puzzle to explain: *Why does it work?*

Additional activities

Students can share their number puzzles with their parents or other adults at home.

Students can complete Workbook page 55.

Answers

Student Book pages 95 and 96

1. **a)** $20 \times 5 \times 18 = 100 \times 18 = 1800$
   b) $15 \times 10 \times 13 = 150 \times 13 = 1950$
   c) $4 \times 25 \times 18 = 100 \times 18 = 1800$
   d) $5 \times 2 \times 15 = 10 \times 15 = 150$
   e) $5 \times 4 \times 26 = 20 \times 26 = 520$

2. $27 \times 6 = 20 \times 6 + 7 \times 6 = 120 + 42 = 162$
   $38 \times 5 = 30 \times 5 + 8 \times 5 = 150 + 40 = 190$
   $58 \times 7 = 50 \times 7 + 8 \times 7 = 350 + 56 = 406$
   $62 \times 9 = 60 \times 9 + 2 \times 9 = 540 + 18 = 558$

3. $21 + 8 = 40 - 11$
   $22 + 8 = 40 - 10$
   $23 + 8 = 40 - 9$
   $2 \times 8 = 12 + 4$
   $2 \times 9 = 12 + 6$

4. Answers will vary as students choose how to change the calculations. Accept any correct solutions.

Workbook page 55

1. 222
2. 430
3. 174
4. 252
5. 6724
6. 693
7. 252
8. 208
9. 296
10. 322
11. 296
12. 492

5 Multiplication and division

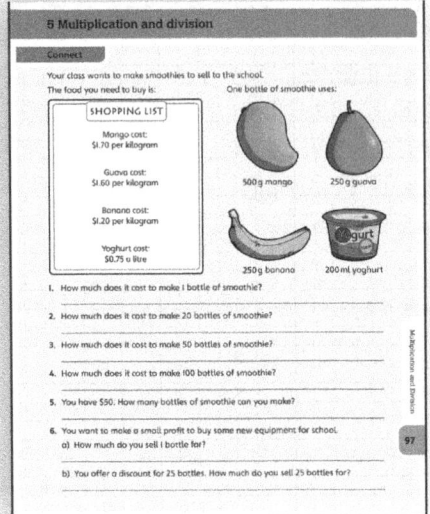
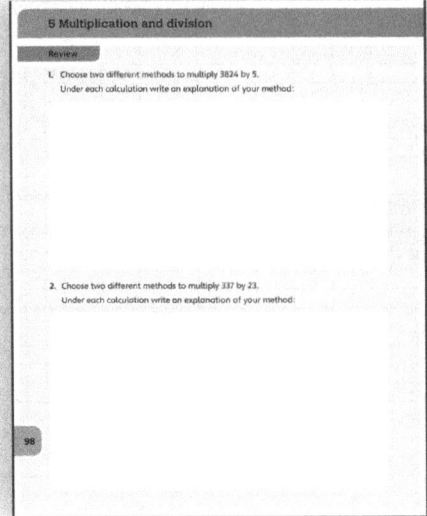
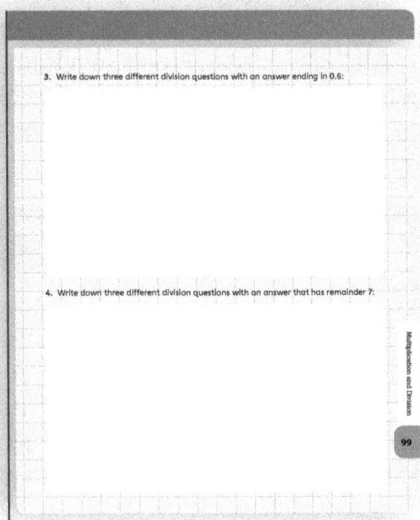

Specific learning foci

- Add or subtract numbers with the same and different numbers of decimal places, including amounts of money.
- Give an answer to division as a mixed number, and a decimal.
- Multiply two-, three- or four-digit numbers (including sums of money) by a single-digit number.
- Divide three-digit numbers by single-digit numbers including those leaving a remainder and divide three-digit numbers by two-digit numbers (no remainder) including sums of money.

Problem solving focus

- Make sense of and solve word problems, single and multi-step.

Key vocabulary

Place value, multiple, product, partition, estimate, double, halve, share, share equally, divide, division, divisor, dividend, remainder, factor, quotient

Resources

- Assessment activity 5– one per student (Resource sheet 5 – see www.oxfordprimary.com/OIPMteacher)

Links to Student Book

See pages 97–99 in Student Book.

Links to Workbook

Workbook page 56

Links to Digital Resource Pack

Digital Resource Pack 6 contains two activities which can be used to support students' multiplication and division of different numbers. On the home page, select 'Multiplication and Division'.

Language support

Use the language of problem solving throughout the activity. Ask, for example:

- *How do you know which calculation to use?*
- *How did you work that out?*
- *Is that answer reasonable?*

 Introductory and Main activity

Ask students to work in mixed-attainment groups of four on the activities on page 97 of the Student Book. Encourage them to try to interpret and begin the activity without any teacher input. his activity is a single extended piece of work. Support each group as they tackle the problem. Allow them thinking time at the beginning to decide on their own strategy. Do not offer help too quickly.

Ask all the groups to share their solutions and their thinking for the final question. Then ask the class to agree: *Which group had the 'best' pricing policy?* Groups should discuss this question carefully before deciding and offer convincing reasons for their choices.

Differentiation

Students should work in mixed-attainment groups to support one another in working through the investigation on page 97 of the Student Book.

When students work through pages 98 and 99 of the Student Book, you may want to help write the answers for those less confident with writing or in speaking English.

Differentiated outcomes
The activities on page 97 of the Student Book are designed to offer differentiation by outcome.

 Learning review

Students should complete the Review activity on pages 98 and 99 of the Student Book as individuals as it is a summative assessment.

Additional activities

The Connect activity is a suitable activity to carry out as a real-life project.

Students can complete Workbook page 56.

Answers

Student Book page 97
1. $1.70
2. $34
3. $85
4. $850
5. 29 bottles
6. Answers will vary as students choose the prices and discounts of the bottles. Accept any well-reasoned answer.

Student Book pages 98 and 99
1. 19 120; students' multiplication methods will vary. Check that the methods are appropriate.
2. 7751; students' multiplication methods will vary. Check that the methods are appropriate.
3. and 4. Students' multiplication methods and division calculations will vary

Workbook page 56
1. $110.50
2. $218.40
3. $13
4. $25.65

Assessment activity 5
1. c) $(53 \times 30) + (53 \times 6)$
2. a) 25
3. b) 18 with 8 left over
4. c) 0.75
5. c) sometimes the same and sometimes less
6. b) $22.50
7. 1, 2, 4, 8, 16, 32, 64, 128, 256, 512 (So I will earn $512 in the tenth week, and $1 027 in total). Yes – I will earn $1 048 576 in the 21st week!

Unit 6 Shapes and Geometry

Overview

Big Idea

The key idea in this unit is using the properties of 2D and 3D shapes to classify and name shapes. Exploring what shapes have in common and what is different about them helps students to understand these properties. You can do this through visualisation and through explanation in discussion. It is vital that students spend time talking about what they notice about shapes. All the activities in this unit require students to describe what they see.

It is also important that students see angle as a dynamic measure. That means that an angle is formed through movement. You can use examples in the classroom, for example the movement of a door, to show that angle is a measurement of the amount of turn.

Possible misconceptions

Students often assume that shapes always appear in familiar orientations and that all shapes are regular. For example, they may assume that all triangles are regular equilateral triangles or that a hexagon refers to a regular six-sided shape rather than any six-sided shape. It is important that students see shapes in many different orientations.

Key vocabulary and language structures

Support students in the use of technical language in this unit. Some terms may seem similar, for example 'parallel' and 'perpendicular'. Model the correct use of terms and create vocabulary lists and glossaries to help students. The key vocabulary for this unit is:

Edge, perimeter, vertex, vertices, face (*How many edges/ vertices/faces does that shape have?*), straight, curved (*How many curved edges does that shape have?*) net, base, regular, irregular, parallel, perpendicular, concave, convex, open, closed, cross-section, 2D, 3D, 2-dimensional, 3-dimensional; polygon, circle, triangle, equilateral triangle, isosceles triangle, scalene triangle, pentagon, hexagon, heptagon, octagon; quadrilateral, kite, parallelogram, rhombus, rectangle, square; cube, cuboid, pyramid, sphere, hemisphere, cone, cylinder, prism, tetrahedron, polyhedron, octahedron, dodecahedron; front elevation, side elevation, plan view, isometric drawing; acute angle, obtuse angle, reflex angle, right angle, interior angle

Coverage in lessons

Learning focus	Learning outcomes
Classifying polygons	Can I classify different polygons?
	Can I recognise whether a 2D shape is a polygon or not?
	Can I identify and describe properties of quadrilaterals including a parallelogram, rhombus and trapezium?
	Can I use properties to classify quadrilaterals?
Properties of 3D shapes	Can I visualise and describe the properties of 3D shapes including faces, edges and vertices?
Making 2D representations of 3D shapes	Can I recognise and make 2D representations of 3D shapes?
Drawing angles and angles in a triangle	Can I estimate and draw acute and obtuse angles?
	Can I use a protractor to measure angles to the nearest degree?
	Can I check that the sum of angles in a triangle is 180°?

Engage

Specific learning foci

- Classify different polygons and understand whether a 2D shape is a polygon or not.
- *Visualise and describe the properties of 3D shapes.*
- Identify and describe properties of quadrilaterals.

Problem solving focus

- Recognise 2D and 3D shapes and their relationships.

Key vocabulary

Edge, perimeter, vertex, vertices, face, straight, curved, net, base, regular, irregular, parallel, perpendicular, concave, convex, open, closed, cross-section, 2D, 3D, 2-dimensional, 3-dimensional, polygon, circle, triangle, equilateral triangle, isosceles triangle, scalene triangle, pentagon, hexagon, heptagon, octagon quadrilateral, kite, parallelogram, rhombus, rectangle, square, cube, cuboid, pyramid, sphere, hemispheres, cone, cylinder, prism, tetrahedron, polyhedron, octahedron, dodecahedron, front elevation, side elevation, plan view, isometric drawing, acute angle, obtuse angle, reflex angle, right angle, interior angle

Resources

- Mini whiteboards and markers
- Index cards
- Selection of magazines and newspapers that students or their families read regularly

Links to Student Book

See page 101 in Student Book.

Language support

Use the posters as Language support for the rest of the unit. It is important that students present the posters to the rest of the class, to enable them to practise speaking the words. Remind students how to pronounce the more unfamiliar words.

 Introductory activity

Ask students to work in mixed-attainment groups of between four and six students. The groups should look at the image on page 101 of the Student Book and list as many shapes as they can see. After 5 minutes ask the groups to feedback. Create a list of all the shapes on the board. Ask each group to write the different shapes on an index card, one shape per card. Then ask the groups to classify the shapes in at least three different ways (for example: **2-dimensional/3-dimensional**, **regular/irregular**, equal sides, equal angles, **straight** sides, **curved**). Ask them to record each classification.

 Main activity

Give each group a selection of newspapers and magazines and ask the group to cut out as many images of shapes as they can find in them. Then ask them to select shapes and to make a poster using as much of the language of shape as they can remember.

Differentiation

All students should contribute to the group discussion and use the vocabulary they can remember. All students will also hear vocabulary that is new to them. Encourage students to ask for definitions of any words that other students use that they don't understand.

Learning review

Ask each group to bring their poster to the front and to share it with the class. Encourage other students to suggest vocabulary that can be added to the poster. Display the posters for the rest of the unit. When new vocabulary is introduced students can add it to the posters.

Additional activities

Students can take photographs of shapes at home or in the locality and use these to make vocabulary posters.

6A Classifying polygons

Discover

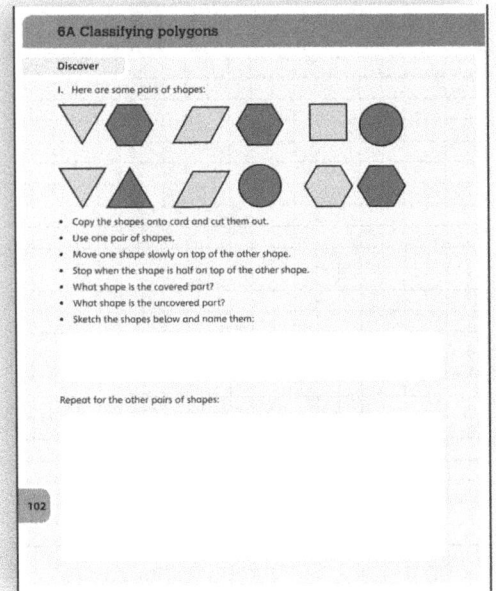
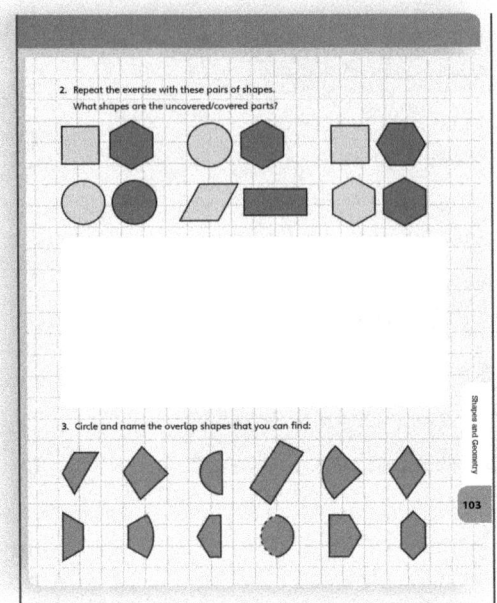

Specific learning foci

- *Classify different polygons and understand whether a 2D shape is a polygon or not.*
- Identify and describe properties of quadrilaterals.

Problem solving focus

- Recognise 2D and 3D shapes and their relationships.

Key vocabulary

Edge, perimeter, vertex, vertices, face straight, curved, regular, irregular, parallel, perpendicular, open, closed, 2-dimensional, polygon, circle, triangle, equilateral triangle, isosceles triangle, scalene triangle, pentagon, hexagon, heptagon, octagon quadrilateral, kite, parallelogram, rhombus, rectangle, square, acute angle, obtuse angle, reflex angle, right angle, interior angle

Resources

- Large equilateral triangle
- Large square
- Card, scissors
- Mathematical dictionary
- Index cards or mini whiteboards and markers

Links to Student Book

See pages 102–103 in Student Book.

Links to Workbook

Workbook page 58

Links to Digital Resource Pack

Digital Resource Pack 6 contains two activities which can be used to support students' recognition and classification of polygons. On the home page, select 'Shapes and Geometry'.

Language support

The game in the Learning review asks students to use the technical vocabulary of shape. Model a wide range of vocabulary and the pronunciation. Encourage students to use the posters from 6 Engage activity as support and to add any new vocabulary.

 **Introductory activity**

Ask two students to come to the front of the class. Ask one student to hold the large **equilateral triangle** and one to hold the large square. Then ask them to gradually overlap the two shapes. Ask them to stop on several occasions. Each time they stop, ask the other students to write down as many properties as they can for the shape they can see in the overlap. Give them one minute to do this. Ask pairs to feedback after each overlap.

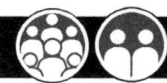 **Main activity**

Ask students to use the scissors and card to make the shapes they need to carry out the activity on pages 102 and 103 of the Student Book. Encourage pairs to use the mathematical dictionary to help them classify any shapes that they do not know, for example: **hexagon**, **heptagon**, **octagon**.

Differentiation

Supporting: Use posters to support students in naming shapes. Ask for properties such a number of sides and **curved** and **straight** edges.

Consolidating: Ask for properties such a number of sides and curved and straight edges and symmetry properties.

Extending: Encourage students to use dictionaries to find names of shapes that they have not met. They should describe a wide range of properties of these shapes.

Differentiated outcomes	
All students	should recognise and name common shapes and describe their properties. They will understand the definition of a polygon.
Most students	will recognise and name most shapes and describe their properties including symmetry.
Some students	will recognise and name all the shapes and describe their properties including symmetry and angle properties.

 **Learning review**

Ask students to draw one of the shapes that they made using the overlap in question 1 on an index card or on their mini whiteboard. Ask them to move around the room (or the class could go outside to play this game). When you say, 'Stop!' ask students to partner with the person next to them. In pairs, ask them to find one thing that their shapes have in common and one difference. Continue this and encourage students to use a wide range of vocabulary.

Additional activities

Students can write instructions to allow someone to make an exact copy of a shape they are thinking about.

Students can complete Workbook page 58.

Answers

Student Book pages 102 and 103

Answers will vary. Accept any accurate answers. Ask students to explain how they know the name of the covered and uncovered parts of the shapes.

Workbook page 58

Answers will vary as students make their own shapes. Check that the names and the properties that the students list match their sketches of their polygons.

6A Classifying polygons

Explore

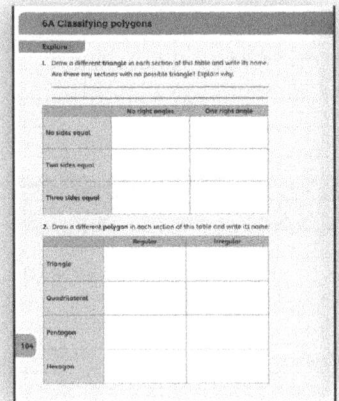 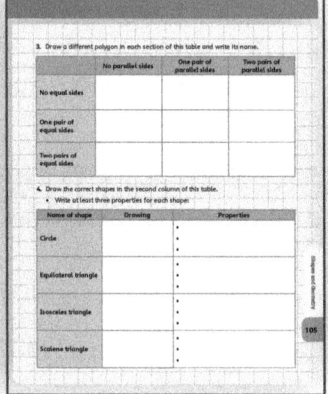 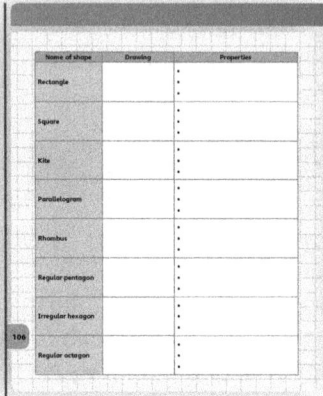 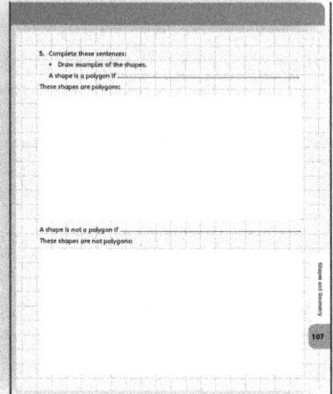

Specific learning foci

- *Classify different polygons and understand whether a 2D shape is a polygon or not.*
- Identify and describe properties of quadrilaterals.

Problem solving focus

- Recognise 2D and 3D shapes and their relationships.

Key vocabulary

Edge, perimeter, vertex, vertices, face straight, curved, regular, irregular, parallel, perpendicular, open, closed, 2-dimensional, polygon, circle, triangle, equilateral triangle, isosceles triangle, right-angled triangle, scalene triangle, pentagon, hexagon, heptagon, octagon quadrilateral, kite, parallelogram, rhombus, rectangle, square, acute angle, obtuse angle, reflex angle, right angle, interior angle

Resources

- Rope (or similar) cut into 12 m lengths
- Flip chart paper

Links to Student Book

See pages 104–107 in Student Book.

Links to Workbook

Workbook page 58

Links to Digital Resource Pack

Digital Resource Pack 6 contains two activities which can be used to support students' recognition and classification of polygons. On the home page, select 'Shapes and Geometry'.

Language support

Encourage students to explain their thinking and to say the vocabulary aloud. Use questions, for example:

- *Are these shapes exactly the same?*
- *What is this shape?*
- *Is this shape a polygon? Why? Why not?*

 Introductory activity

Take the class outdoors or into a large space such as a hall. Ask the class to work in groups of 12 if possible. Give each group a piece of rope. Explain that they are going to make various shapes by holding the rope in different ways and using their bodies and the rope to form the shape. Ask them to make the following shapes:

- A square
- A rectangle
- A different rectangle
- A **triangle**
- An **equilateral triangle**
- A **right-angled triangle**
- An **isosceles triangle**
- A **scalene triangle**
- A **hexagon**

After each shape, ask one student from each group to sketch the shape they made on a large piece of flip-chart paper. At the end of the activity ask the groups to share their results. Ask: *Are your shapes exactly the same?*

 Main activity

Ask students to work in pairs on the activities on pages 104–107 of the Student Book. Encourage the pairs to discuss their answers and to draw and name various triangles and polygons separately first before drawing them in the correct section of the classification tables. Remind students that a **polygon** is a closed **2-dimensional** (2D) shape with **straight** sides. Any shape with a **curved** side, or any shape with a gap in the perimeter (an open shape) is not a polygon. If necessary, remind students about **parallel** sides and **perpendicular** sides.

Remind students that they should be specific when they name the shapes in question 2. For example, they may use an 'equilateral triangle' for a regular triangle or a 'square' for a regular **quadrilateral**. A regular **pentagon** should be written simply as 'regular pentagon' to emphasise that a 'regular pentagon' is a subset of the set 'pentagon'.

Differentiation

Supporting: Use posters to support students in naming shapes. Ask for properties such as number of sides and curved and straight edges.

Consolidating: Ask for properties such as number of sides and curved and straight edges and symmetry properties.

Extending: Encourage students to use dictionaries to find names of shapes that they have not met. They should describe a wide range of properties of these shapes.

Differentiated outcomes	
All students	should classify common shapes and describe their properties. They will understand the definition of a polygon.
Most students	will classify a wide range of shapes and describe their properties including symmetry.
Some students	will recognise and name all the shapes and describe their properties including symmetry and angle properties.

 Learning review

Draw a large table on the board like this:

	Polygon	Not a polygon
Contains only **right angles**		
Contains at least one **obtuse angle**		
Contains at least one **reflex angle**		

Ask students to come up to the board one at a time and to draw a shape in one of the boxes on the table. Remind students of the meanings of the terms acute, obtuse and reflex.

Additional activities

Students can take photographs of shapes around the school. They can use the tables in questions 1 or 2 to classify them.

Students can complete Workbook page 58.

Answers

Student Book pages 104–107

Answers will vary as students choose their own shapes to draw in the tables and the properties of their shapes. Check that students' properties match their shapes.

Workbook page 58

Answers will vary as students make their own shapes. Check that the names and the properties that the students list match their sketches of their polygons.

6B Properties of 3D shapes

Discover

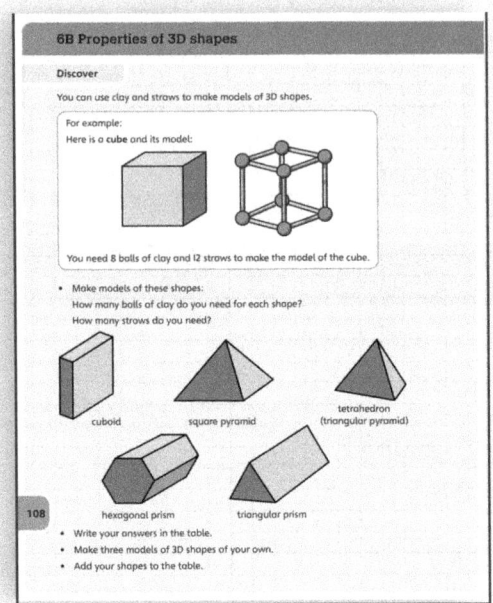
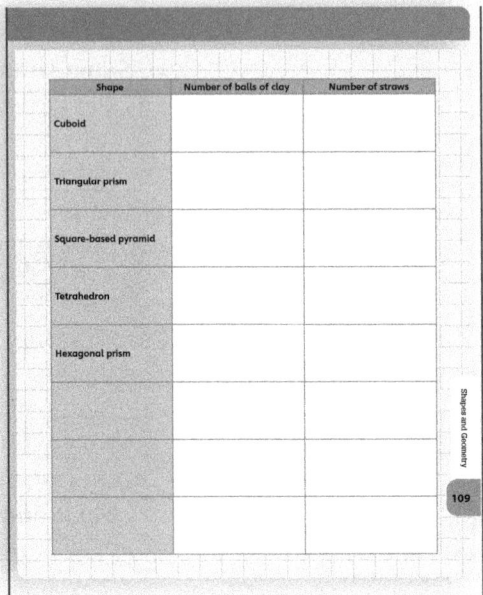

Specific learning foci

- *Visualise and describe the properties of 3D shapes.*
- Recognise 2D representations of 3D shapes.

Problem solving focus

- Recognise 2D and 3D shapes and their relationships.

Key vocabulary

Edge, perimeter, vertex, vertices, face, parallel, perpendicular, cross-section, 3D, 3-dimensional, cube, cuboid, pyramid, sphere, hemisphere, cone, cylinder, prism, tetrahedron, polyhedron, octahedron, dodecahedron

Resources

- Modelling clay or adhesive putty such as Blu-tack
- Modelling straws

Links to Student Book

See pages 108–109 in Student Book.

Links to Workbook

Workbook page 59

Links to Digital Resource Pack

Digital Resource Pack 6 contains two activities which can be used to support students' recognition of the properties of polygons. On the home page, select 'Shapes and Geometry'.

Language support

Encourage students to use the appropriate technical vocabulary, for example: vertices, edges and faces.

Remind students that the plural of vertex is vertices. It is important that students realise that there are lots of different prisms, pyramids and cylinders, and that these are classified by the shape of their base. Remind students that the base of a prism is its cross-section.

Ask questions, for example:

- *How many vertices/edges/faces does that shape have?*
- *What shape is the base?*

 **Introductory activity**

Ask a student to come to the front of the class. The other students are going to give this student instructions to make a cube, using modelling clay and straws, as shown on page 108 of the Student Book. Each student can give only one instruction; then it is the next student's turn.

Write the key instructions on the board as a model for the exercises on pages 108 and 109 of the Student Book, for example: *Attach two straws to one ball of clay. Put the straws at right angles to one another.*

 **Main activity**

Ask students to work on the activity on pages 108 and 109 of the Student Book in pairs to encourage discussion.

Ask: *What do you notice about the relationship between the straws and balls of clay and the numbers of **vertices** and **edges** of the shape?* The students should name the shapes that they are making and describe other properties of the shapes.

There are three additional rows in the table on page 109 for students to make their own **3D shapes**.

Differentiation

Supporting: Ask students to show you how they are counting vertices, edges and **faces.**

Consolidating: Ask students to name the new shapes they are making and to tell you their properties.

Extending: Encourage students make complex shapes of their own and find their names.

Differentiated outcomes	
All students	should make the shapes and count faces, angles and vertices.
Most students	will make shapes of their own and find their names.
Some students	will make complex shapes of their own and find their names.

 **Learning review**

Ask one of the pairs to describe the 3-dimensional (3D) shape that they created for themselves. They need to describe it so that you can exactly copy the shape. As they describe the shape, ask questions and model phrases using the vocabulary of shape to model the correct pronunciation, for example: *How many faces does this shape have? This shape has five faces. What shape are the faces? The two faces at each end are equilateral triangles. They are the same size.*

Additional activities

Students can bring examples of 3D shapes from home to share with the class. Alternatively, they can take photographs of 3D shapes in the locality to create posters.

Students can complete Workbook page 59.

Answers

Student Book pages 108 and 109

Shape	Number of balls of clay	Number of straws
Cuboid	8	12
Triangular prism	6	9
Square-based pyramid	5	8
Tetrahedron	4	6
Hexagonal prism	12	8

Workbook page 59

Answers will vary as students choose their own shapes to analyse. Check that they have recorded the correct numbers of faces, vertices and edges.

6B Properties of 3D shapes

Explore

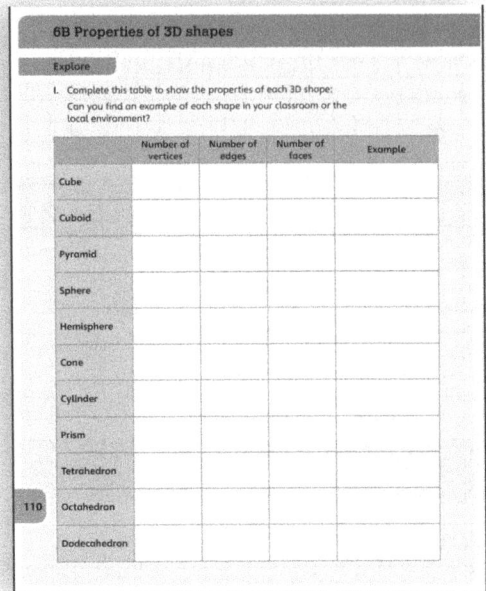

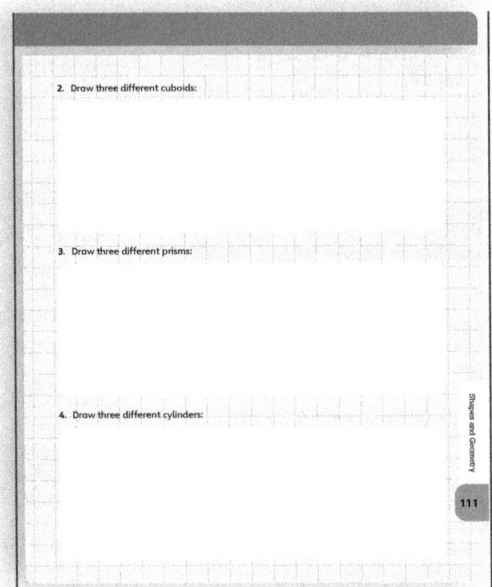

Specific learning foci

- *Visualise and describe the properties of 3D shapes.*
- Recognise 2D representations of 3D shapes.

Problem solving focus

- Recognise 2D and 3D shapes and their relationships.

Key vocabulary

Edge, perimeter, vertex, vertices, face, parallel, perpendicular, cross-section, 3D, 3-dimensional, cube, cuboid, pyramid, sphere, hemisphere, cone, cylinder, prism, tetrahedron, polyhedron, octahedron, dodecahedron

Resources

- A range of different 3D shapes

Links to Student Book

See pages 110–111 in Student Book.

Links to Workbook

Workbook page 59

Links to Digital Resource Pack

Digital Resource Pack 6 contains two activities which can be used to support students' recognition of the properties of polygons. On the home page, select 'Shapes and Geometry'.

Language support

Encourage students to use the appropriate technical vocabulary, for example: vertices, edges and faces. Remind students that the plural of vertex is vertices.

It is important that students realise that there are lots of different prisms, pyramids and cylinders and that these are classified by the shape of their base. Ask questions, for example:

- *How many vertices/edges/faces does that shape have?*
- *What shape is the base?*

For the Learning review, students need to ask questions with a yes or no answer, for example:

- *Does the shape have six faces?*
- *Does the shape have any curved faces?*

138

 Introductory activity

Have a **3-dimensional** container in a bag on the desk. Describe one property of the shape. For example, for a **cube** you can say: *It has six faces*. Ask pairs to write down any possible shapes with this property. Repeat this until the students 'guess' the shape. Repeat two or three times using different 3D shapes. Then encourage students to describe the properties.

 Main activity

Ask students to work in pairs on the activity on pages 110 and 111 of the Student Book to encourage discussion.

Encourage students to find a 3D shape and see where it fits in the grid rather than try to fill in the grid from top to bottom. You could bring a range of books into the classroom for students to explore for examples, including more unusual or complex examples such as **tetrahedron, polyhedron, octahedron, dodecahedron**.

Differentiation

Supporting: Focus on accurately counting the faces, **vertices** and **edges** of basic 3D shapes.

Consolidating: Encourage students to find examples of all the 3D shapes in the table and count faces, edges and vertices.

Extending: Encourage students to find examples of all the 3D shapes that do not appear in the table and to describe their properties.

Differentiated outcomes	
All students	should find examples of basic 3D shapes and count faces, edges and vertices.
Most students	will find examples of all the 3D shapes in the table and count faces, edges and vertices.
Some students	will find examples of all the 3D shapes in the table as well as others and count faces, edges and vertices.

 Learning review

Ask a student to come to the front of the classroom and to choose one of the 3D shapes they can see in the room without saying which it is. Ask the other students to ask questions (for example: 'Does it have six faces?'), one at a time, to help them guess the shape. The student can only answer 'Yes' or 'No' to each question.

Additional activities

Students can bring examples of 3D shapes from home to share. Alternatively, they can take photographs of 3D shapes in the locality to create posters.

Students can complete Workbook page 59.

Answers

Student Book pages 110 and 111

	Number of vertices	Number of edges	Number of faces
Cube	8	12	6
Cuboid	8	12	6
Pyramid	Dependent on the example they use		
Sphere	0	0	1
Hemisphere	0	1	2
Cone	1	1	2
Cylinder	0	2	3
Prism	Dependent on the example they use		
Tetrahedron	4	6	4
Octahedron	6	12	8
Dodecahedron	20	30	12

Workbook page 59

Answers will vary as students choose their own shapes to analyse. Check that they have recorded the correct numbers of faces, vertices and edges.

Discover

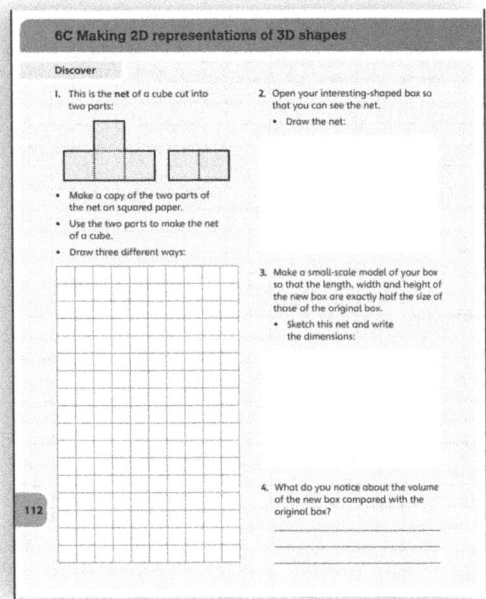

Specific learning focus

- Recognise and make 2D representations of 3D shapes including nets.

Problem solving focus

- Recognise 2D and 3D shapes and their relationships.

Key vocabulary

Net, base, 3D, 2-dimensional, 3-dimensional, polygon, circle, triangle, equilateral triangle, isosceles triangle, scalene triangle, pentagon, hexagon, heptagon, octagon, quadrilateral, kite, parallelogram, rhombus, rectangle, square, cube, cuboid, pyramid, sphere, cone, cylinder, prism, tetrahedron, polyhedron, octahedron, dodecahedron

Resources

- Squared paper
- A selection of boxes including different-shaped cuboids, different-shaped cylinders, prisms and pyramids
- Card, scissors, sticky tape

Links to Student Book

See page 112 in Student Book.

Links to Workbook

Workbook page 60

Links to Digital Resource Pack

Digital Resource Pack 6 contains two activities which can be used to support students' recognition of the faces of 3D shapes. On the home page, select 'Shapes and Geometry'.

Language support

Throughout this activity ask students to explain their answers. Model the use of the key mathematical vocabulary, for example: length, width, height, faces, edges, as well as the names of shapes.

Ask students to find as many different ways as possible of arranging five squares, with at least one edge of each square touching the edge of another square. For example:

After 10 minutes, collect as many examples as you can. Ask students to draw these examples on the board. Then ask students to decide: *Which can you fold up into an open box? Which can you not fold up into an open box?* Ask students to explain their answers. Remind students that the shapes that can be folded to form an open cube are called **nets** of a cube.

Ask students to work in pairs on the activity in the Student Book to encourage discussion. Give each pair a different box. (You could ask students to bring in their own boxes from home for this activity.)

Differentiation

Supporting: Encourage students to find all possible arrangements of the squares and to describe the properties of their net.

Consolidating: Ask students to describe the process of making a scale model.

Extending: Ask students to explore a general rule to predict which will form nets of **cubes** and general rules linking lengths, areas and volumes

Differentiated outcomes	
All students	should find a range of ways to arrange the squares and draw a net of their box.
Most students	will find all the ways to arrange the cubes and will visualise which are cubes of nets and make accurate scale models.
Some students	will find a general rule to predict which will form nets of cubes and general rules linking lengths, areas and volumes.

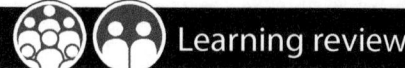

Take feedback from students. Ask: *What did you notice about the difference in volume between the scale model and the original box?* Write these sentences on the board and ask students to complete them by looking at their models:

I double the dimensions of a box. The new length is ___ times the original length.

I double the dimensions of a box. The new area of a face is ___ times the original area of a face.

I double the dimensions of a box. The new volume is ___ times the original volume.

Note that while volume is beyond the scope of the framework for Stage 6, students are likely to have a natural understanding of volume, particularly when working with 3D models.

Additional activities

Students can make boxes out of card, to hold presents. Encourage them to make some boxes which are not cuboids.

Students can complete Workbook page 60.

Answers

Student Book page 112

Answers will vary as students draw their own nets and make their own models. Accept any correct answers. While students make their models, ask them what they notice about the size of their models compared to the size of the original shapes.

Workbook page 60

Answers will vary as students choose different boxes to make their own 3D shapes. Accept any correct answers.

6C Making 2D representations of 3D shapes

Explore

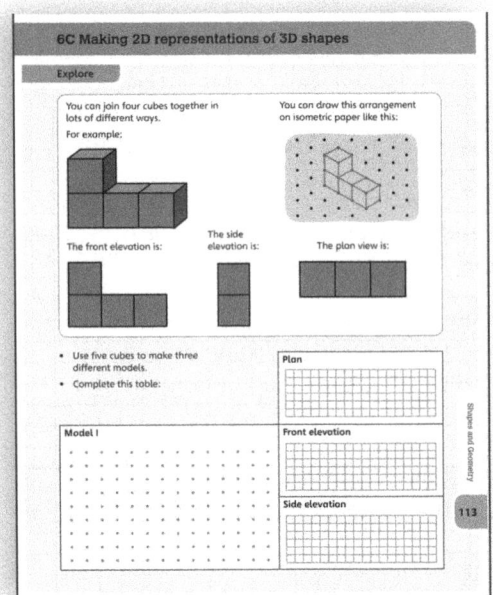

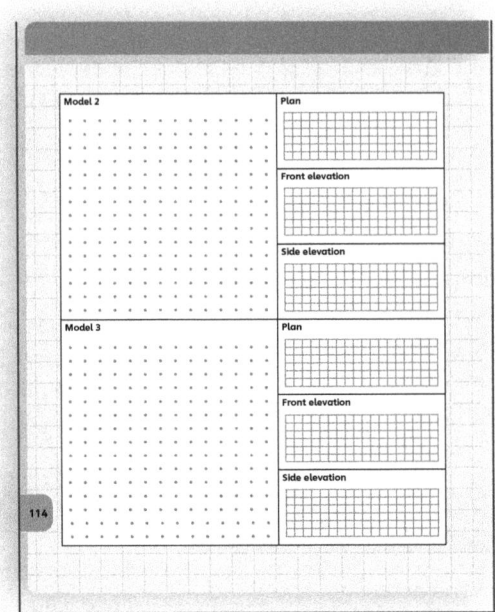

Specific learning focus

- Recognise and make 2D representations of 3D shapes including nets.

Problem solving focus

- Recognise 2D and 3D shapes and their relationships.

Key vocabulary

Edge, vertex, vertices, net, base, 3-dimensional, rectangle, square, cube, cuboid, front elevation, side elevation, plan view, isometric drawing

Resources

- Linking cubes
- Large box
- Isometric paper
- Squared paper

Links to Student Book

See pages 113–114 in Student Book.

Links to Workbook

Workbook page 60

Links to Digital Resource Pack

Digital Resource Pack 6 contains two activities which can be used to support students' recognition of the faces of 3D shapes. On the home page, select 'Shapes and Geometry'.

Language support

The Introductory activity demands a high level of language skills. You may need to model the use of relevant vocabulary, for example:

The ball is............. the bag.

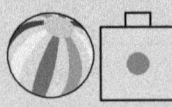
next to

on top of

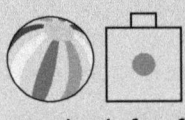
to the left of

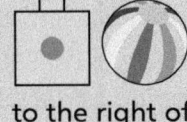
to the right of

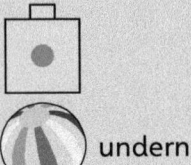
underneath

Introductory activity

Ask two students to come to the front. Ask one student to make a model out of five linking cubes. Put it in the large box so that the other students cannot see it. Then ask the student to give instructions so that their partner exactly replicates the model. This should include matching colours. Repeat this activity three times with different students. Use the last model to draw a **front elevation**, then a **side elevation** and finally a **plan view** on the board. Write these terms on the board. For support, students can make copies of the models so that they can see the three views clearly for themselves.

 Main activity

Ask students to work in pairs on the activity on pages 113 and 114 of the Student Book to encourage discussion. Students may need additional support in carrying out the **isometric drawing**. Use peer support for this.

Differentiation

Supporting: Offer students support from other students to use isometric paper.

Consolidating: Ask students to support other students in using isometric paper.

Extending: Ask students to draw more complex plans, using isometric paper.

Differentiated outcomes	
All students	should recognise the different views and use isometric paper with support.
Most students	will recognise the different views and support other students to use isometric paper.
Some students	will draw more complex plans.

 Learning review

Ask one of the pairs to come to the front and draw the plan view for one of their shapes. Ask the other students: *Is this enough information to replicate the model?* Then ask the pair to draw the front elevation. The other students make any changes to their models that they need to. Finally, ask the pair to draw the side elevation. Ask the other students: *Is your model an exact copy?* Repeat this activity if necessary.

Additional activities

Students can use isometric paper to sketch a wide range of 3D shapes.

Students can complete Workbook page 61.

Answers

Student Book pages 113 and 114

Answers will vary as students use the cubes to make their own shapes. Check that students' drawing match their models. Observe students while they're working and note who is able to record their shapes on isometric paper and who needs more practice.

Workbook page 61

Answers will vary because students draw their own triangles on the 'pin boards'. Check that students have labelled the acute angles, obtuse angles and right angles correctly.

Discover

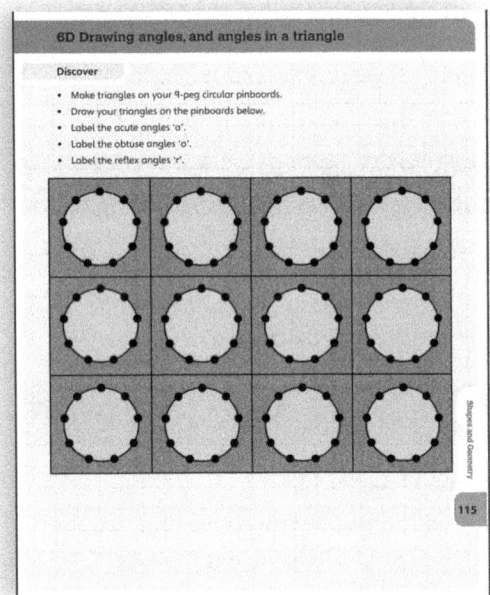

Specific learning foci

- Estimate, recognise and draw acute and obtuse angles and use a protractor to measure to the nearest degree.
- *Check that the sum of angles in a triangle is 180°.*

Problem solving focus

- Make, test and refine hypotheses, explain and justify methods, reasoning, strategies, results or conclusions orally.

Key vocabulary

Perimeter, vertex, vertices, triangle, equilateral triangle, isosceles triangle, right-angled triangle, scalene triangle, acute angle, obtuse angle, reflex angle, right angle, interior angle

Resources

- 9-peg circular pinboards and elastic bands (if possible) or printed circles with 9 dots equally spaced around the circumference
- Large protractor

Links to Student Book

See page 115 in Student Book.

Links to Workbook

Workbook page 60

Links to Digital Resource Pack

Digital Resource Pack 6 contains two activities which can be used to support students' recognition of different types of triangle. On the home page, select 'Shapes and Geometry'.

Language support

Challenge students to make triangles with particular properties.

Ask questions, for example:

- *Can you find a triangle with an obtuse angle?*
- *Can you find a triangle with a reflex angle?*
- *Can you find a triangle with a right angle?*

Encourage students to classify the triangles using examples of equilateral, isosceles, right-angled and scalene triangles.

Support students with the pronunciation of the names of triangles.

 ## Introductory activity

Draw five 9-pin circular pinboards on the board. Ask five different students to come to the front of the class and draw a **triangle**. Each triangle should be different from the previous one. Ask pairs of students to discuss the properties and the names of the triangles. Take feedback and label the different types of triangles and the different angles on the board for students to refer to throughout the Main activity.

If any of the key vocabulary isn't listed, ask a student to draw a triangle that will give an example of that vocabulary.

 ## Main activity

Give out the pinboards and elastic bands. Ask each student in the group to make a different triangle on their pinboard. Then ask them to record the triangles in the Student Book. As you work with groups encourage them to look carefully at the triangles to check that 'different' triangles are not the same triangle in a different orientation. They can check this by measuring angles.

Differentiation

Supporting: Encourage students to draw examples of **equilateral**, **isosceles**, **right-angled** and **scalene triangles.**

Consolidating: Encourage students to name examples of equilateral, isosceles, right-angled and scalene triangles.

Extending: Encourage students to measure and label the angles in the triangles.

Differentiated outcomes	
All students	should make and name a range of triangles.
Most students	will make all the different triangles and label angles correctly.
Some students	will understand that interior angles of all triangles add up to 180° by estimating and measuring angles.

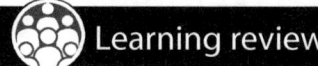 ## Learning review

Ask a student from each group to come to the front and to sketch one of their triangles on the board. Use a large protractor to check that the **interior angles** add up to 180°. This helps to remind students how to use a protractor for 6D Explore. Try to find examples of equilateral, isosceles, right-angled and scalene triangles.

Additional activities

Students can use the pinboards to explore different shapes. For example: How many quadrilaterals can they make? How many pentagons?

Students can complete Workbook page 60.

Answers

Student Book page 115

Answers will vary as students draw their own triangles on the pinboards. Check that students have labelled the acute angles, obtuse angles and reflex angles correctly.

Workbook page 60

Answers will vary as students choose different boxes to make their own 3D shapes. Accept any correct answers.

Explore

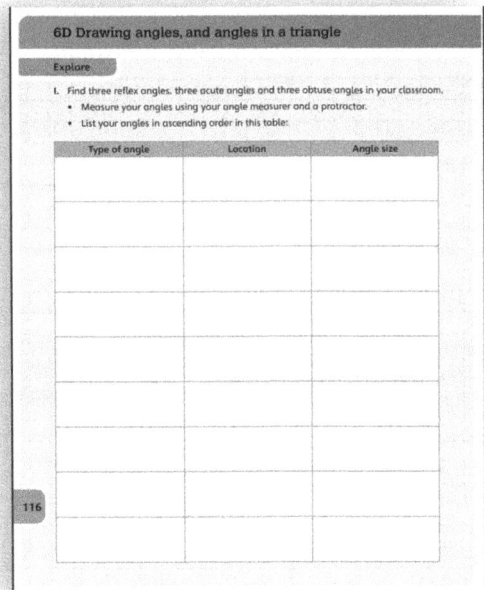
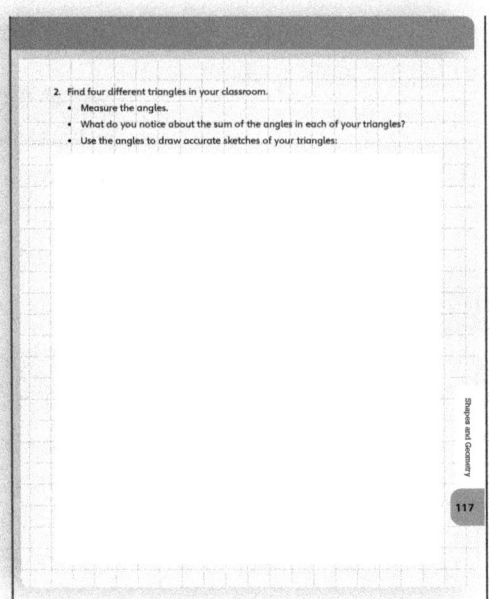

Specific learning foci

- *Estimate, recognise and draw acute and obtuse angles and use a protractor to measure to the nearest degree.*
- Check that the sum of angles in a triangle is 180°.

Problem solving focus

- Make, test and refine hypotheses, explain and justify methods, reasoning, strategies, results or conclusions orally.

Key vocabulary

Perimeter, vertex, vertices, triangle, equilateral triangle, isosceles triangle, right-angled triangle, scalene triangle, acute angle, obtuse angle, reflex angle, right angle, interior angle

Resources

- Protractors
- Strips of card
- Scissors
- Paper fasteners

Links to Student Book

See pages 116–117 in Student Book.

Links to Workbook

Workbook page 61

Links to Digital Resource Pack

Digital Resource Pack 6 contains two activities which can be used to support students' recognition of different types of triangle. On the home page, select 'Shapes and Geometry'.

Language support

As you work with the students, ask them to classify the triangles. Ask questions, for example:

- *What type of triangle is that?*
- *Is it equilateral, isosceles, right-angled or scalene?*
- *How do you know?*

 ## Introductory activity

Ask each student to make an angle measurer by putting a paper fastener through the corner of two pieces of card. It will look like this:

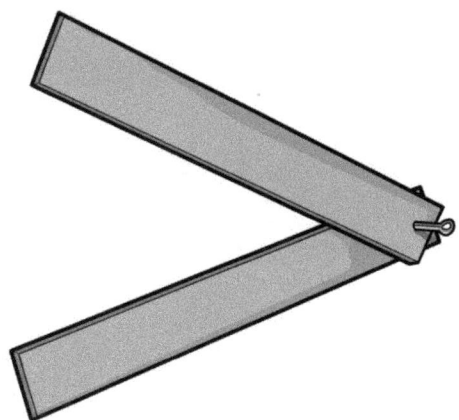

Ask students to show you an angle of 60°, then 140° and finally 230°. They should check their angles with a partner first and agree who is correct if they have different angles. Remind students of the meanings of the terms **acute**, **obtuse** and **reflex**. Hand out protractors to pairs of students. Ask one of the pair to challenge the other student to make a specific angle with their angle measurer. Then the first student checks the angle with their protractor. Remind students of the importance of using the cross as the zero point.

 ## Main activity

Ask students to work in the same pairs on the activity on pages 116 and 117 of the Student Book. Students can explore the environment around the classroom or outside to give them more choice of triangles and angles. They should take it in turns to complete a row in the table on page 116 of the Student Book.

Differentiation

Supporting: Encourage students to draw examples of **equilateral**, **isosceles**, **right-angled** and **scalene triangles.**

Consolidating: Encourage students to name examples of equilateral, isosceles, right-angled and scalene triangles.

Extending: Encourage students to measure and label the angles in the triangles.

Differentiated outcomes	
All students	should find and sketch triangles and understand the terms acute, obtuse and reflex.
Most students	will measure angles accurately with support.
Some students	will estimate angles accurately and support other students in using protractors.

 ## Learning review

Ask a student from each group to come to the front and to sketch one of their triangles on the board. Check that the interior angles add up to 180°. Try to find examples of equilateral, isosceles, right-angled and scalene triangles.

Additional activities

Students can use their angle measurers to help them make scale models of triangular structures that they find in the environment.

Students can complete Workbook page 61.

Answers

Student Book pages 116 and 117

Answers will vary as students find different angles and triangles in the classroom. Check that students' examples seem reasonable and that each angle type fits the measured size of the angle.

Workbook page 61

Answers will vary because students draw their own triangles on the 'pin boards'. Check that students have labelled the acute angles, obtuse angles and right angles correctly.

6 Shapes and geometry

Connect and Review

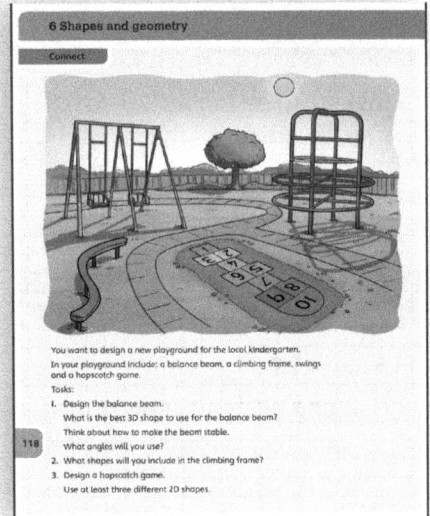

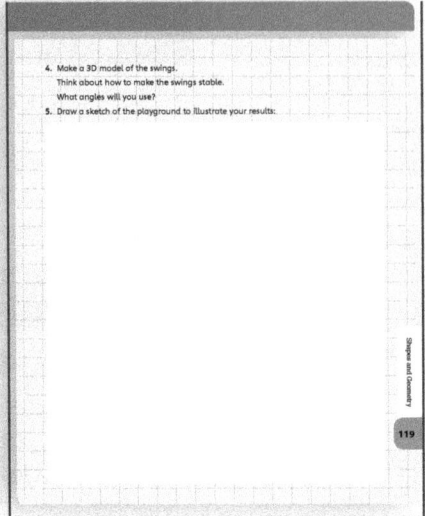

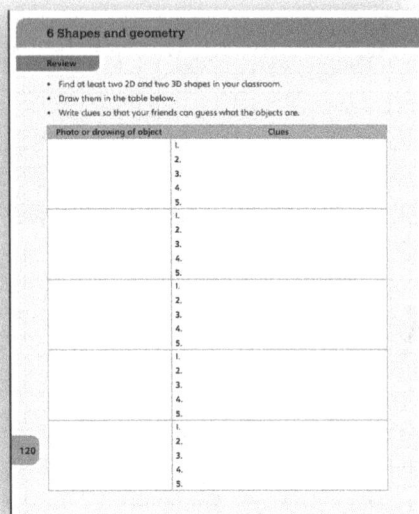

Specific learning foci

- Classify different polygons and understand whether a 2D shape is a polygon or not.
- Visualise and describe the properties of 3D shapes.
- Identify and describe properties of quadrilaterals.
- Recognise and make 2D representations of 3D shapes including nets.
- Estimate, recognise and draw acute and obtuse angles and use a protractor to measure to the nearest degree.

Problem solving focus

- Recognise 2D and 3D shapes and their relationships.

Key vocabulary

Edge, perimeter, vertex, vertices, face straight, curved, base, regular, irregular, parallel, perpendicular, concave, convex, open, closed, cross-section, 2D, 3D, 2-dimensional, 3-dimensional, polygon, circle, triangle, equilateral triangle, isosceles triangle, scalene triangle, pentagon, hexagon, heptagon, octagon quadrilateral, kite, parallelogram, rhombus, rectangle, square, cube, cuboid, pyramid, sphere, hemisphere, cone, cylinder, prism, tetrahedron, polyhedron,, octahedron, dodecahedron, acute angle, obtuse angle, reflex angle, right angle, interior angle

Resources

- Modelling materials
- Card, scissors, glue, sticky tape, string, coloured pencils

Links to Student Book

See pages 118–120 in Student Book.

Links to Workbook

Workbook page 62

Links to Digital Resource Pack

Digital Resource Pack 6 contains two activities which can be used to support students' understanding of 2D and 3D shapes. On the home page, select 'Shapes and Geometry'.

Language support

The presentation is an important way to ensure students are articulating the key vocabulary. Work with students to prepare these presentations. Focus on pronunciation of the key vocabulary from this unit.

 Introductory and Main activity

Either visit a local park or use a video of children playing in a park. Ask each mixed-attainment group of four to six to make a list of important features in a successful play area. Take feedback on this to support the designs that groups will make. Display this feedback list throughout the activity.

Ask students to work in their small groups to design their play park following the instructions on pages 118 and 119 of the Student Book. Give them a variety of materials to work with as suggested in the Resources. It may be appropriate to extend this activity over a number of lessons.

At the end of the activity ask each group to present a report on their design. As a class, agree on a set of criteria you can use to assess the designs. Use the list that you created in the Introductory activity as a basis for these criteria.

Differentiation

Students should work in mixed attainment groups to support one another in working through the investigation on pages 118 and 119 of the Student Book.

For the activity on page 120 of the Student Book, you may want to help write the answers for those less confident with writing or in speaking English.

Differentiated outcomes
The activity on pages 118 and 119 of the Student Book designed to offer differentiation by outcome.

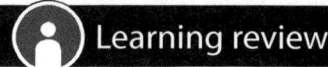 Learning review

Students should complete the Review activity as individuals as it is a summative assessment.

Additional activities

Students can explore other architectural features. For example: they can find designs that are predominantly circular, triangular, and so on.

Students can complete Workbook page 62.

Answers

Student Book pages 118 and 119

Answers will vary as students design their own playground and play apparatus. Check that students' answers seem reasonable – the shapes they use should be appropriate for each piece of play apparatus.

Student Book page 120

Answers will vary as students choose to draw their own 2D and 3D shapes from the classroom. Check that students' clues for each shape seem reasonable.

Workbook page 62

Answers will vary as students choose which properties to give for each shape. Check that the properties are correct.

Assessment activity 6

1. **b)** It has two pairs of parallel sides.

2. **a)** Triangular prism

3. **b)** Pyramids come to a point and prisms have the same cross-section all along their length.

4. **c)** Rhombus

5. 75°

6. Accept accurate answer to within 1 degree.

7. The sum of the interior angles is $(n - 2) \times 180$. Accept any form of this formula.

Unit 7 Position and Movement

Overview

Big Idea

The Big Idea in this unit is how we use mathematics to describe the position or the movement of an object. Coordinates describe position. Transformations (reflections, rotations and translations) describe movement. After an object moves, the coordinates that describe its position are different. It is vital that students are able to learn actively. They need to experience the movement in order to notice how position changes. Instead of using mirrors for reflection, for example, you can make cut-outs of the shapes to be rotated, translated or reflected. This allows students to physically move the objects.

Possible misconceptions

Students may forget the order of coordinates. Some teachers use the phrase 'You go along the hall and then up the stairs.' This reminds students that the first coordinate (the x-coordinate) describes position along the horizontal (x-axis), and the second coordinate (the y-coordinate) describes the position up and down the vertical axis (y-axis).

Key vocabulary and language structures

Origin, coordinates; first, second, third, fourth quadrants; symmetry, line of symmetry, axis of symmetry; vertex, vertices; parallel, perpendicular; acute, obtuse, reflex angles; mirror line, reflect, reflection; rotate, rotation; translate, translation; transformation; clockwise, anti-clockwise

Coverage in lessons

Learning focus	Learning outcomes
Reading and plotting coordinates	Can I use coordinates to describe position on a grid?
Reflections, translations and rotations	Can I tell where a polygon will be after a reflection when the sides of the shape are not parallel to the mirror line?
	Can I tell where a polygon will be after a translation or a rotation through 90° about one of its vertices?

7 Position and Movement

Engage

7 Position and Movement

Specific learning foci

- *Read and plot coordinates in all four quadrants.*
- Predict where a polygon will be after one reflection, one translation or rotation through 90 degrees about one of its vertices.

Problem solving focus

- Recognise 2D and 3D shapes and their relationships.

Key vocabulary

Origin, coordinates, first, second, third, fourth quadrants, symmetry, line of symmetry, axis of symmetry, vertex, vertices, parallel, perpendicular, acute, obtuse, reflex angles, mirror line, reflect, reflection, rotate, rotation, translate, translation, transformation, clockwise, anti-clockwise

Resources

- Magazines or books of illustrations which use symmetry
- Digital cameras

Links to Student Book

See page 121 in Student Book.

Language support

As students give you the instructions in the Introductory activity, make a note of all the vocabulary they use on the whiteboard. Include all the words from the key vocabulary listed above.

Introductory activity

Arrange the class in mixed-attainment groups of four to six. Ask each group to look at the image on page 121 of the Student Book. Tell them to try to describe the shape as clearly as possible. They should imagine they are having a telephone conversation with someone who cannot see the image but who wants to make an exact copy. You may need to use a vocabulary box on the board to help students with the language (see Key vocabulary).

Ask one of the groups to read their instructions to the class. As they read their instructions, another student should try recreate the image on the whiteboard.

Main activity

Instruct students, working in the small groups, to find an example of a Rangoli pattern, a piece of Islamic art or any appropriate design or pattern that uses **symmetry**. Alternatively, they can find photograph examples of patterns which use symmetry (either natural patterns or patterns within architectural designs around the school). Then tell the pairs to use these designs to create posters explaining key vocabulary listed in the overview.

Differentiation

All students should contribute to this activity through using their current vocabulary to describe shapes. You should work with the groups and model key vocabulary that you do not hear the students using.

It is likely that all students will hear a range of new or unfamiliar words which will build their vocabulary.

Learning review

Ask the groups to share their posters with the class. Decide on one poster to display for the rest of the unit. Students can use this poster and their own ideas to complete the position and movement words in the glossary on pages 192 to 204 of the Student Book.

Additional activities

Students can find similar examples of patterns at home, in their places of worship, or other places they visit.

Discover

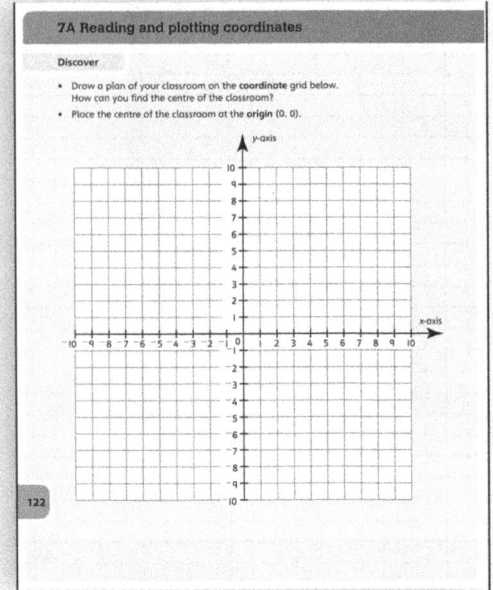
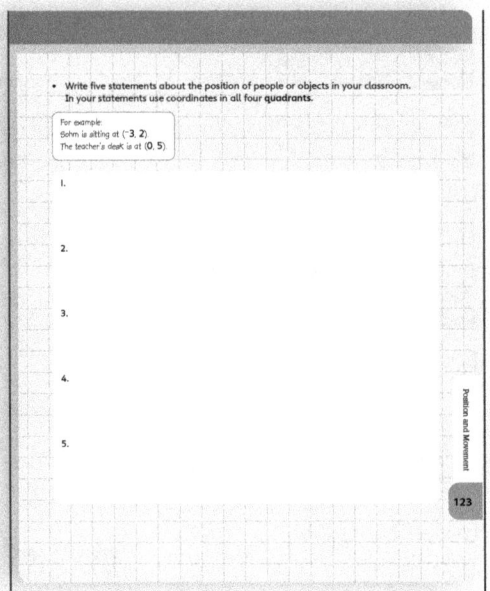

Specific learning focus

- Read and plot coordinates in all four quadrants.

Problem solving focus

- Understand everyday systems of measurements in length.

Key vocabulary

Origin, coordinates, first, second, third, fourth quadrants

Resources

- Tape measures
- Squared paper

Links to Student Book

See pages 122–123 in Student Book.

Links to Workbook

Workbook page 64

Links to Digital Resource Pack

Digital Resource Pack 6 contains two activities which can be used to support students' understanding of coordinates and symmetry. On the home page, select 'Position and Movement'.

Language support

Model the language of coordinates by asking questions. For example:

- *Which students are in the third quadrant?*
- *Where is the origin in the classroom?*
- *How do you remember the order of coordinates?*

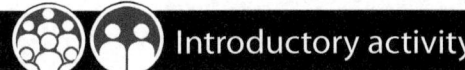
Introductory activity

Ask students in pairs to list all the facts they can remember about **coordinates** and plotting coordinates on a grid. After 5 minutes, take feedback from the class. Tell them that they are going to make a plan of the classroom. As a group, they need to decide:

- *What is the best scale to use?*
- *Will you draw a scale plan of the class?*
- *Will you plot the position of people?*
- *Will you plot the position of objects?*

Main activity

Tell students to work in small groups on the activity on pages 122 and 123 of the Student Book. This ensures that students discuss the work. Students can also check one another's decisions. This activity depends on the previous experience of students. You may choose to group by prior attainment and ask some groups to create a scale plan and others to simply plot points.

Differentiation

Supporting: Ask students to plot points on the grid which represent objects in the classroom.

Consolidating: Ask students to plot points on the grid which accurately represent objects in the classroom.

Extending: Ask students to plot points on the grid which represent objects in the classroom to scale.

Differentiated outcomes	
All students	should plot points accurately in the grid.
Most students	will create a plan of the classroom, using points on the grid.
Some students	will create a scale plan of the classroom, using points on the grid.

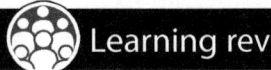
Learning review

Ask each group to ask one of their five statements about the positions of people or objects in the classroom as a question.

For example:

- *Who is sitting at point $(-3, +4)$?*
- *How many students are in the **first quadrant**?*

Additional activities

Students can make similar plans of rooms at home.

Students can complete Workbook page 64.

Answers

Student Book page 122 and 123

Answers will vary because students draw plans of the classroom on the coordinate grids. Check that their statements about the positions of objects and people in the plan are correct and that the coordinates are accurate.

Workbook page 64

Answers will vary because students draw plans of a room in their home on the coordinate grids. Check that the coordinates that they give for items in the room are accurate.

Explore

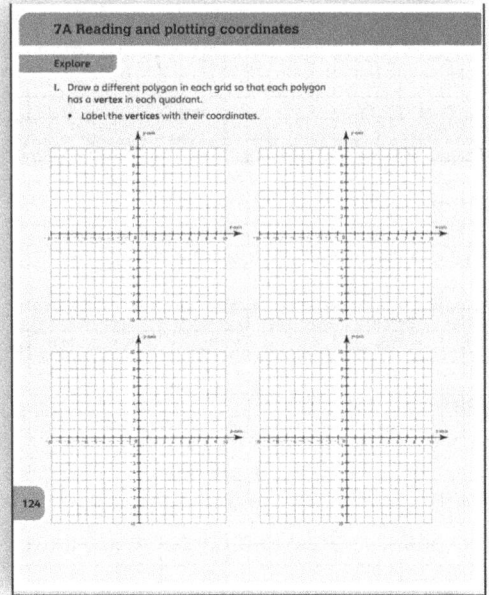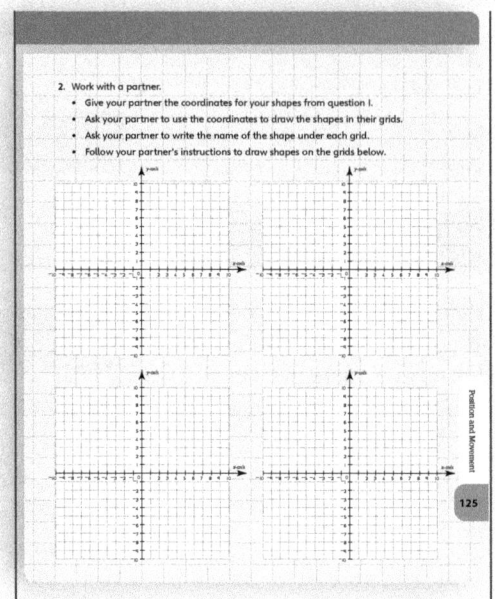

Specific learning focus

● Read and plot coordinates in all four quadrants.

Problem solving focus

● Understand everyday systems of measurements in length.

Key vocabulary

Origin, coordinates, first, second, third, fourth quadrants, polygon, vertex, vertices, regular, irregular, parallel, perpendicular, acute, obtuse, reflex

Resources

● Two polygons drawn on a large Cartesian grid, which you have prepared before the activity
● Squared paper
● Mini whiteboards and markers

Links to Student Book

See pages 124–125 in Student Book.

Links to Workbook

Workbook page 65

Links to Digital Resource Pack

Digital Resource Pack 6 contains two activities which can be used to support students' understanding of coordinates and coordinate grids. On the home page, select 'Position and Movement'.

Language support

As students are working, ask questions to encourage the use of the language of properties of polygons. For example:

● *Are there any parallel/perpendicular lines?*
● *What sort of symmetry does that shape have?*
● *Are there any acute/obtuse/reflex angles?*

 Introductory activity

Use one of the **polygons** that you prepared before the activity. Read the **coordinates** of each **vertex** in turn. Tell students to mark the **vertices** on their squared paper to recreate the polygon. Then ask students to talk to a partner and to list as many properties of the shape as they can, including the name of the shape. Repeat for your second shape. Use one **regular** and one **irregular** shape.

 Main activity

Ask students to work in pairs on the activity on pages 124 and 125 of the Student Book. Each student prepares four different polygons to share with their partner. They may need to refer to the posters from Unit 6 to remind them of the names of different polygons.

Differentiation

Supporting: Ask students to name the coordinates of points.

Consolidating: Ask students to name the coordinates of points and the shapes.

Extending: Ask students to name the coordinates of points and describe the properties of the shapes.

Differentiated outcomes	
All students	should use coordinate pairs to describe the position of their shapes.
Most students	will use coordinate pairs to describe the position of their shapes and use a range of shapes that they can name.
Some students	will use coordinate pairs to describe the position of their shapes and use a wide range of shapes that they can name.

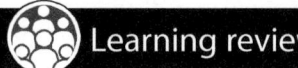 Learning review

Ask students to give you instructions to allow you to recreate their shape. Then model the use of language by naming as many properties of the shape as you can.

Additional activities

You can ask students to draw more complex designs on their mini whiteboards, for example: open shapes, or shapes including curved lines.

Students can complete Workbook page 65.

Answers

Student Book pages 124 and 125

Answers will vary as students choose their own shapes to draw on the coordinate grids. Check that students have labelled the vertices of each shape with the correct coordinates.

Workbook page 65

Answers will vary as students choose where to draw a hexagon on the coordinate grids. While students are working, observe who can read and plot coordinates accurately and those who require more practice.

7B Reflections and rotations

Discover

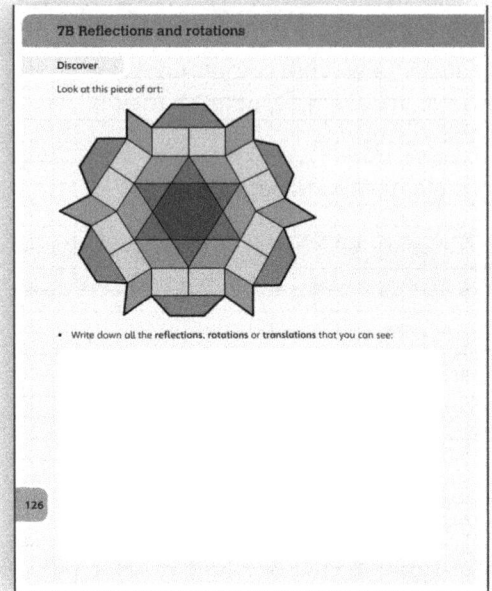 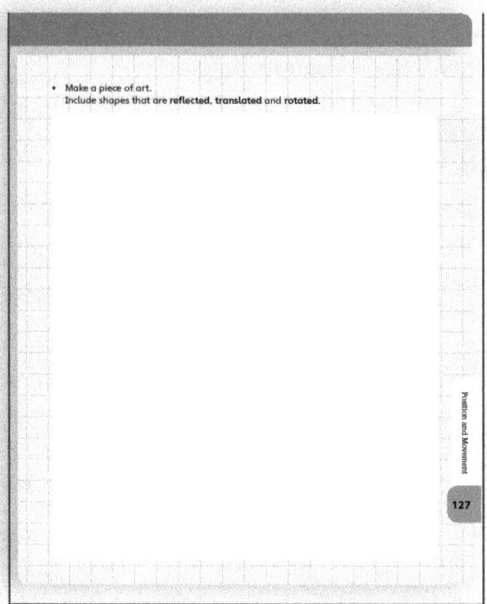

Specific learning foci

- *Predict where a polygon will be after one reflection, one translation or a rotation through 90 degrees about one of its vertices.*
- Identify and describe properties of quadrilaterals.

Problem solving focus

- Deduce new information from existing information and realise the effect that one piece of information has on another.

Key vocabulary

Mirror line, reflect, reflection, rotate, rotation, translate, translation, transformation, clockwise, anti-clockwise

Resources

- Large cut-out rectangle and equilateral triangle
- Glue, card, scissors
- Prepared Cartesian grid (axes labelled from −10 to 10) on the whiteboard
- Prepared cards with the following instructions:
    - *Reflect about the x-axis.*
    - *Reflect about the y-axis.*
    - *Rotate through 90° clockwise about a vertex.*
    - *Rotate through 90° anti-clockwise about a vertex.*
    - *Translate 3 units in the positive x-direction.*
    - *Translate 4 units in the negative y-direction.*

Links to Student Book

See pages 126–127 in Student Book.

Links to Workbook

Workbook page 66

Links to Digital Resource Pack

Digital Resource Pack 6 contains two activities which can be used to support students' understanding of reflection. On the home page, select 'Position and Movement'.

Language support

As students are working, ask them to talk about the type of transformation they are using:

- *Is that a reflection, a rotation or a translation?*
- *Where is the mirror line for that reflection?*

 Introductory activity

Attach the rectangle to the grid on the board. Draw round the rectangle to mark its position. Ask a student to come to the front. Tell them to pick a card, carry out the instruction and mark the new position of the rectangle on the grid. Repeat this three more times with different students, each time moving the previous shape. Repeat with the triangle. This time let the first student select a starting position for the triangle. Move the triangle four times. This creates a pattern of rectangles and triangles.

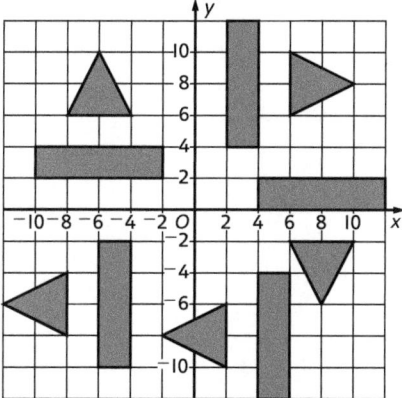

 Main activity

Students work in pairs on the activity on pages 126 and 127 of the Student Book to support discussion. Ask them to create their own artworks using simple polygons as the base. First ask them to cut out the shapes they are using as the basis of the artwork. Then tell them to use different **transformations – rotations**, **translations** and **reflections** – of these shapes to create their final artwork.

Differentiation

Supporting: Point out the transformations so that you model the vocabulary.

Consolidating: Ask students to describe the transformations to you.

Extending: Encourage the students to use multiple transformations.

Differentiated outcomes	
All students	should use simple transformations.
Most students	will use examples of rotations, reflections and translations.
Some students	will use a wide range of transformations and name them.

 Learning review

Select some of the final artworks to share. Model the use of language by describing what you can see. For example:

- *I can see a reflection in the x-axis here.*
- *You translated this shape here.*
- *Can you see a rotation in this pattern?*

Additional activities

Students can find similar patterns at home or in the local environment and write descriptions.

Students can complete Workbook page 66.

Answers

Student Book pages 126 and 127

Check that students have identified the different possible reflections, rotations and translations.

Workbook page 66

Check that students have coloured the pattern so that it contains reflections, rotations and translations.

7B Reflections and rotations

Explore

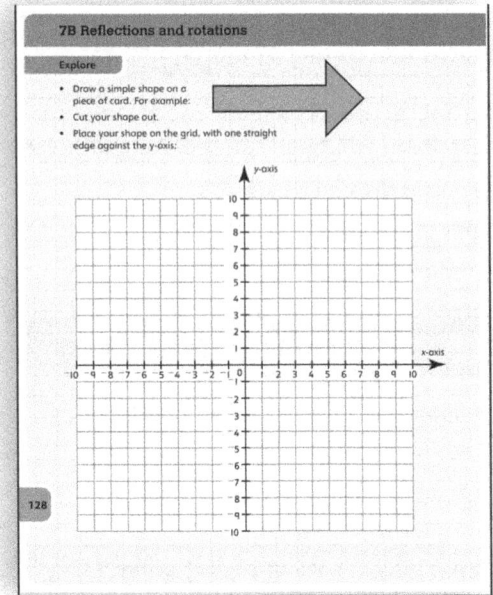

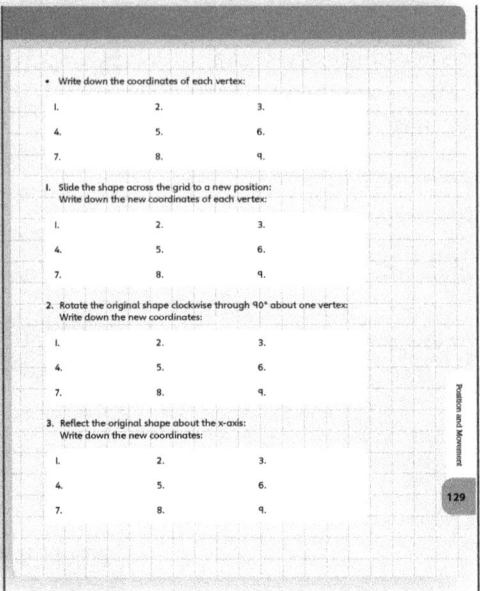

Specific learning foci

- *Predict where a polygon will be after one reflection, one translation or a rotation through 90 degrees about one of its vertices.*
- Identify and describe properties of quadrilaterals.

Problem solving focus

- Deduce new information from existing information and realise the effect that one piece of information has on another.

Key vocabulary

Mirror line, reflect, reflection, rotate, rotation, translate, translation, transformation, clockwise, anti-clockwise, coordinates

Resources

- Prepared 'maze' using chalk or small cones in a large open space
- Coloured card, scissors
- Mini whiteboards and markers

Links to Student Book

See pages 128–129 in Student Book.

Links to Workbook

Workbook page 67

Links to Digital Resource Pack

Digital Resource Pack 6 contains two activities which can be used to support students' understanding of reflection. On the home page, select 'Position and Movement'.

Language support

Ask students to give instructions. This helps you to work with individuals on pronunciation and accuracy of vocabulary. Model useful instructions, for example:

- *Walk forward five paces.*
- *Turn clockwise through 90 degrees.*

Introductory activity

Before the activity, prepare a 'maze' on the ground/floor with chalk or small cones. Include left and right turns through 90°.

 Start

Fnish
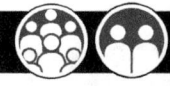

Ask a student to stand at the entrance to the maze. Blindfold them. Ask the other students to take it in turns to give the student instructions to guide them through the maze. These instructions may be, for example:

● *Walk forward 4 paces.*

● *Turn 90° **anti-clockwise**.*

You could create two or three mazes and turn this activity into a competition. For example, the winner could be the team who completes the maze in the quickest time.

Main activity

Ask students in pairs to complete the activity on pages 128 and 129 of the Student Book. They should draw different shapes and carry out the **transformations** individually and then check one another's answers. Encourage students to use shapes which are not simple quadrilaterals. They should draw shapes of an appropriate size which will fit onto the grid.

Differentiation

Supporting: Ask students to name the **coordinates** of points.

Consolidating: Ask students to describe the **transformations** using the coordinate grid.

Extending: Ask students to carry out multiple transformations.

Differentiated outcomes	
All students	should plot coordinates accurately and name the different transformations.
Most students	will use more complex shapes and name coordinates of points accurately after the transformations.
Some students	will use complex shapes, name their properties and name coordinates of points accurately after the transformations.

Learning review

Draw a set of axes and coordinate grid on the whiteboard. Ask a student to draw their initial shape on the grid. Then ask them to give the coordinates of the shape after their translation for question 1 on page 129 of the Student Book. Ask another student to draw the new shape. Ask the other students to write the transformation on their mini whiteboards. After 1 minute, ask them to show you their boards all at the same time. Show students with an incorrect transformation what the effect of their transformation would be, so that they can see their mistake. Repeat for an example of question 2 and question 3.

Additional activities

Students can use computer software to create and guide objects through mazes.

Students can complete Workbook page 67.

Answers

Student Book pages 128 and 129

Answers will vary because students choose where to place their shape on the coordinate grid and where to move it to. While students are working, observe how they record the coordinates of their shape. Note who can reflect, rotate and slide their shapes correctly and who needs more practice.

Workbook page 67

Answers will vary because students draw their own shape on a coordinate grid. Check that they have reflected the shape correctly in the ways required.

7 Position and movement

Connect and Review

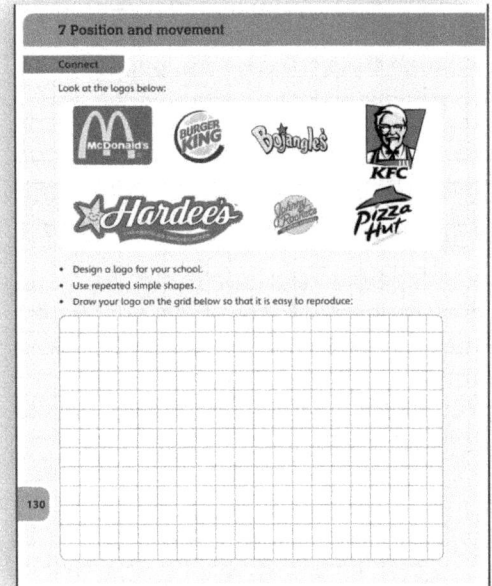

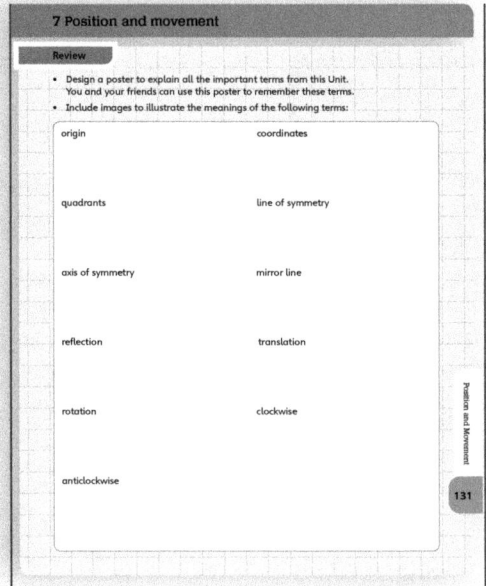

Specific learning foci

- Read and plot coordinates in all four quadrants.
- Predict where a polygon will be after one reflection, one translation or a rotation through 90 degrees about one of its vertices.

Problem solving focus

- Recognise 2D and 3D shapes and their relationships.

Key vocabulary

Symmetry, line of symmetry, axis of symmetry, vertex, vertices, parallel, perpendicular, mirror line, reflect, reflection, rotate, rotation, translate, translation, transformation, clockwise, anti-clockwise

Resources

- Examples of logos
- Squared paper for drafting and planning
- Assessment activity 7 – one per student (Resource sheet 7 – see www.oxfordprimary.com/OIPMteacher)

Links to Student Book

See pages 130–131 in Student Book.

Links to Workbook

Workbook page 68

Links to Digital Resource Pack

Digital Resource Pack 6 contains two activities which can be used to support students' understanding of coordinates and symmetry. On the home page, select 'Position and Movement'.

Language support

Engage in discussions with each group as they design their logos. Ask questions, for example:

- *What shape is that?*
- *Where is that shape reflected?*
- *What makes this an effective logo?*

Introductory and Main activity

For Connect activities, ask students to work in mixed-attainment groups of four. Encourage them to try to interpret and begin the activity without any teacher input.

Look at examples of logos. Ask students, in groups, to list the elements of an 'effective' logo. Take feedback from the groups. Make a list of criteria for 'effective' logos. Explain that they will use these criteria to assess the logos at the end of the session. Groups should then create their own logos. Each member of the group designs a logo for the school.

The group look at each logo in turn. They list the positives and what they would change.

The group pick their 'favourite' logo and work on it together to improve it.

Ask each group to present their logo. The rest of the class assess each group's logo. The class then use the criteria from the introduction to decide on the best logo.

Differentiation

Students should work in mixed-attainment groups to support one another in working through the investigation. You may want to help write the answers for those less confident with writing or in speaking English.

Differentiated outcomes
The activity on page 130 of the Student Book is designed to offer differentiation by outcome.

Learning review

Students should complete the Review activity on page 131 of the Student Book as individuals as it is a summative assessment.

Additional activities

Students can find a wide range of logos and rank them according to the effectiveness criteria from the Introductory activity. Students can use their criteria to design alternative logos for their favourite brands.

Students can complete Workbook page 68.

Answers

Student Book page 130

Answers will vary as students draw their own logo.

Student Book page 131

Answers will vary as students draw their own examples of each term and key word. Check that students have understood the vocabulary correctly.

Workbook page 68

Answers will vary as students draw their own patterns check that the patterns include reflections, rotations and translations.

Assessment activity 7

1. **b)** $(3, -2)$

2. **d)** negative x- and negative y-coordinates

3. **c)** $(0, 0)$

4. **b)** You always write the x-coordinate before the y-coordinate

5. **b)** A translation of -2 in the x-direction

6. **c)** A reflection in the x-axis

7.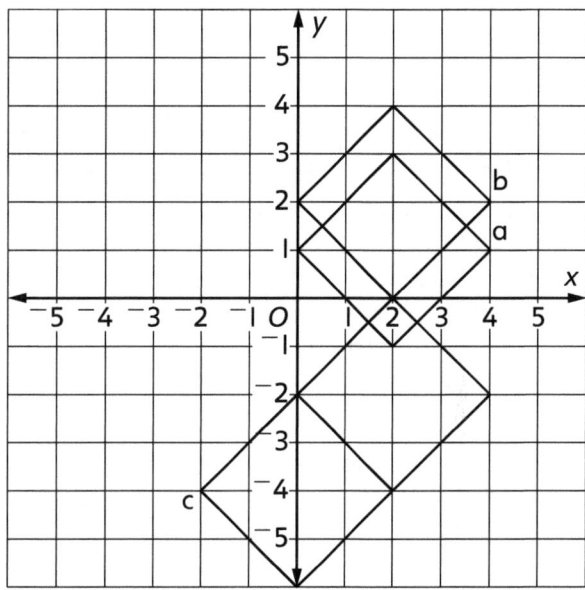

Unit 8 Length, Mass and Capacity

Overview

Big Idea

By this stage, students should have a good understanding of length, mass and capacity. They should know that an object in any orientation has the same length. They should also understand that, because of its density, a small object can sometimes be heavier than a larger object.

Students need to use their understanding of place value and their knowledge of decimals to help them convert between units of measure. In this unit, the students will develop their knowledge of scales. This will help them to use measures to an appropriate degree of accuracy. Introduce students to the idea that measure is always only accurate to a chosen degree of accuracy. We can never measure a line exactly. The measurement is always to the nearest mm, cm, m, and so on. Students need to decide an appropriate degree of accuracy to use.

Possible misconceptions

Students may find it difficult to understand that a measure such as 230 cm is the same as 2.3 m. They may think they are different because 230 is a larger number. You can use measuring equipment that is calibrated in both cm and m, or l and ml, in practical activities to show students how to convert between units.

Students may also not know Imperial units. These are introduced in this unit. You can use a video or visit a setting in which Imperial units are used to show these units in context.

Key vocabulary and language structures

Units of measure;

kilometre (km), metre (m), centimetre (cm), millimetre (mm);

mile, yard, feet, foot, inches, inch;

ruler, metre stick, tape measure, trundle wheel;

mass, weight; tonne, kilogram (kg), gram (g), milligram (mg) pounds, ounces;

capacity; litre (l), centilitre (cl), millilitre (ml) pint, gallon;

investigation, hypothesis, conclusion, results;

... is as long as ...; ... is as heavy as ... , ... is the same height/weight as ...; ... is longer/heavier than ...;

weigh/weight, high/height, long/length, wide/width; measure, measurement, to the nearest ...

Coverage in lessons

Learning focus	Learning outcomes
Selecting and using appropriate units of measure	Do I know which units to use?
	Can I explain what Imperial units are?
	Can I explain when I use Imperial units?
Converting units of measurement	Can I convert between kg and g and litres and millilitres?
	Can I use my knowledge of decimals to help convert units?
Using scales and measuring accurately	Can I use different scales to measure quantities?
	Can I use this knowledge to help me construct objects using measures?

8 Length, Mass and Capacity

Engage

Specific learning foci

- Select and use standard units of measure.
- Know imperial units still in common use, e.g. the mile, and approximate metric equivalents.

Problem solving focus

- Understand everyday systems of measurement in length, weight and capacity.

Key vocabulary

kilometre (km), metre (m), centimetre (cm), millimetre (mm) mile, yard, feet, foot, inches, inch, tonne, kilogram (kg), gram (g), milligram (mg) pounds, ounces litre (l), centilitre (cl), millilitre (ml) pint, gallon

Resources

- Mini whiteboards and markers

Links to Student Book

See page 133 in Student Book.

Language support

During the presentations listen carefully to students' pronunciation of the units of measurement. Model the correct pronunciation. Make a display of all the units. Students can refer to this during the unit.

 Introductory activity

Ask students to talk in pairs. Ask: *When have you used measurement this week?* After 5 minutes, take feedback from the pairs. List all the units of measure that they mention on the whiteboard. Students can refer to this list when working on the main activity. If they do not mention units, prompt them, asking: *What units did you measure in?* Refer to the vocabulary list above. For any of these units that students haven't used, ask: *Has anyone measured in … this week?*

 Main activity

Organise students into mixed-attainment groups of four. Ask: *Which occupations use measuring? What sort of measuring do they need to use?* After 10 minutes, list all these occupations on the whiteboard. Ask each group to select a different occupation and to plan a short role-play which shows them carrying out measurements at work. They can present these role-plays during the Learning review.

Differentiation

Supporting: Encourage students to contribute to the discussion by inviting them to take part and suggest some units of measurement and occupations.

Consolidating: Ask students to think of examples for units of measurement and occupations that have not yet been used.

Extending: Ask students to think of examples for all the units of measurement in the vocabulary list.

 Learning review

During the presentations, ask every group to make a list of all the units of measurement that are used in the presentations. Discuss units that are not mentioned, including Imperial units such as **mile**, **yard**, **foot**, **inch**, **pint**, **gallon**, **pound**, **ounce**. Ask: *Why are some units used more commonly than others?*

Additional activities

Students can interview their parents or other adults about their jobs, or their everyday routines. They can find out how these adults use measurement in their everyday lives.

8A Selecting and using appropriate units of measure

Discover

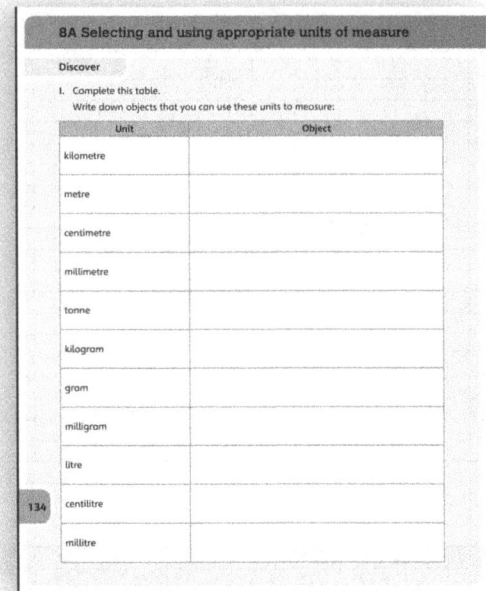
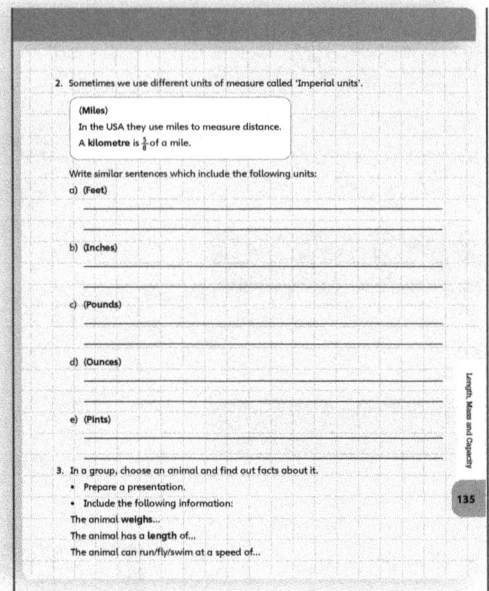

Specific learning focus

- Select and use standard units of measure.

Problem solving focus

- Understand everyday systems of measurement in length, weight and capacity.

Key vocabulary

Kilometre (km), metre (m), centimetre (cm), millimetre (mm), mile, yard, feet, foot, inches, inch, tonne, kilogram (kg), gram (g), milligram (mg), pounds, ounces, litre (l), centilitre (cl), millilitre (ml), pint, gallon

Resources

- Scissors
- Large sheets of paper
- Local newspapers or magazines that students have regular access to

Links to Student Book

See pages 134–135 in Student Book.

Links to Workbook

Workbook pages 70 and 71

Links to Digital Resource Pack

Digital Resource Pack 6 contains two activities which can be used to support students' understanding of measurement. On the home page, select 'Length, Mass and Capacity'.

Language support

Encourage students to read the results of their research aloud to you. Focus particularly on the units. You may need to model the language for students so that they hear the correct pronunciation.

 Introductory activity

Ask students to look through the magazines and newspapers and cut out articles or advertisements that use units of measure related to length, mass or capacity. They can use these to create a poster. In their poster, tell them to highlight the unit and list all units used in the article they have selected.

 Main activity

Ask students to work in pairs to answer the first two questions on pages 134 and 135 of the Student Book. Students take it in turns to find an object that is measured in the given unit. If possible, students can use the Internet or Resources for research to find the equivalent measurements for the Imperial units in question 2.

Students then work in small groups to prepare a presentation (question 3 on page 135 of the Student Book). They can use the Internet or Resources for research to find the measurements for their chosen animal. For example, the National Geographic website states that blue whales grow up to 100 **feet** (30 **metres**) long and weigh about 200 **tonnes**, their tongues weigh as much as an elephant and their hearts weigh as much as a car.

Differentiation

Supporting: Prompt students to think of examples for units that they might know.

Consolidating: Prompt students to think of examples for all the units.

Extending: Prompt students to think of a range examples for all the units.

Differentiated outcomes	
All students	should think of objects to represent some units.
Most students	will think of objects to represent most of the units.
Some students	will think of a range of objects to represent all the units.

 Learning review

Ask the groups to present their research into their animal. After the presentations, students can find the longest/shortest, heaviest/lightest, fastest/ slowest animal.

Additional activities

Students can make 'Top Trumps' style cards using the information on the animals. These are cards with an image of the animal and a bulleted list of length, mass, speed. To play with the cards, players pick a category from their card which they think will 'beat' that category on all other players' cards.

Blue Whale

•Length: 30 metres
• Mass: 200 tonnes
•Speed: 50 km/h

Students can complete Workbook page 70.

Answers

Student Book pages 134 and 135

1. Answers will vary as students choose their own objects as examples of units of measure.

2. Answers will vary as students give their own definitions and examples of the imperial units and relationships between the imperial and metric units. Check that students have correctly understood the imperial units.

3. Answers will vary as the students prepare a presentation about an animal of their choice.

Workbook pages 70 and 71

Shanghai Tower 695.2 yards

Monitor lizard 64 inches

Elephant 5060 pounds

Large drinking glass 0.81 pints

Human being 1397 pounds

River Nile 2612.5 miles

Can of fizzy drink 0.594 pint

Small cat 6.38 pounds

Distance from London to Dubai 3437.5 miles

Smallest adult 22 inches

8A Selecting and using appropriate units of measure

Explore

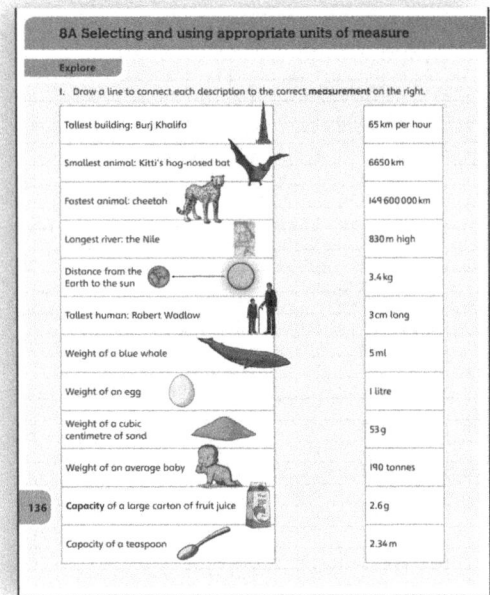

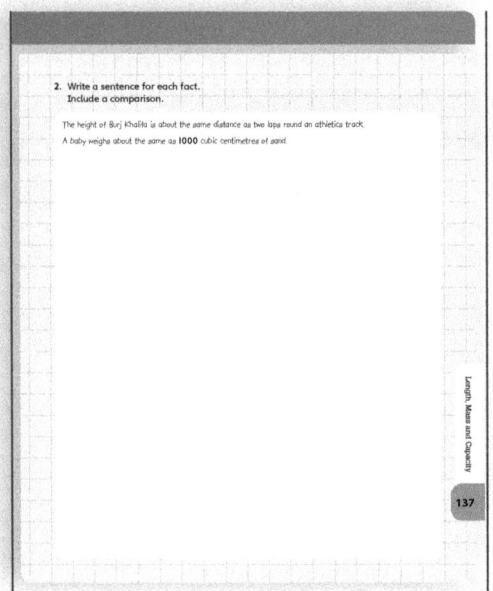

Specific learning focus

● Select and use standard units of measure.

Problem solving focus

● Understand everyday systems of measurement in length, weight and capacity.

Key vocabulary

Kilometre (km), metre (m), centimetre (cm), millimetre (mm) mile, yard, feet, foot, inches, inch, tonne, kilogram (kg), gram (g), milligram (mg) pounds, ounces litre (l), centilitre (cl), millilitre (ml) pint, gallon

Resources

● Mini whiteboards and markers

Links to Student Book

See pages 136–137 in Student Book.

Links to Workbook

Workbook page 71

Links to Digital Resource Pack

Digital Resource Pack 6 contains two activities which can be used to support students' understanding of measurement. On the home page, select 'Length, Mass and Capacity'.

Language support

Refer back to the vocabulary list of units. Encourage students to use the units in their responses. Pick five students who are confident in their use of language for the Learning review to act as models for the use of language. For example:

● *What unit can we use to measure the length of the classroom?*

● *What units can we use to measure the amount of fruit juice in a bottle?*

● *What units do we use to measure our weight?*

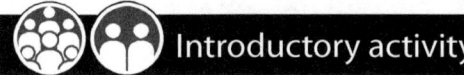 Introductory activity

Ask students to discuss in pairs and to write an object or measurement that fits each of the following descriptions (read them out to students):

- *Something that is 1.5 **mm** long*
- *Something that weighs 2 **kg***
- *A place that is 15 **km** away*
- *The width of the classroom*
- *The capacity of a can of cola.*

Ask: *Which units were easy to find examples for? Which were more difficult?* To support students, you can prepare examples before the lesson.

 Main activity

Students should work in pairs on the activities on pages 136 and 137 of the Student Book to support one another and to aid discussion. As students work on the activities, ask:

- *How do you know that is correct?*
- *Can you show me how long that is?*
- *Did that surprise you?*

For the final part of the activity (writing comparison statements), prepare examples to support students. For example, you may have something that weighs 1 kg for students to use for comparisons. Select five students who have interesting comparisons for the Learning review.

Differentiation

Supporting: Support students in matching units by asking probing questions.

Consolidating: Ask students to explain and justify their answers.

Extending: Encourage students to think of interesting comparisons.

Differentiated outcomes	
All students	should match units to objects with support.
Most students	will match objects to units, supporting others.
Some students	will find interesting comparisons.

 Learning review

Ask the five students you selected during the Main activity to come to the front. They can ask questions that prompt their comparison. For example, a student who wrote 'The classroom is as high as Robert Wadlow' may ask 'What is the same height as the classroom?' Tell the other students to write down the answer on their whiteboards.

Additional activities

Students can research one of the topics, for example 'Tall buildings'. They can use these measurements to create scale drawings of the buildings and then make a comparative diagram.

Students can complete Workbook page 70.

Answers

Student Book pages 136 and 137

1.

Tallest building	830 m high
Smallest animal	3 cm long
Fastest animal	65 km per hour
Longest river	6650 km
Distance from Earth to Sun	149 600 000 km
Tallest human	2.34 m
Weight of blue whale	190 tonnes
Weight of an egg	53 g
Weight of a cubic centimetre of sand	2.6 g
Weight of an average baby	3.4 kg
Capacity of a large carton of fruit juice	1 litre
Capacity of a teaspoon	5 ml

2. Answers will vary because students write their own sentences for each fact in question 1. Check that students' sentences are reasonable.

Workbook pages 70 and 71

Shanghai Tower 695.2 yards

Monitor lizard 64 inches

Elephant 5060 pounds

Large drinking glass 0.81 pints

Human being 1397 pounds

River Nile 2612.5 miles

Can of fizzy drink 0.594 pint

Small cat 6.38 pounds

Distance from London to Dubai 3437.5 miles

Smallest adult 22 inches

8B Converting units of measurement

Discover

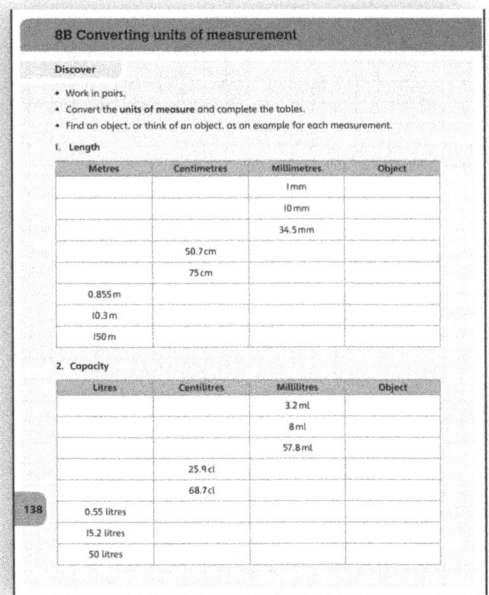 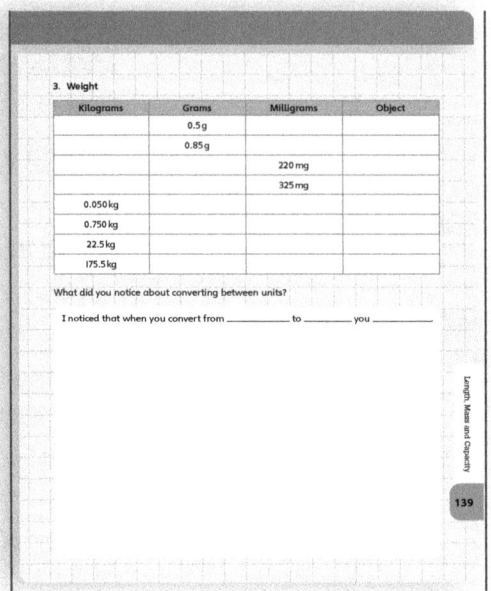

Specific learning foci

- Convert between units of measurement, using decimals to three places.
- Recognise and use decimals with up to three places in the context of measurement.

Problem solving focus

- Understand everyday systems of measurement in length, weight and capacity and use these to perform simple calculations.

Key vocabulary

Kilometre (km), metre (m), centimetre (cm), millimetre (mm) mile, yard, feet, foot, inches, inch, tonne, kilogram (kg), gram (g), milligram (mg), pounds, ounces, litre (l), centilitre (cl), millilitre (ml), pint, gallon

Resources

- Range of measuring equipment and items to measure
- Calculators

Links to Student Book

See pages 138–139 in Student Book.

Links to Workbook

Workbook page 72

Links to Digital Resource Pack

Digital Resource Pack 6 contains two activities which can be used to support students' understanding of measurement. On the home page, select 'Length, Mass and Capacity'.

Language support

During the Main activity, ask students to explain their thinking about multiplying and dividing by 100 and 1000. You can use place value grids to remind them that they are not 'adding zeros' but moving the digits across the decimal point. For example:

- *What is the value of the '3' in 5430?*
- *What is the value of the '7' in 98.7?*
- *When I multiply 89.7 by 100, what is the new value of the '8'?*

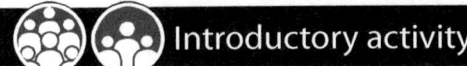 **Introductory activity**

Prepare a series of measuring activities using everyday objects, which involve measuring length, finding the capacity of containers and weighing objects. Ask each group to find the measurement in the most sensible unit and then convert this to other units. For example:

'My hand span is 12 **cm**. This is equivalent to 120 **mm**, 0.12 **m** and 0.00012 **km**.'

You may need to remind students of the conversion factors and that milli means 1000. For example: *There are 1000* **millilitres** *in 1* **litre**.

Use mixed-attainment groups so that students can discuss the measurements and that more confident learners can model the vocabulary to less confident learners.

 **Main activity**

Ask students to discuss the conversion of the units for the Student Book activity as a group and then complete the tables individually. If they do not agree, they can check using a calculator. When they try to think of objects, ask them to start with objects they can visualise easily. They may not be able to complete them all. To support students, find objects that students are familiar with before the lesson to demonstrate every measurement. As students complete the tables, select three or four objects to use in the Learning review.

Differentiation

Supporting: Support students in measuring objects accurately and converting units.

Consolidating: Ask students to explain their thinking when they convert units.

Extending: Ask students to think of good examples for each of the measurements in the tables.

Differentiated outcomes	
All students	should measure objects accurately and convert units with support.
Most students	will measure objects accurately and convert units.
Some students	will measure objects accurately and convert units and think of good examples.

 **Learning review**

Have on display the three or four the objects you selected during the Main activity. State a measurement for one of the objects, from which it is difficult to recognise the object. For example: *This object has a capacity of 1000 ml.* (A large carton of fruit juice)

Students can decide in pairs what the object might be.

Additional activities

Students can carry out the same activity but start with objects. For example: *Find the capacity and height of a can of cola and write the units in different ways.*

Students can complete Workbook page 72.

Answers

Student Book pages 138 and 139

1. Check that the objects that students suggest for each measurement are appropriate.

Metres	Centimetres	Millimetres
0.001 m	0.1 cm	1 mm
0.01 m	1 cm	10 mm
0.0345 m	3.45 cm	34.5 mm
0.507 m	50.7 cm	507 mm
0.75 m	75 cm	750 mm
0.855 m	85.5 cm	855 mm
10.3 m	1030 cm	10 300 mm
150 m	15 000 cm	150 000 mm

2. Check that the objects that students suggest for each measurement are appropriate.

Litres	Centilitres	Millilitres
0.0032 l	0.32 cl	3.2 ml
0.008 l	0.8 cl	8 ml
0.0578 l	5.78 cl	57.8 ml
0.259 l	25.9 cl	259 ml
0.687 l	68.7 cl	687 ml
0.55 l	55 cl	550 ml
15.2 l	1520 cl	15 200 ml
50 l	5000 cl	50 000 ml

3. Check that the objects that students suggest for each measurement are appropriate.

Kilograms	Grams	Milligrams
0.0005 kg	0.5 g	500 mg
0.000 85 kg	0.85 g	850 mg
0.000 22 kg	0.22 g	220 mg
0.000 325 kg	0.325 g	325 mg
0.050 kg	50 g	50 000 mg
0.750 kg	750 g	750 000 mg
22.5 kg	22 500 g	22 500 000 mg
175.5 kg	175 500 g	175 500 000 mg

Workbook page 72

1. 1 km = 1000 m   1 litre = 10 cl   1 kg = 1000 g
   1 m = 100 cm   1 litre = 1000 ml   1 g = 1000 mg
   1 cm = 10 mm   1 cl = 100 ml

2. a) 8700 m   **e)** 845 ml   **i)** 9.85 litres
   b) 875 cm   **f)** 8950 g   **j)** 6.75 kg
   c) 895 mm   **g)** 9650 mg
   d) 55 cl 50 ml   **h)** 5.5 km

Explore

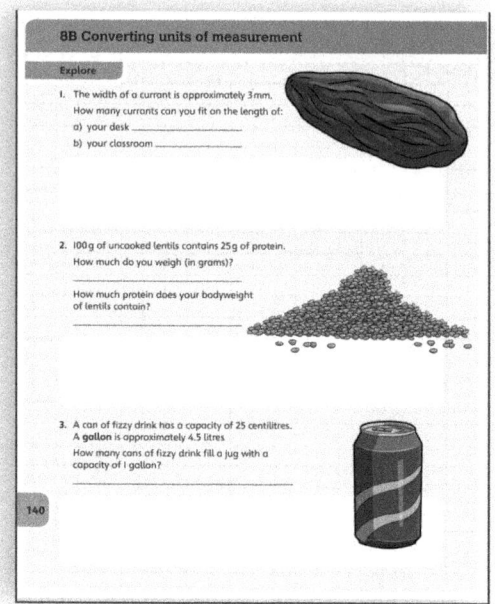
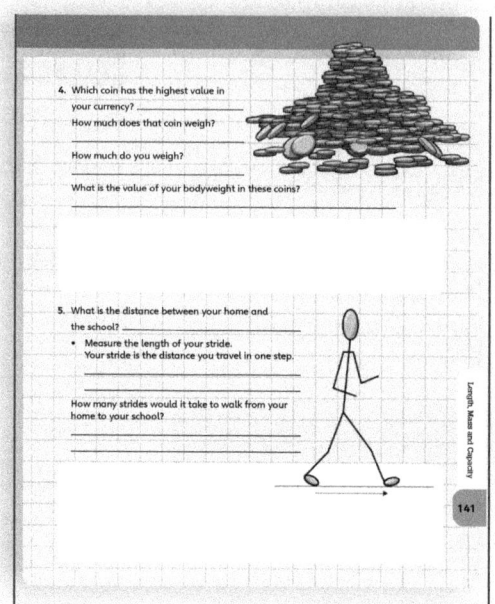

Specific learning foci

- *Convert between units of measurement, using decimals to three places.*
- Recognise and use decimals with up to three places in the context of measurement.

Problem solving focus

- Understand everyday systems of measurement in length, weight and capacity and use these to perform simple calculations.

Key vocabulary

Kilometre (km), metre (m), centimetre (cm), millimetre (mm), mile, yard, feet, foot, inches, inch, tonne, kilogram (kg), gram (g), milligram (mg), pounds, ounces, litre (l), centilitre (cl), millilitre (ml), pint, gallon

Resources

- Range of measuring equipment
- Calculators

Links to Student Book

See pages 140–141 in Student Book.

Links to Workbook

Workbook page 73

Links to Digital Resource Pack

Digital Resource Pack 6 contains two activities which can be used to support students' understanding of measurement. On the home page, select 'Length, Mass and Capacity'.

Language support

Support students with the language of comparison, for example:

- *… is as long as …*
- *… is as heavy as …*
- *… is the same height/weight as …*

As students work on the word problems remind them to check their answers. Ask: *Does that answer make sense?*

 Introductory activity

Ask the class to imagine building a human tower by standing on one another's shoulders. Ask: *How tall would the tower be?* Write some of the estimates on the board. Ask students to work in pairs to measure one another using a tape measure. List all the heights on the board.

Give four students calculators. Read out all the measurements. Ask the four students to total them using the calculators. Make sure that the students agree on the total. Then write down the answer and compare it to the estimates. Try to think of something that is the same height as the total height of their human tower. Alternatively, you can measure out this distance with a trundle wheel. Carry out the initial calculation in cm using an estimate for a person's height in cm, and then carry out the conversion into m and km. This will involve three places of decimals. Briefly discuss rounding to the nearest m or km in this context.

 Main activity

Split the class into five mixed-attainment groups. Each group should work on a different problem from pages 140 and 141 of the Student Book.

Encourage the groups to break down each problem into small steps.

For example, for question 1 they can measure the desk and divide that measurement by 10. They can then find out how many currants fit into that measure and multiply this answer by 10 to find the answer.

For question 4, it may be easier to give students the mass of the highest value coin.

For question 5, students may need help in working out the distance between their home and the school. For the questions involving bodyweight, you may find it more appropriate to give the groups an average bodyweight of a Stage 6 student.

Encourage students to estimate when they see three places of decimals. Encourage them to make sense of the decimals up to three decimal places in the context of these measurements. Encourage individual students to ask questions if they do not understand what someone else is saying.

Differentiation

Students will bring a range of experience to the task which they can share.

Differentiated outcomes
All students will benefit from working in groups on these activities and from hearing the solutions presented. Less confident students will hear vocabulary modelled by other students and gain problem solving skills. More confident students benefit from having to explain their thinking and the problem-solving process.

 Learning review

Ask each group to present the solution to their problem. Encourage other groups to ask questions to make sure all students understand the solution. After each presentation, the rest of the students can complete the answers in their Student Books.

Additional activities

Students can set their own word problems for one another.

Students can complete Workbook page 73.

Answers

Student Book pages 140 and 141

Answers will vary as the measures are related to the students' lives. Check that the conversions are reasonable.

Workbook page 73

1. Answers will vary as the distance is dependent on the students' homes. Check that the destination is reasonable.

2. Answers will vary as the age is dependent on the students' ages. Check that the age is reasonable.

3. 50 g

4. Answers will vary as the amount is dependent on how many breaths students calculate they breathe in a week. Check that the students' methods are reasonable.

Discover

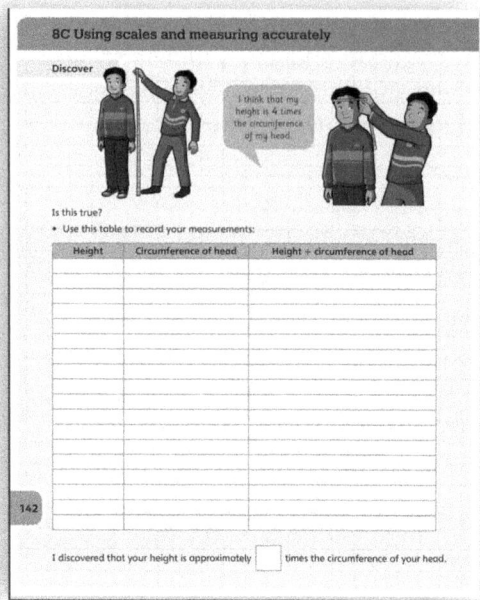

Specific learning foci

- Select and use standard units of measure.
- *Interpret readings on different scales.*

Problem solving foci

- Understand everyday systems of measurement in length and use these to perform simple calculations.
- Make, test and refine hypotheses, explain and justify methods, reasoning, strategies, results or conclusions orally.

Key vocabulary

Metre (m), centimetre (cm), millimetre (mm)

Resources

- Tape measures
- Calculators

Links to Student Book

See page 142 in Student Book.

Links to Workbook

Workbook pages 74 and 75

Links to Digital Resource Pack

Digital Resource Pack 6 contains two activities which can be used to support students' understanding of measurement. On the home page, select 'Length, Mass and Capacity'.

Language support

Check that students round to the nearest centimetre accurately. Ask: *When do you round up and when do you round down?* You can also develop the vocabulary of investigation, for example:

- *What was your hypothesis?*
- *Was your hypothesis correct?*

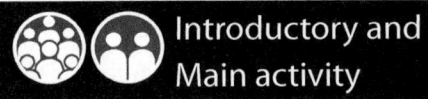

Introductory and Main activity

Ask the class this question:

Imagine I measure the distance around my head.

What do we call this measurement? (Circumference)

How many times the circumference of my head is my height?

Write all students' estimates on the whiteboard. During the lesson, students will find out which of these estimates is the most accurate. Ask students to measure the height of their partner and the circumference of their partner's head. Agree as a class which measurement around the head you will use (for example: just above the ears) so that this measurement is consistent. Remind students to measure to the nearest centimetre and to record both measurements in centimetres. Students then list all these measurements on the main whiteboard in a large table.

Height	Circumference of head
152 cm	48 cm

Students then copy these measurements into the table in the Student Book and work out the ratio of height to circumference for each using a calculator.

Differentiation

Students will bring a range of experience to the task which they can share.

Differentiated outcomes
All students will benefit from working on this investigation and from hearing the solutions presented. Less confident students will hear vocabulary modelled by other students and gain problem solving skills. More confident students benefit from having to explain their thinking and the findings.

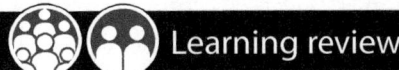

Learning review

Ask students to give you their conclusions and to justify their results.

Additional activities

Students can use the table of measurements to construct a scattergram and draw a line of best fit to answer the question. They can also include more data, for example: they can measure adults or children from the kindergarten to see if the ratio is the same.

Students can complete Workbook pages 74 and 75.

Answers

Student Book page 142

The actual ratio will be closer to 3 : 1

Workbook pages 74 and 75

Answers will vary as students measure objects around them. Check that students' measurements are reasonable.

Explore

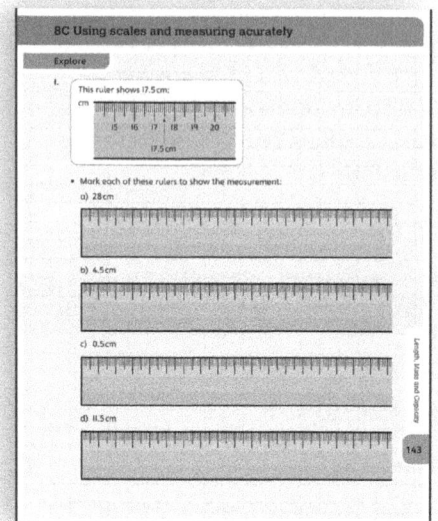

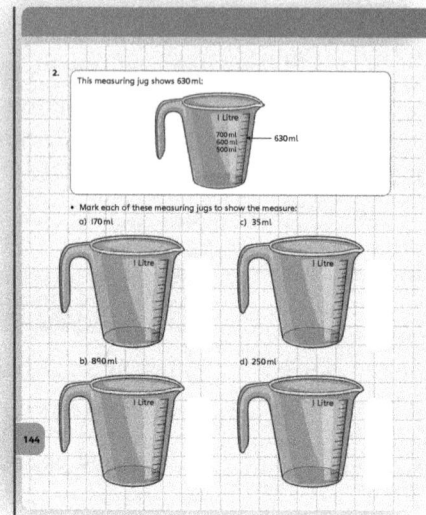

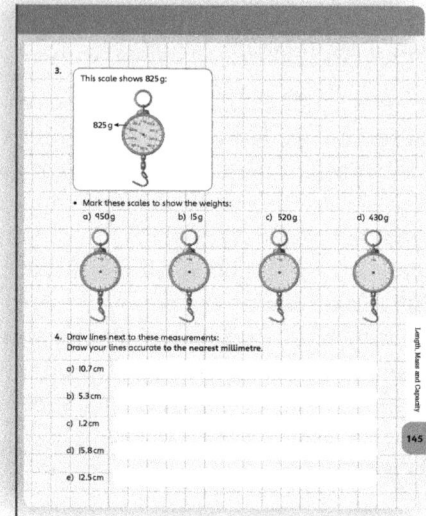

Specific learning foci

- *Interpret readings on different scales.*
- Draw and measure lines to the nearest centimetre and millimetre.

Problem solving focus

- Understand everyday systems of measurement in length, weight and capacity and use these to perform simple calculations.

Key vocabulary

Kilometre (km), metre (m), centimetre (cm), millimetre (mm), mile, yard, feet, foot, inches, inch, tonne, kilogram (kg), gram (g), milligram (mg) pounds, ounces litre (l), centilitre (cl), millilitre (ml), pint, gallon

Resources

- Rulers or metre sticks
- Measuring jugs
- Weighing scales
- Range of objects to measure

Links to Student Book

See pages 143–145 in Student Book.

Links to Workbook

Workbook page 75

Links to Digital Resource Pack

Digital Resource Pack 6 contains two activities which can be used to support students' understanding of measurement. On the home page, select 'Length, Mass and Capacity'.

Language support

Support students by focusing on the language of units and accuracy, for example:

- *Are you measuring to the nearest centimetre or millimetre?*
- *Are you measuring to the nearest gram or milligram?*
- *Are you measuring to the nearest centilitre or millilitre?*
- *I am measuring to the nearest …*

Introductory and Main activity

Set up a range of activities in the classroom. On one table place a range of objects and some rulers/metre sticks to measure length; on another table place a range of containers and some measuring jugs to measure capacity; and on a third table a range of objects and weighing scales to measure mass. Ask the groups to move around the tables measuring the objects in turn and making a note of the longest item, the heaviest item and the container with the greatest capacity. Ask: *What degree of accuracy will you use when you measure?*

After all the groups have measured all the items, ask groups to feed back. Check their measurements. Discuss the degrees of accuracy they used. Now ask them to write their measurements to different degrees of accuracy, for example:

- *To the nearest **metre***
- *To the nearest **litre***
- *To the nearest **kilogram.***

Differentiation

Supporting: Support students to measure accurately, modelling the process.

Consolidating: Ask students to tell you the degree of accuracy they are using.

Extending: Ask students to support other students.

Differentiated outcomes	
All students	should measure items accurately with support.
Most students	will measure items to different degrees of accuracy.
Some students	will check other's measurements and correct them.

Learning review

Ask students to use their measuring skills to complete the questions on pages 143 to 145 of the Student Book. They should work in pairs so that they can check one another's answers.

Additional activities

Students can find the longest/widest object in their house. They can bring the measurements in to school to compare with those of other students. Similarly, they can find the largest container or the heaviest object.

Students can complete Workbook pages 74 and 75.

Answers

Student Book pages 143 to 145

1. Check that students have marked the correct lengths on the rulers.
2. Check that students have marked the correct capacities on the measuring jugs.
3. Check that students have marked the correct weights on the scales.
4. Check that students have drawn the lines to the correct lengths.

Workbook pages 74 and 75

Answers will vary as students measure objects around them. Check that students' measurements are reasonable.

8 Length, mass and capacity

Connect and Review

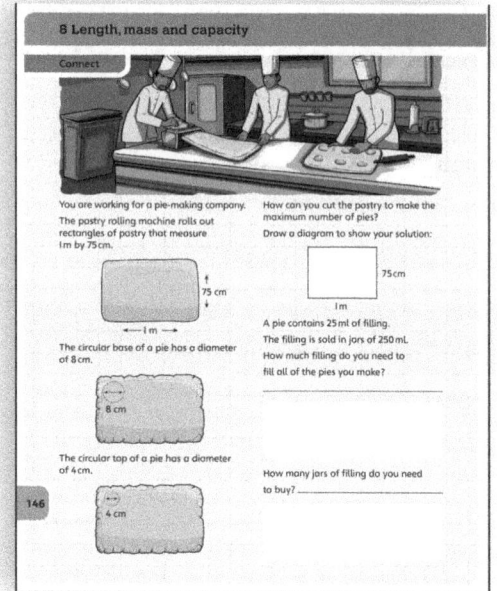

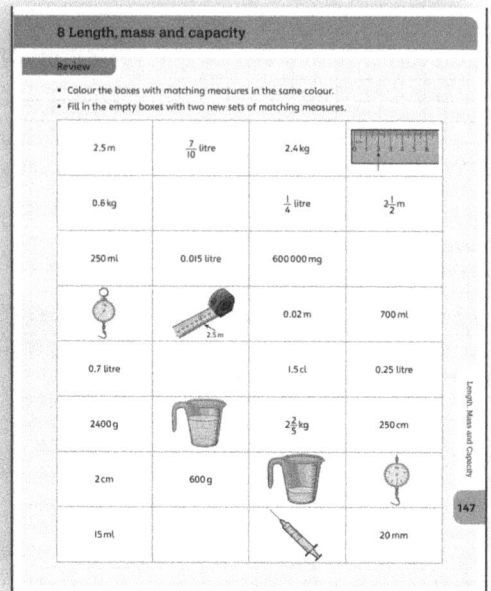

Specific learning foci

- Select and use standard units of measure.
- Convert between units of measurement.
- Draw and measure lines to the nearest centimetre and millimetre.

Problem solving foci

- Understand everyday systems of measurement in length, weight and capacity and use these to perform simple calculations.
- Use logical reasoning to explore and solve number problems.
- Make sense of and solve word problems.
- Solve simple word problems involving ratio and direct proportion.

Key vocabulary

Centimetre (cm), millimetre (mm), kilogram (kg), gram (g), milligram (mg), litre (l), centilitre (cl), millilitre (ml)

Resources

- Rulers
- Squared paper
- Pairs of compasses
- Assessment activity 8 – one per student (Resource sheet 8 – see www.oxfordprimary.com/OIPMteacher)

Links to Student Book

See pages 146–147 in Student Book.

Links to Workbook

Workbook page 76

Links to Digital Resource Pack

Digital Resource Pack 6 contains two activities which can be used to support students' understanding of measurement. On the home page, select 'Length, Mass and Capacity'.

Language support

Develop the language of problem solving, for example:

- *Are there other possible arrangements?*
- *How do you know that this is the best arrangement?*

Introductory and Main activity

Ask students to work in groups of four on the activities on page 146 of the Student Book. Encourage them to try to interpret and begin the activity without any teacher input.

It is important that the groups of students decide how to solve the problem created on page 146 of the Student Book without support. Give each group squared paper, rulers and compasses. Give them time to think through the problem and work out their approach before you offer help. If a group is struggling to start, suggest that they 'visit' a group that has found a way to start. The best way to approach the solution is to draw a section of the pastry (say 25 cm × 25 cm) and make cut-outs of pie 'bases' and 'tops'. These can then be rearranged on the 'pastry'.

Ask groups to present their solutions. It is useful to present alternative solutions so that the class can discuss which solution and method they think is best.

Differentiation

Students should work in mixed-attainment groups to support one another in working through the investigation on page 146 of the Student Book.

For the activity on page 147 of the Student Book, you may want to help write the answers for those less confident with writing or in speaking English.

Differentiated outcomes
This is an activity designed to offer differentiation by outcome.

Learning review

Students should complete the Review activity on page 147 of the Student Book as individuals as it is a summative assessment.

Additional activities

The activity on page 146 of the Student Book is a great activity to carry out practically. Students can roll pastry and then reroll the pastry when the first set of bases and tops have been made. The class can also sell the pies and think about budgeting and appropriate selling prices.

Students can complete Workbook page 76.

Answers

Student Book page 146

Accept any sensible diagrams.

Student Book page 147

$2.5\,\text{m} = 2\frac{1}{2}\,\text{m}$

$\frac{7}{10}\,\text{litre} = 700\,\text{ml}$

$2.4\,\text{kg} = 2400\,\text{g}$

$\text{ruler} = 2\,\text{cm} = 20\,\text{mm}$

$0.6\,\text{kg} = 600\,000\,\text{mg}$

$\frac{1}{4}\,\text{litre} = 250\,\text{ml}$

$0.015\,\text{litre} = 1.5\,\text{cl}$

weighing scales $= 600\,\text{g}$

measuring tape $= 250\,\text{cm}$

$0.02\,\text{m} = 2\,\text{cm}$

measuring jug $= 700\,\text{ml} = 0.7\,\text{litres}$

syringe $= 15\,\text{ml}$

Workbook page 76

1. 9.9 litres
2. 15.5 kg; 2.5 kg
3. $15

Assessment activity 8

1. **a)** g and mg
2. **a)** multiply by 100
3. **b)** 0.33 litres
4. **b)** 10
5. **a)** 1250 ml
6. Accept any accurate answers.

Unit 9 Time

Overview

Big Idea

The only new idea for students in this unit is that of different time zones. Usually, students who travel have an understanding of this concept but some may find it very difficult to understand that it is not the same time in every place in the world. It is helpful to remind students that, because the world turns on its axis, it is night in half the world when it is day in the other half. Midday in one part of the world is midnight in an opposite part of the world.

Possible misconceptions

A very common misconception is in using the 24-hour clock. Students are used to a decimal place value system based on 10, so they often forget that an analogue clock is based on 12 hours, with 24 hours in one day. The best way to overcome this is practice. Remind students that 20:00 is 8 p.m. and not 10 p.m. – to work out 12-hour clock times from 24-hour clock times from 13:00 onwards, we subtract 12 from the 24-hour clock times. Converting 23:00 hours to 12-hour clock time can be helpful when discussing this, since it cannot be expressed as a 12-hour clock time plus 10. It is 23:00 – 12 = 11p.m.

Key vocabulary and language structures

Millisecond, second; hour, day, week, month, year, decade, century, millennium; a.m., p.m.; midday, midnight; timetable; arrive, depart; 24-hour clock, 12-hour clock; digital times, analogue times; digital watch/clock, analogue watch/clock; international time zones

Coverage in lessons

Learning focus	Learning outcomes
Converting between units of time	Can I convert between different units of time?
	Can I explain the difference between analogue and digital clocks and watches?
Using the 24-hour clock and timetables	Can I use the 24-hour clock to read timetables?
Calculating time intervals including time zones	Do I know what the time is in a different time zone?

9 Time

Engage

Specific learning foci

- *Recognise and understand the units form, measuring time.*
- Tell the time using digital and analogue clocks.
- Compare times on digital/analogue clocks.
- Calculate time intervals using digital and analogue times.

Problem solving focus

- Understand everyday systems of measurement in time.

Key vocabulary

Millisecond, second, hour, day, week, month, year, decade, century, millennium, a.m., p.m., midday, midnight, timetable, arrive, depart, 24-hour clock, 12-hour clock, international time zones, analogue, digital

Resources

- Large sheets of paper
- Marker pens

Links to Student Book

See page 149 in the Student Book.

Language support

Work with each group in turn as they create their posters. Ask individual students to read out parts from the poster. This allows you to both check and model correct pronunciation. Refer back to the vocabulary list to encourage students to use the correct vocabulary.

 Introductory activity

Organise students into mixed-attainment groups of four. Ask them to write down as many ways that they use time as possible. Ask them to try to classify this list using a mind map. After 10 **minutes** rotate the sheets of paper to the next group so that each group begins to add to each poster. After 30 minutes select one of the posters. Ask the group to present this.

Main activity

Ask each group to select one of the discussion starters from page 149 of the Student Book. Groups can choose to discuss the same question. Listen to students as they discuss these questions. Make a note of the mathematical vocabulary that they are using. Write this on the whiteboard for the Learning review.

Differentiation

Students will all use and hear new vocabulary and all hear pronunciation modelled by other students. As this is an Introductory activity, listen carefully to the discussions so that you can plan for your future teaching.

Learning review

Look at the mathematical vocabulary that you listed on the board. Ensure it includes most of the vocabulary at the top of this page. Ask groups to make posters with definitions of the words. They can refer to this throughout the unit.

Additional activities

Students can keep a diary during the week of all the ways in which they use time and tell the time.

9A Converting between units of time

Discover

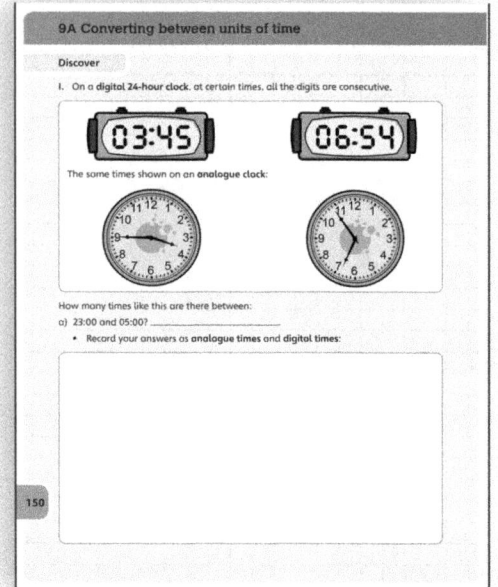 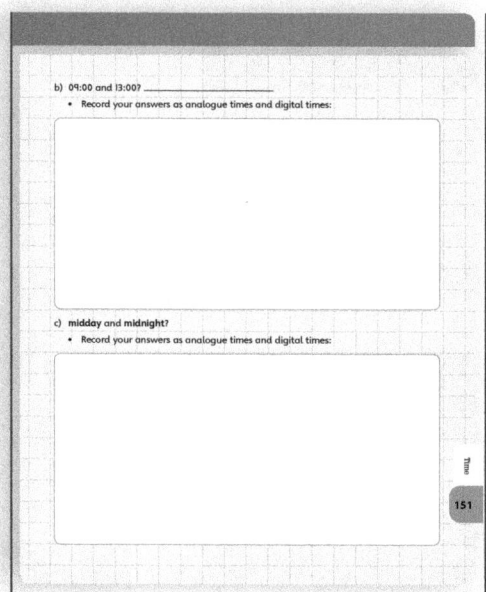

Specific learning foci

- Tell the time using digital and analogue clocks.
- Compare times on digital/analogue clocks.

Problem solving focus

- Understand everyday systems of measurement in time.

Key vocabulary

a.m., p.m., midday, midnight, 24-hour clock, 12-hour clock, digital, analogue

Resources

- Large analogue clock big enough for whole class use
- Mini whiteboards and markers
- Analogue watches or clocks for individual use if possible

Links to Student Book

See pages 150–151 in Student Book.

Links to Workbook

Workbook page 78

Links to Digital Resource Pack

Digital Resource Pack 6 contains two activities which can be used to support students' understanding of time. On the home page, select 'Time'.

Language support

Asking students to speak out their thinking in the introduction and in the Learning review is important. Encourage students to develop extended responses, saying, for example: *Tell me a bit more about that. How do you know that is the correct answer?* Encourage students to use the 'analogue' form, for example:

- *ten past one*
- *quarter to five.*

Compare this with the digital forms, for example:

- *one ten*
- *four forty-five.*

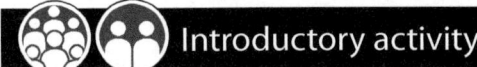 Introductory activity

Ask: *How many of you have* **analogue** *watches or analogue clocks at home?* Discuss the differences between analogue times and digital times, including the use of **a.m.** and **p.m.** Use the large analogue clock at the front of the class to show students a range of times. Each time you show a time, ask students to write the same time using the digital **24-hour clock** form on mini whiteboards. Use the following times, moving the hands on by the specified time intervals:

- 09.24 a.m.
- 45 minutes later (10:09)
- 2 hours 15 minutes later (12:24)
- 1 hour 30 minutes later (13:54)
- 5 hours 20 minutes later (19:14)

After each time, ask: *How did you calculate the new time?* Use any errors as a teaching point. Work with students to identify where they made the mistake. This can also help other students to avoid making the same mistakes

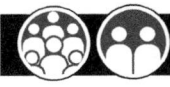 Main activity

Students work through the activities in pairs to support one another and to check answers. It may be helpful for students to have access to analogue clocks on their tables. They can use these to turn the hands to make the times that they write initially as digital times. You may need to remind students to look carefully at the position of the minute hand.

Differentiation

Supporting: Ask students to say the times as they write them down.

Consolidating: Ask students to find how long it is between some of the times they are writing down.

Extending: Ask students to find how long it is between all the times they are writing down and to explore the patterns.

Differentiated outcomes	
All students	should find time differences, using the clocks as support.
Most students	will find time differences, using the clocks.
Some students	will use the clocks, using mental methods.

 Learning review

Ask students to discuss the following question with a partner: *What are the most important things to remember when writing digital times as analogue times?* After 2 minutes, take feedback from the pairs. List all the feedback somewhere where it can be referred to for the rest of the unit.

Additional activities

Students can list all the places where they see an analogue clock. They can keep a diary and write down the time (analogue and digital) it was when they saw each clock.

Students can complete Workbook page 78.

Answers

Student Book pages 150 and 151

1. **a)** 23:45, 01:23, 02:10, 02:34, 03:21, 03:45, 04:32, 04:56
   b) 12:34
   c) 12:34, 23:45

Workbook page 78

2. 14:46; clock face shows 46 minutes past two
3. 22:10; clock face shows ten past ten
4. 02:45; clock face shows quarter to three
5. 07:34; clock face shows thirty-four minutes past seven

9A Converting between units of time

Explore

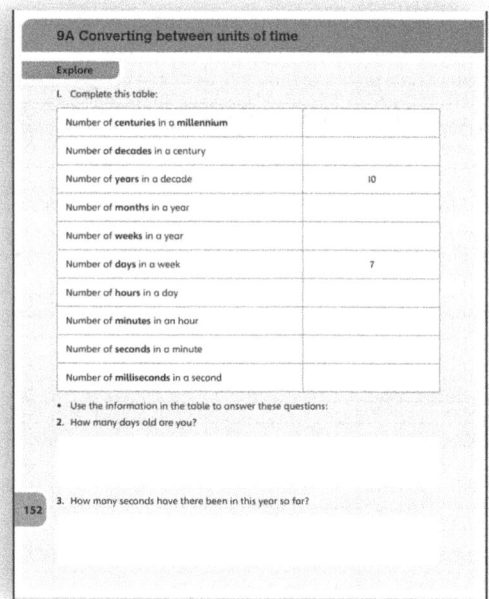

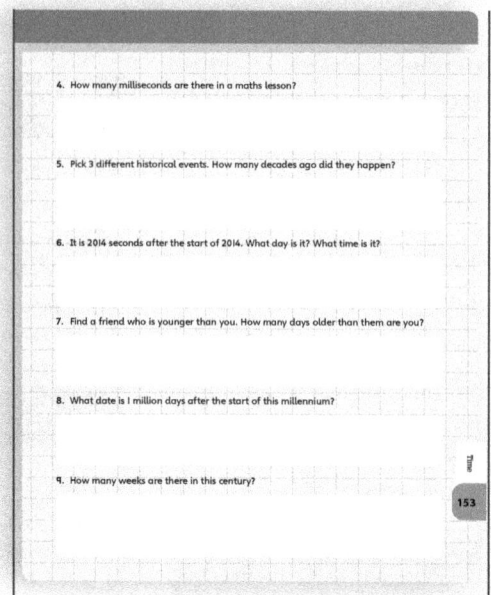

Specific learning foci

- Tell the time using digital and analogue clocks.
- Compare times on digital/analogue clocks.

Problem solving focus

- Understand everyday systems of measurement in time.

Key vocabulary

Millisecond, second, hour, day, week, month, year, decade, century, millennium

Resources

- Flashcards with the following 'units of time' vocabulary on them:
  millennium, century, decade,
  year, month, week, day,
  hour, minute, second, millisecond
- Pot of lollipop sticks with each student's name on a separate stick
- Calculators
- Calendar

Links to Student Book

See pages 152–153 in Student Book.

Links to Workbook

Workbook page 79

Links to Digital Resource Pack

Digital Resource Pack 6 contains two activities which can be used to support students' understanding of time. On the home page, select 'Time'.

Language support

As you work with the pairs encourage them to explain their working. Ask, for example:

- *How are you doing the calculation?*
- *Why are you multiplying by: 24 or 60?*

Encourage students to talk to one another about their answers so that they can check that their answers make sense. Students are all probably a similar number of days old, for example. They may ask one another:

- *How many days old are you?*
- *How many milliseconds are there in a second?*

 Introductory activity

Pick a lollipop stick out of the pot. Ask the named student to come to the front and pick a flashcard. Repeat with other students. When each student picks a flashcard, ask them to stand in ascending order (with **millisecond** at one end and **millennium** at the other end). Each time a student picks a card, ask them to state one fact they know about that unit of time, for example: 'There are 100 years in a **century**.' or 'There are 60 **seconds** in 1 **minute**.'

 Main activity

Ask students to work in pairs to discuss and complete the table on page 152 of the Student Book. When students have completed the table go through the answers so that all students have the correct information before they move on to the questions. Check any errors with students to find out what mistakes they made.

You may choose to group the students by prior attainment for the activities on page 153 so that you can support them in carrying out the calculations. Students can use calculators to do calculations.

Differentiation

Supporting: Model the calculation for the students explaining how to carry out the calculation.

Consolidating: Support the students in carrying out the calculations.

Extending: Ask students to share their strategies.

Differentiated outcomes	
All students	should complete the table on page 152 accurately.
Most students	will answer the questions on page 153 with support.
Some students	will answer the questions on page 153 and share their strategies.

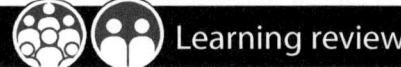 Learning review

Ask students to work in mixed-attainment pairs. Pick two flashcards at random. Ask: *How many of the smaller unit are there in the larger unit?* The more confident partner should explain to the less confident partner how to work this out. Take feedback from one of the pairs, asking:

How did you carry out the calculation?

Repeat as many times as you think is necessary.

Additional activities

Students can set questions for members of their family to answer using important time-related facts about the family.

Students can complete Workbook page 79.

Answers

Student Book pages 152 and 153
1.

Number of centuries in a millennium	10
Number of decades in a century	10
Number of years in a decade	10
Number of months in a year	12
Number of weeks in a year	52
Number of days in a week	7
Number of hours in a day	24
Number of minutes in an hour	60
Number of seconds in a minute	60
Number of milliseconds in a second	1000

2. –3. Answers will vary. Check that students' answers are reasonable.

Workbook page 79

Answers will vary. Check that students' answers are reasonable.

Discover

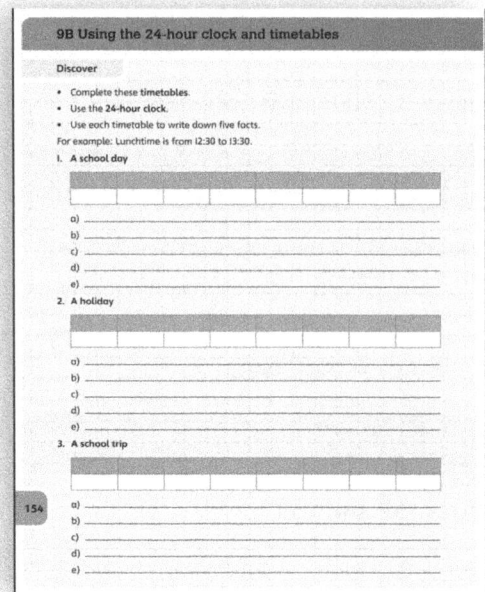

Specific learning focus

- Read and use timetables using the 24-hour clock system.

Problem solving focus

- Use ordered lists or tables to help solve problems systematically.

Key vocabulary

a.m., p.m., midday, midnight, timetable

Resources

- Mini whiteboards and markers
- Lollipop sticks with students' names (from 9A Explore)

Links to Student Book

See page 154 in Student Book.

Links to Workbook

Workbook page 80

Links to Digital Resource Pack

Digital Resource Pack 6 contains two activities which can be used to support students' understanding of time. On the home page, select 'Time'.

Language support

Ask questions to support students and to assess their understanding of calculating time intervals, for example:

- *How long after …?*
- *How much time is there between …?*

Encourage students to use the vocabulary of time. Model the use of the 24-hour clock saying, for example: *oh five seventeen* for 05:17.

 Introductory activity

Ask each pair to write down on their mini whiteboards two times that relate to an event from yesterday. This can be any event, for example: the time they woke up, the time they left their home to go to school, the time they finished their homework, the time they arrived home after temple. Tell them to include one time from the morning and one time from the afternoon or evening.

Use the lollipop sticks to select six students. Ask them to arrange themselves in a line at the front of the class in ascending order, from the earliest event to the latest event. Ask students to work in pairs to calculate the time gaps between the events. Take feedback from pairs asking them to describe their strategies. Discuss the idea of a timetable.

 Main activity

Students work in pairs to create timetables for the activity on page 154 of the Student Book. Encourage students to use times which are not simply half and quarter hours, particularly on the school trip and the holiday timetables. In their lists of related facts, ask students to include facts which are about time gaps, not simply stating the times, for example:

I am asleep for 8 hours 35 minutes.

Differentiation

Supporting: Ask students to create timetables to the nearest quarter-hour.

Consolidating: Ask students to create timetables to the nearest 5 minutes.

Extending: Ask students to create timetables to the nearest minute.

Differentiated outcomes	
All students	should create timetables to the nearest quarter-hour.
Most students	will create timetables to the nearest 5 minutes.
Some students	will create timetables to the nearest minute.

 Learning review

Ask one pair with an interesting holiday timetable to come to the front. Ask them to write their timetable on the board. Each pair should create a question based on this timetable and swap it with another pair.

Additional activities

Students can keep diaries of the day's or week's events. They can create a timetable to show the activities.

Students can complete Workbook page 80.

Answers

Student Book page 154

Answers will vary as students create their own timetables. Check that the facts that students have written about their timetables are reasonable.

Workbook page 80

Answers will vary as students wrote their own school timetables. Check that the facts that they wrote about the timetables are appropriate.

Explore

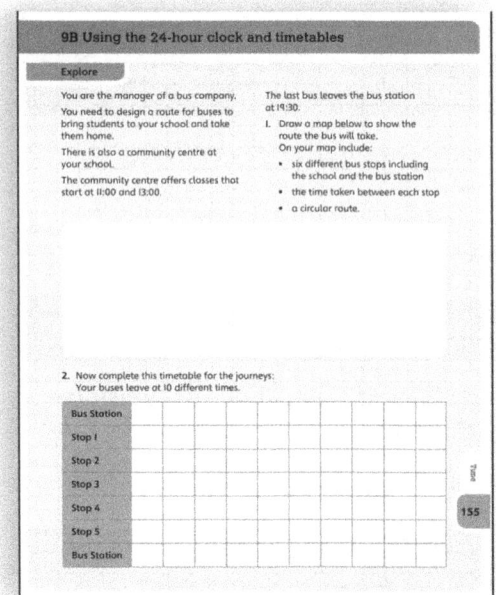

Specific learning focus

- Read and use timetables using the 24-hour clock system.

Problem solving focus

- Use ordered lists or tables to help solve problems systematically.

Key vocabulary

a.m., p.m., midday, midnight, timetable, arrive, depart

Resources

- Large sheets of paper and pens

Links to Student Book

See page 155 in Student Book.

Links to Workbook

Workbook page 81

Links to Digital Resource Pack

Digital Resource Pack 6 contains two activities which can be used to support students' understanding of time. On the home page, select 'Time'.

Language support

Encourage students to give specific feedback on the routes. If there is time in the Main activity, students can look at other groups' routes and offer comments before each group completes a final version based on the comments of the other students. They can check, for example, that timings are accurate based on the sketch maps or that the bus stops at the most important places on the map.

 Introductory activity

Work with the whole class to model the activity on page 155 of the Student Book. First list six possible places that need a bus stop in the local area (one of which is the 'bus station'). Draw a simple sketch map starting (and ending) at a 'bus station' and joining these places together. Take suggestions from students. Ask: *How long does it take a bus to travel between … and …?* Write these times on the sketch map. Then, starting at the bus station with a starting time of 08:45, write down the times that the bus **arrives** at, and **departs** from, each stop.

 Main activity

Ask students to work in mixed-attainment groups, using paper and pens, to make the maps of their bus route and then the bus timetable for their route. When they are sure that they have an accurate map and **timetable** ask them to describe their routes and timetables to you. They can then each make an individual copy on page 155 of the Student Book.

Differentiation

Supporting: Ask students to explain how they are constructing the timetable.

Consolidating: Ask students to explain how they know what the time intervals should be.

Extending: Ask students to create word problems based on the timetable.

Differentiated outcomes	
All students	should understand how a timetable is constructed.
Most students	will use the timetable to calculate time intervals.
Some students	will create word problems based on the timetable.

 Learning review

Choose one group to present their route and timetable to the rest of the class. Ask the other students to ask questions and to give feedback on the effectiveness of their route.

Additional activities

Students can find bus timetables for the local area. They can write a series of questions based on these timetables.

Students can complete Workbook page 81.

Answers

Student Book page 155

Accept any sensible answers.

Workbook page 81

Answers will vary as students design their own flight timetables. Check that these seem reasonable.

Discover

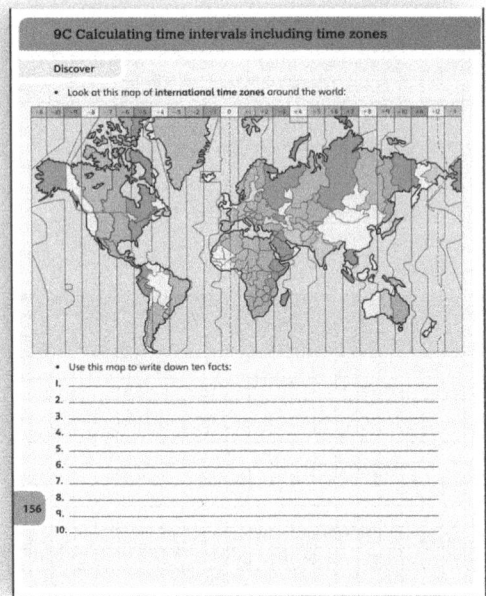

Specific learning focus

- Appreciate how the time is different in different time zones around the world.

Problem solving focus

- Use ordered lists or tables to help solve problems systematically.

Key vocabulary

a.m., p.m., midday, midnight, 24-hour clock, 12-hour clock, international time zones

Resources

- Large map of the world showing time zones
- Mini whiteboards and markers
- Lollipop sticks with students' names

Links to Student Book

See page 156 in Student Book.

Links to Workbook

Workbook page 82

Links to Digital Resource Pack

Digital Resource Pack 6 contains two activities which can be used to support students' understanding of time. On the home page, select 'Time'.

Language support

Use language of comparison, for example:

- *How much earlier?*
- *How much later?*
- *How many hours before?*
- *How many hours after?*

 Introductory activity

Ask students, in pairs, to list on their mini whiteboards all the different places in the world that they have visited or where their family members live. Select students by picking lollipop sticks. Ask each selected student to choose a place off their list. Find the place on the large world map and work out the current time in that place using the **international time zones**. Keep a list of all the times and places on the board.

 Main activity

Ask the students to work in the same pairs as for the Introductory activity. Encourage them to write down a range of facts. Share any interesting facts with the whole class as a model of good practice.

Differentiation

Supporting: Ask students who have experience of time zones to support students who do not have this experience.

Consolidating: Ask students to share their strategies for finding time differences.

Extending: Ask students to create two-step word problems.

Differentiated outcomes	
All students	should appreciate how the time is different in different time zones around the world.
Most students	will find time differences in different time zones.
Some students	will create word problems based on different time zones.

 Learning review

Use the lollipop sticks again to select students. Ask each student to share one of their facts. Ask the other students in the group to check that this fact is correct. Then ask each pair to create a word problem based on their facts. They should exchange this problem with another pair.

Additional activities

Students can use airline timetables or airline tickets to explore time zones. In particular, they can look at journeys when you appear to arrive before you leave.

Students can complete Workbook page 82.

Answers

Student Book page 156

Accept any sensible answers.

Workbook page 82

1. 15:25
2. 11:30
3. 17:45
4. 14:15
5. 22:25
6. 17:30
7. 21:00
8. 02:00

Explore

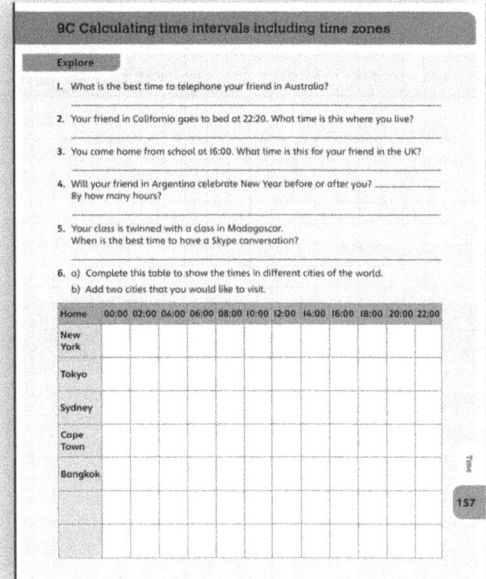

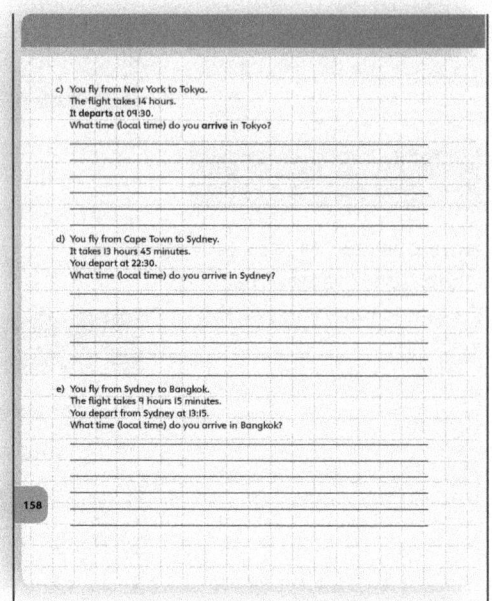

Specific learning focus

- Appreciate how the time is different in different time zones around the world.

Problem solving focus

- Use ordered lists or tables to help solve problems systematically.

Key vocabulary

a.m., p.m., midday, midnight, 24-hour clock, 12-hour clock, international time zones

Resources

- Large map of the world showing time zones
- Mini whiteboards and markers
- Lollipop sticks with students' names

Links to Student Book

See pages 157–158 in Student Book.

Links to Workbook

Workbook page 83

Links to Digital Resource Pack

Digital Resource Pack 6 contains two activities which can be used to support students' understanding of time. On the home page, select 'Time'.

Language support

When students talk in pairs during the Learning review, listen to their conversations. You can use students who are confident in English to act as models for others in the class.

 Introductory activity

Use the list of times that you created in 9C Discover, or repeat the activity to create a new set of times and places. Ask pairs of students:

- *Imagine you want to telephone <one of the places> now.*
- *What might be happening there now?*
- *What might be happening there 8 hours later than now?*

Repeat for three different time zones.

Main activity

Students should work in the same pairs. Where possible these should include a student with experience of time zones. Students may need to use the map of the world to locate places within time zones. Encourage students to share answers with one another to check that they are carrying out calculations accurately.

Differentiation

Supporting: Ask students who have experience of time zones to support students who do not have this experience.

Consolidating: Ask students to share their strategies for finding time differences.

Extending: Ask students to create two-step word problems.

Differentiated outcomes	
All students	should appreciate how the time is different in different time zones around the world.
Most students	will find time differences in different time zones.
Some students	will create their own word problems based on different time zones.

 Learning review

Ask students to discuss the following in pairs:

- *What have you learnt in 9C Discover and 9C Explore?*
- *What have you learnt that is new?*
- *What are you surprised about?*
- *What did you already know?*

Take feedback from each pair in turn.

Additional activities

Students can keep diaries of their activities and link them to those of students in other countries. For example:

- *What are students in Sudan doing when you are going to school?*

This is a great activity for schools that are twinned with a school in another country.

Students can complete Workbook page 83.

Answers

Student Book pages 157 and 158

1–5 Accept any sensible answers.

6. **c)** 12.30 the next day

   d) 20.15 the next day

   e) 19.30 the same day

Workbook page 83

Dhaka 17:40

Tokyo 02:55 (the next day)

Nairobi 18:00

Phnom Penh 01:35 (the next day)

Kuala Lumpur 06:40 (the next day)

Toronto 04:10 (the next day)

Anchorage 03:55 (the next day)

London 02:05 (the next day)

9 Time

Connect and Review

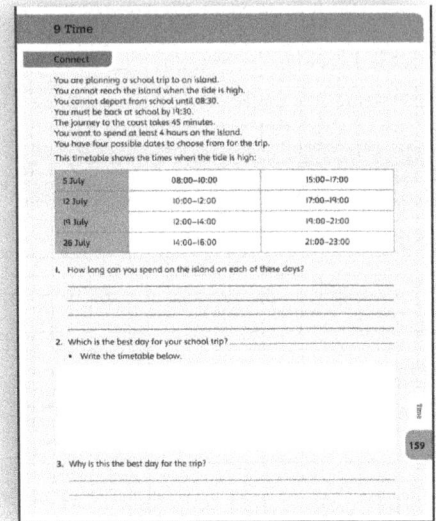 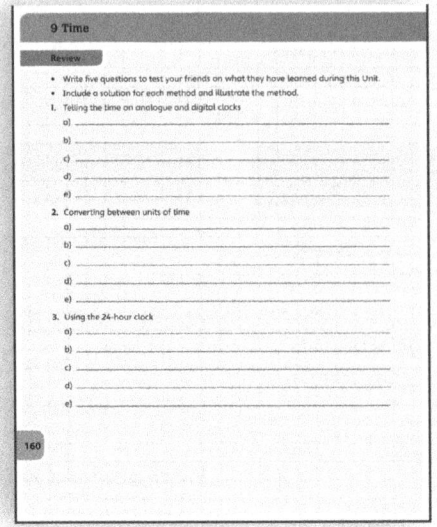 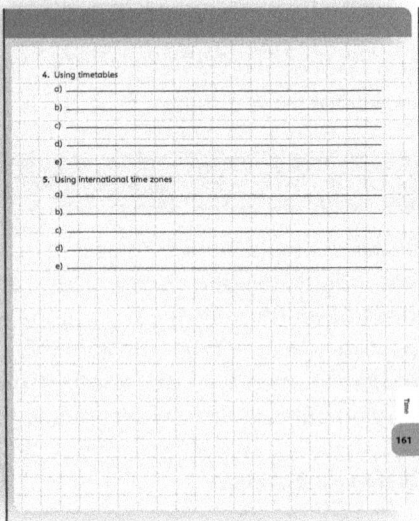

Specific learning foci

- Recognise and understand the units for measuring time.
- Read and use timetables using the 24-hour clock system.
- Calculate time intervals using digital times.

Problem solving focus

- Understand everyday systems of measurement in time and use these to perform simple calculations.

Key vocabulary

Millisecond, second, hour, day, week, month, year, decade, century, millennium, a.m., p.m. midday, midnight, timetable, arrive, depart, 24-hour clock, 12-hour clock, international time zones

Resources

- Large sheets of paper for drafting out solutions to the problem
- Assessment activity 9 – one per student (Resource sheet 9 – see www.oxfordprimary.com/OIPMteacher)

Links to Student Book

See pages 159–161 in Student Book.

Links to Workbook

Workbook page 84

Links to Digital Resource Pack

Digital Resource Pack 6 contains two activities which can be used to support students' understanding of time. On the home page, select 'Time'.

Language support

As the groups prepare their presentations, remind them of key vocabulary they can use. For example:

- *We will leave school at …*
- *We will spend … hours on the island.*
- *We will leave the island at …*

 Introductory and Main activity

Ask students to work in mixed-attainment groups of four on the activities on page 159 of the Student Book. Keep the introduction short. It is important that students try to understand the problem on page 159 of the Student Book for themselves, including thinking about how they might represent the problem and the solution. After the students have had 5 minutes interpreting the problem, you may wish to clarify the meaning of any of the vocabulary that students do not understand.

For groups that are struggling to start the problem, you can suggest using a timetable to 'map out' the visit. Students may need help in understanding low and high tide if this is a concept that they have not met before: You can shade in the times when there is a high tide. You can use a different colour to show the travelling time. As you work with the groups, select two groups with different solutions to present at the end.

Ask the two selected groups to present their recommendations. The other students can then decide which recommendation they think is best.

Differentiation

Students should work in mixed attainment groups to support one another in working through the investigation on page 159 of the Student Book.

For the activity on pages 160 and 161 of the Student Book, you may want to help write the answers for those less confident with writing or in speaking English.

Differentiated outcomes
This is an activity designed to offer differentiation by outcome.

Learning review

Students should complete the Review activity on pages 160 and 161 of the Student Book as individuals as it is a summative assessment.

Additional activities

Students can plan a class trip that the class will take.

Students can complete Workbook page 84.

Answers

Student Book page 159

1. 5 July – 8 hours 45 mins
   12 July – 7 hours 45 mins
   19 July – 9 hours 30 mins
   26 July – 9 hours 30 mins
2. 5 July:
   09:15 – depart from school
   10:00 – arrive at island
   15:00 – depart from island
   15:45 – arrive at school

Student Book pages 160 and 161

Answers will vary as students write their own test questions on time. Check that their answers are correct.

Workbook page 84

1. 15:20
2. 20:30
3. 20:14
4. 604 800 seconds

Assessment activity 9

1. c) Populations of cities
2. a) 12:00
3. b) 13:30 my time
4. c) 16:02
5. b) 1440
6. c) 3 000 000 000
7. Answers will vary as students write their own timetables. Accept any sensible answers.

Overview

Big Idea

The Big Idea here is the use of standard units. Remind students that we use square centimetres and so on for measuring area. The area is simply a count of how many squares cover the shape. We use centimetres and metres for measuring the perimeter. This is a measure of distance.

Students have met all the key ideas before. This unit expects them to apply their knowledge in a range of investigational situations.

Possible misconceptions

Students may still confuse area and perimeter. This is an issue of language rather than a misconception within the mathematics. Thinking about the other meanings of the words can help. For example, students may understand area as a 'place'. For example, they may say, 'I live in the downtown area'. This suggests coverage, rather than something that surrounds, as in 'perimeter fence'.

You may observe students with a misconception about the conservation of area. For example, they may not see that when they rearrange a rectangle by cutting it up, the area of the new shape remains the same. Carrying out activities which involve rearranging shapes to conserve area is the best way to support students in overcoming this misconception (see the diagram opposite).

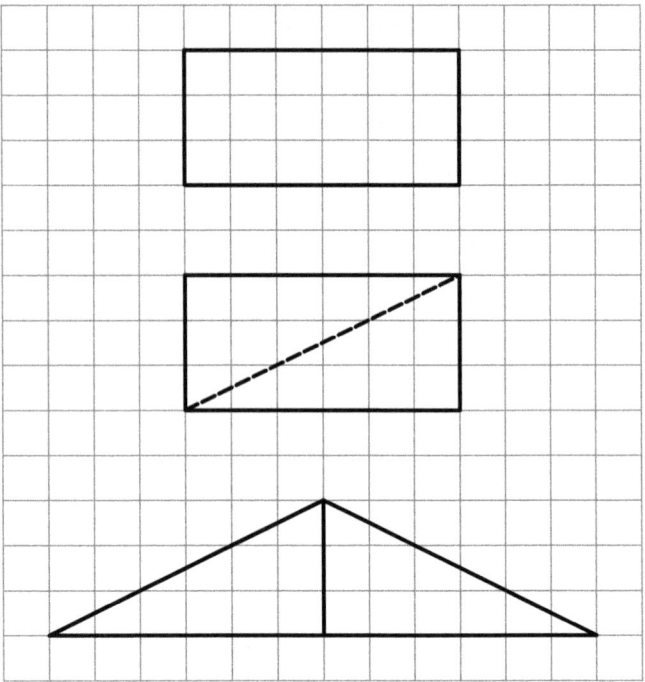

Finally, students may think that there is only one possible area for a given perimeter. This misconception is dealt with in the Engage activity.

Key vocabulary and language structures

Length, width, height, depth, breadth; edge, perimeter, circumference; area, surface, face, surface area; square centimetre (cm²), square metre (m²), square millimetre (mm²); rectilinear, scattergram, correlation

Coverage in lessons

Learning focus	Learning outcomes
Area and perimeter of rectilinear shapes	Can I measure the area and perimeter of rectilinear shapes?
Estimating areas of irregular shapes by counting squares	Can I find approximate areas by counting squares?
Calculating areas and perimeters of compound shapes	Can I use what I know to find the areas and perimeters of compound shapes?

Engage

Specific learning focus

- Measure and calculate the perimeter and area of rectilinear shapes.

Problem solving focus

- Understand everyday systems of measurement in length and use these to perform simple calculations.

Key vocabulary

Length, width, height, depth, breadth, edge, perimeter, circumference, area, surface, square centimetre (cm²), square metre (m²), square millimetre (mm²), rectilinear

Resources

- Mini whiteboards and markers
- Squared paper

Links to Student Book

See page 163 in the Student Book.

Language support

Model the use of the vocabulary that you listed as you work with groups during the Main activity. As the groups report back, model the correct use of the vocabulary, for example:

What is the width /length /height /breadth /depth?

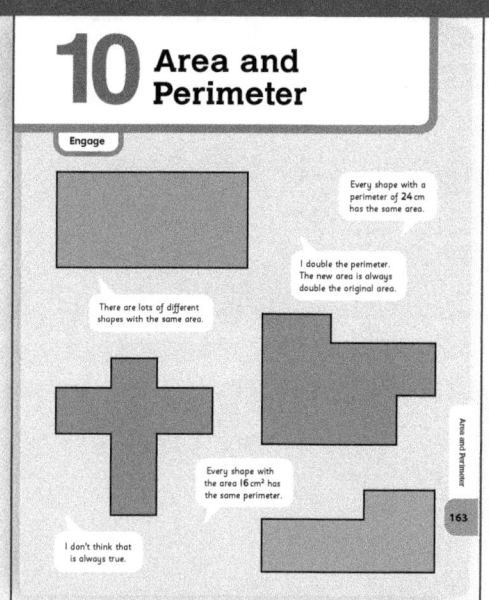

 Main activity

Arrange students into mixed-attainment groups of four or five. Tell each group to explore one of the statements in the speech bubbles on page 163 of the Student Book. Different groups can explore the same question. Encourage students to try examples (using the squared paper and mini whiteboards) to see if the statements are always true, sometimes true or never true. Two students from each group can report back to the rest of the class.

Differentiation

All students will engage in the investigation that their groups have chosen. Students will bring different prior experience to the group and you should encourage all students to contribute to the discussion. Less experienced students will benefit from hearing other students talk about their understandings and from hearing the key vocabulary used by other students. More experienced students will consolidate their understanding through explaining to others. Listen carefully to group discussions and introduce key vocabulary as necessary.

Learning review

Select a group to report back on each question. Encourage them to use the vocabulary that you listed at the beginning of the lesson.

Introductory activity

Ask pairs to talk for 5 minutes and to consider the question: *What do you know about **area** and **perimeter**?* After 5 minutes, take one piece of feedback from each pair in the class.

During the feedback, list key vocabulary on the whiteboard. Include, for example: **length**, **width**, **height**, **depth**, **breadth**, **edge**, **perimeter**, **circumference**, **area**, **surface**, face, **square centimetre (cm²)**, **square metre (m²)**, **square millimetre (mm²)**

Additional activities

Students can explore similar statements linked to volume. They can consider questions, for example:

- *You double the dimensions of a cuboid. What happens to the volume?*

Note again that volume is beyond the scope of the Stage 6 framework, but students are likely to have an intuitive understanding of volume, and these Additional activities are useful as extension work.

Discover

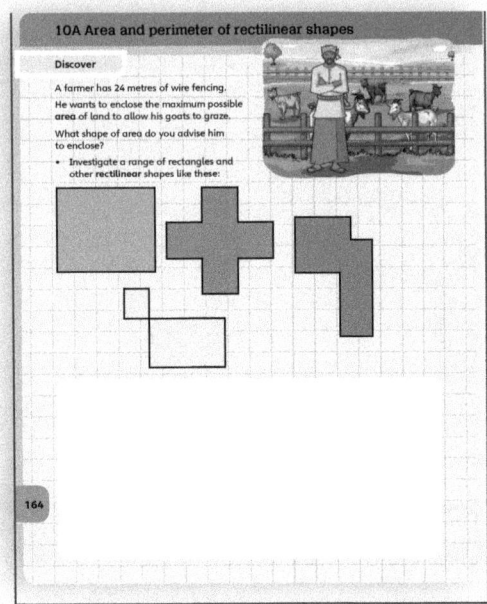

Specific learning focus

- Measure and calculate the perimeter and area of rectilinear shapes.

Problem solving focus

- Understand everyday systems of measurement in length and use these to perform simple calculations.

Key vocabulary

Length, width, height, depth, breadth, edge, perimeter, area, square centimetre (cm^2), square metre (m^2), square millimetre (mm^2), rectilinear

Resources

- Mini whiteboards and markers
- Squared paper

Links to Student Book

See page 164 in the Student Book.

Links to Workbook

Workbook page 86

Links to Digital Resource Pack

Digital Resource Pack 6 contains two activities which can be used to support students' understanding of the area and perimeter of rectilinear shapes. On the home page, select 'Area and Perimeter'.

Language support

During the reporting back in the Learning review, focus on the vocabulary developed in the activity. As you work with groups in the main activity, model the use of the key vocabulary. For example:

- *The width of this field is …*
- *The length of this field is …*
- *The area of this field is …*

 Introductory activity

If possible, use a large open space for this activity. Ask students to join hands and form a rectangle. Allow them to organise this for themselves. Ask: *What is the perimeter*? (Take the answer in units of arm spans.) Now ask them to form a different rectangle. Again ask: *What is the perimeter?* (The perimeter remains the same whatever rectangle they form.)

After you have repeated this several times, ask pairs to sketch the rectangles that they formed and to find what the **areas** of these rectangles are. They may be surprised that the areas are different (although a similar activity was covered in Stage 5).

 Main activity

Remind students that a rectilinear shape is a polygon made of straight lines that meet at right angles. Ask each student to draw two **rectilinear** shapes with a perimeter of 24 on their whiteboard. Tell the pairs to work out the areas of their four shapes initially, then to try the activity on page 164 of the Student Book. The pairs can explore different shapes to try to find the maximum area. As you support the groups, find a pair who are able to explain their solution as a good model to the rest of the class. Support them by asking them to practise their reporting back with you.

Differentiation

Supporting: Support students to find areas.

Consolidating: Ask students how they are finding the areas and which shapes are giving them the largest areas.

Extending: Ask students to explore a wider range of shapes.

Differentiated outcomes	
All students	should find areas of a range of rectilinear shapes.
Most students	will find an area that they can recommend.
Some students	will explore other shapes.

 Learning review

Ask the pair you selected to report back to the group. Encourage them to talk through the whole process and not to just give you their answer. Compare this solution with other solutions. As a class, agree on the best solution.

Additional activities

Students can extend the activity in the Student Book to look beyond rectilinear shapes. The maximum area is actually made by a circle of circumference 24 m.

Students can complete Workbook page 86.

Answers

Student Book page 164

Answers will vary as students draw their own rectangles and rectilinear shapes. Check that students have worked out the areas correctly.

Workbook page 86

Answers will vary as students draw plans of their own playgrounds that have areas of 40 square metres. Check that the areas shown are all equal.

Explore

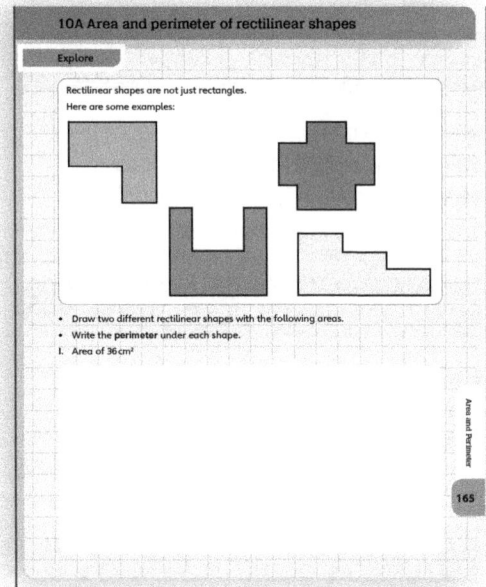
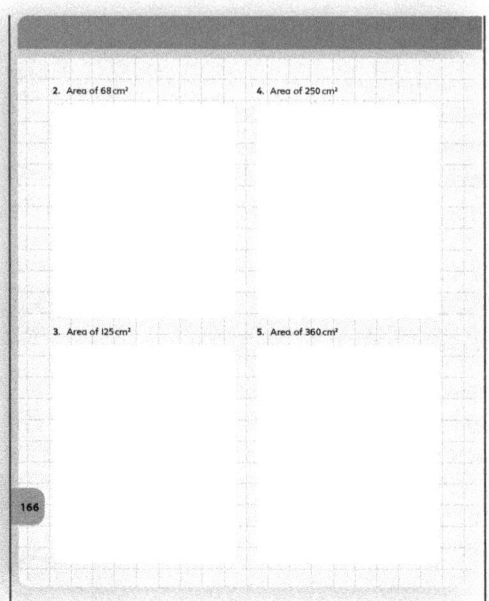

Specific learning focus

- Measure and calculate the perimeter and area of rectilinear shapes.

Problem solving focus

- Understand everyday systems of measurement in length and use these to perform simple calculations.

Key vocabulary

Length, width, height, depth, breadth, edge, perimeter, area, square centimetre (cm²), square metre (m²), square millimetre (mm²), rectilinear

Resources

- Mini whiteboards and markers
- Squared paper

Links to Student Book

See pages 165–166 in the Student Book.

Links to Workbook

Workbook page 87

Links to Digital Resource Pack

Digital Resource Pack 6 contains two activities which can be used to support students' understanding of the area and perimeter of rectilinear shapes. On the home page, select 'Area and Perimeter'.

Language support

During the reporting back in the Learning review, focus on the vocabulary developed in the activity. As you work with students in the Main activity, model the use of key vocabulary, for example:

- *What are the dimensions of your shapes?*
- *What is the length?*
- *What is the width?*

 Introductory activity

Draw a rectangle on the whiteboard. Tell students: The **area** of this rectangle is 48 cm².

Then ask: *What are possible dimensions for the **length** and **width**?* Ask pairs to write their answers on their whiteboards. Emphasise that the sketch is not to scale. Ensure you get all possible answers (1 × 48, 2 × 24, 3 × 16, 4 × 12, 6 × 8). Repeat this with a cross shape, made up of five squares, with a total area of 100 cm².

 Main activity

Ask students as pairs to explore the activity on pages 165 and 166 of the Student Book. They should create their own shapes and then their partner should check that their calculations are correct. Ask individuals to explain how they decided on the dimensions of the shapes. Make the link to factors where appropriate.

Differentiation

Supporting: Support students to find areas.

Consolidating: Ask students how they are finding the areas and how they are deciding on the dimensions of the rectangles.

Extending: Ask students to explore a wider range of shapes with the given areas.

Differentiated outcomes	
All students	should find areas and **perimeters** of **rectilinear** shapes.
Most students	will explain their strategies carefully.
Some students	will explore other shapes with the given areas.

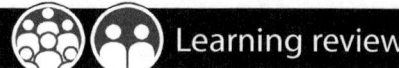 Learning review

Take one solution for each question from students in the group.

Ask: *Can you remember any quick ways to find the areas of rectangles?*

Remind them of the formula: Area = base × height

Additional activities

You can extend the activity to work with other polygons, particularly with triangles.

Students can complete Workbook page 87.

Answers

Student Book pages 165 and 166

Answers will vary as students draw their own rectilinear shapes for the given areas. Check that the perimeters are correct for each shape.

Workbook page 87

Answers will vary as students draw their own rectilinear shapes for the given perimeters and areas. Check that the students' shapes do have the required properties.

10B Estimating areas of irregular shapes by counting squares

Discover

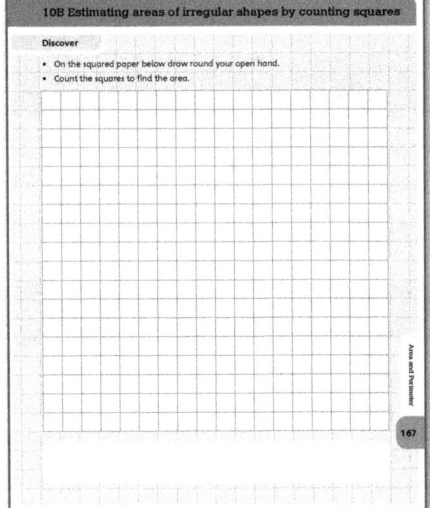

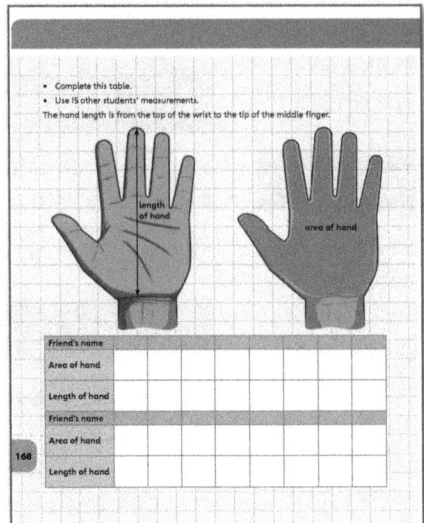

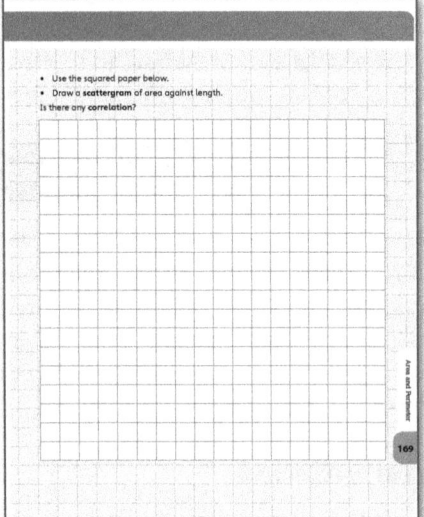

Specific learning focus

- Estimate the area of an irregular shape by counting squares.

Problem solving focus

- Understand everyday systems of measurement in length and use these to perform simple calculations.

Key vocabulary

Area, square centimetre (cm^2), square metre (m^2), square millimetre (mm^2), scattergram, correlation

Resources

- Mini whiteboards and markers
- Photocopy of your handprint on cm-squared paper
- Squared paper

Links to Student Book

See pages 167–169 in the Student Book.

Links to Workbook

Workbook page 88

Links to Digital Resource Pack

Digital Resource Pack 6 contains two activities which can be used to support students' estimating of area of rectilinear shapes. On the home page, select 'Area and Perimeter'.

Language support

The key new ideas here are the scattergram and correlation. Model the use of these words.

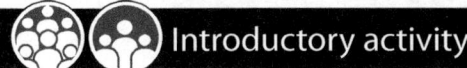 Introductory activity

Ask each student to estimate the **area** of your handprint in square centimetres. Tell them to write their estimates on their whiteboards. Give out your handprint. Ask each group of four or five students to estimate the area by counting squares. Tell students in each group to count separately and then to agree on their group estimate. This emphasises that this method is not accurate and can only provide an estimate. Ask students how they counted 'part squares'. Discuss which was the best method of dealing with 'part squares'. One method is to count every square which is more than half covered as 'one' and to not count any square which is less than half covered.

 Main activity

Ask students to find the area of their own hand in the same way. They draw round their hand on page 167 of the Student Book, count squares to find the area and then measure the length of their hand. They then complete the table using other students' measurements. Students complete the **scattergram** after the Learning review.

Differentiation

Supporting: Observe students counting squares and suggest ways to count part squares.

Consolidating: Ask students to share their strategies for counting part squares.

Extending: Ask students to explore the relationship between hand area against hand length.

Differentiated outcomes	
All students	should estimate areas by counting squares.
Most students	will suggest a sensible strategy for counting part squares.
Some students	will explore the relationship between hand area against hand length.

 Learning review

As students work on the Main activity draw a set of axes on the whiteboard. Ask students to come up one at a time to the board and then mark their hand area and length of hand on the set of axes. This enables you to show the **correlation** (relationship) between length of hand and hand area. In this case, the longer the hand length, the larger the hand area. You may need to support some students in finding the correct place for their cross.

When you have completed the scattergram, you can ask students to complete it in their textbook if appropriate. You may choose to set this as an extension activity.

Additional activities

Students can repeat the activity with other groups, for example: very young children, or male and female. They can consider the question: Is the correlation different?

Students can complete Workbook page 88.

Answers

Student Book pages 167 to 169

Answers will vary as students find the areas of their hands and the hands of their friends. Check that the areas seem reasonable.

Workbook page 88

Answers will vary as students find the areas of leaves by drawing round them and counting squares and part squares. Check that the areas are correct.

Explore

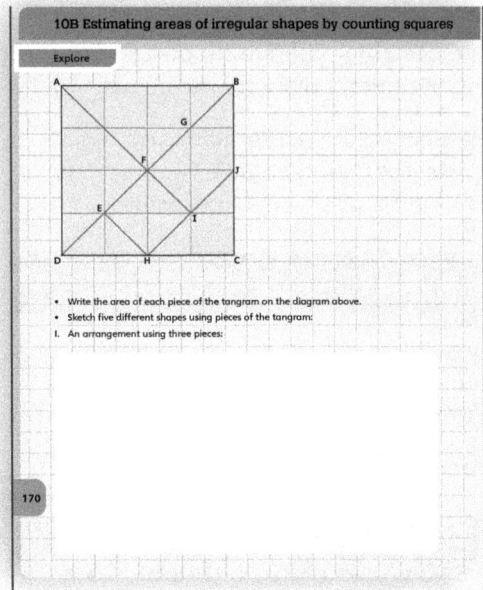

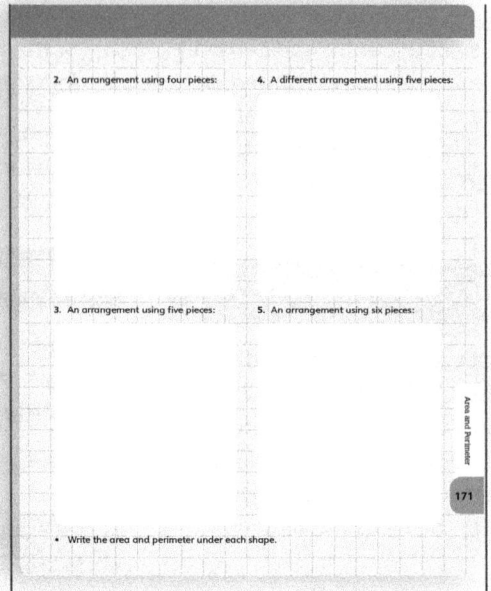

Specific learning focus

- Estimate the area of an irregular shape by counting squares.

Problem solving focus

- Understand everyday systems of measurement in length and use these to perform simple calculations.

Key vocabulary

Area, square centimetre (cm²), square metre (m²), square millimetre (mm²), tangram

Resources

- Squared paper or card
- Scissors

Links to Student Book

See pages 170–171 in the Student Book.

Links to Workbook

Workbook page 89

Links to Digital Resource Pack

Digital Resource Pack 6 contains two activities which can be used to support students' estimating of area of rectilinear shapes. On the home page, select 'Area and Perimeter'.

Language support

Remind students that:

- *Perimeter is a length. We measure perimeter in centimetres.*
- *Area is a 'count' of the number of square centimetres covered by the shape.*
- *We measure area in square centimetres.*

 Introductory activity

Make a large copy of the **tangram** from page 170 of the Student Book on your whiteboard. Ask students to work in pairs to calculate the **area** of each piece of the tangram. Take feedback and write the area of each part on your whiteboard. Note that the squares on page 170 of the Student Book are slightly bigger than 2 cm × 2 cm. For the purposes of this activity, say that they are exactly 2 cm × 2 cm.

 Main activity

Ask each student to make their own version of the tangram on squared paper or card. They then use this to find answers to the questions on pages 170 and 171 of the Student Book. Encourage students to create their own shapes and then to get a partner to check their answers.

Differentiation

Supporting: Support students to find perimeters and areas of the shapes they make.

Consolidating: Ask students to explain how they are quickly finding areas and perimeters.

Extending: Ask students to find the fraction of the total area of the square that each shape makes.

Differentiated outcomes	
All students	should make a range of shapes using tangram pieces.
Most students	will find the areas and perimeters of the shapes.
Some students	will explore fractions using the tangram pieces.

 Learning review

Take feedback from pairs to find the largest and smallest perimeters for the shapes for each answer. Ask individual students to draw these shapes on the board. Link this back to the earlier lesson. Ask: *Why do they think these shapes have the largest/smallest perimeters?*

Additional activities

Students can draw round complex shapes onto squared paper. They can estimate and then calculate the areas.

Students can complete Workbook page 89.

Answers

Student Book pages 170 and 171

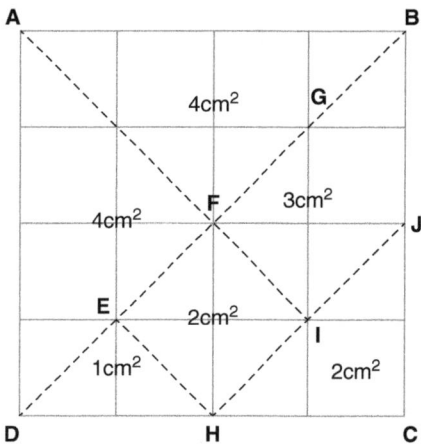

Answers will vary as students make their own arrangements of the tangram pieces. Check that the areas and perimeters of each of the students' shapes are correct.

Workbook page 89

Answers will vary as students draw their own leaves. Check that leaf A has an area of 38 cm^2, B has an area of 46 cm^2, and leaf C has an area of 19 cm^2.

10C Calculating areas and perimeters of compound shapes

Discover

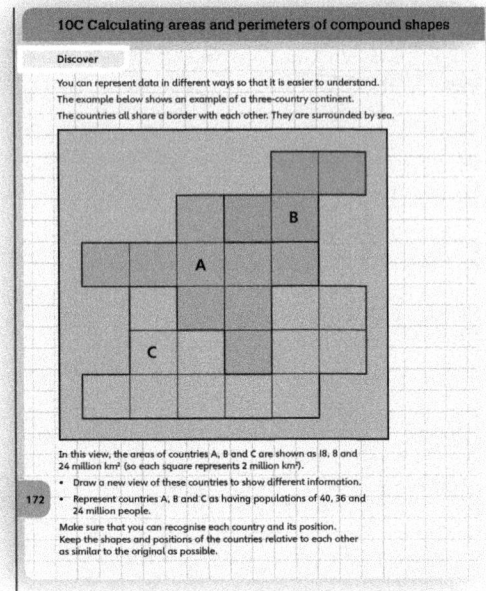
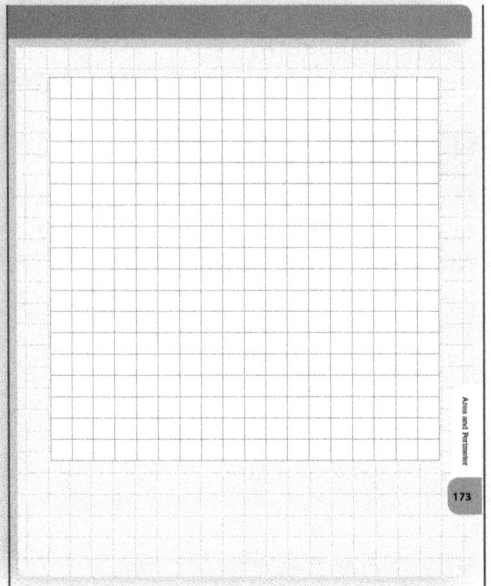

Specific learning focus

- Calculate perimeter and area of simple compound shapes that can be split into rectangles.

Problem solving focus

- Solve simple word problems involving ratio and direct proportion.

Key vocabulary

Length, width, area, square centimetre (cm²), square metre (m²), square millimetre (mm²)

Resources

- Large sheets of squared paper
- Coloured pencils

Links to Student Book

See pages 172–173 in the Student Book.

Links to Workbook

Workbook page 90

Links to Digital Resource Pack

Digital Resource Pack 6 contains two activities which can be used to support students' understanding of calculating the area and perimeter of rectilinear shapes. On the home page, select 'Area and Perimeter'.

Language support

Encourage students to explain their thinking. Ask, for example:

- *How did you decide to start?*
- *Are you certain that is correct?*
- *What do you think you will do next?*

 Introductory and Main activity

Prepare for this activity by working through the investigation yourself.

This activity should be carried out as a small-group investigation. Ask students to work in mixed-attainment groups of four to six. For this activity, allow groups to try to make sense of the investigation for themselves. Give out large sheets of squared paper. Encourage the groups to explore a wide range of possible arrangements. As students are working on the investigation, encourage them to speak out their thinking to you and to recap on their thinking process so far. Choose one of the groups who can do this well to present their solution at the end of the lesson.

Differentiation

Join in with group discussions and encourage all students to make a contribution. You should also encourage students to explain their ideas carefully so that all the other members of the group understand.

Differentiated outcomes
All students should contribute to the group discussion, and all will learn and develop their understanding through listening to the ideas of other students.

 Learning review

Take feedback from the group that you have selected. Encourage them to talk through the whole investigational process, including errors that they made and things they tried which didn't work.

You may want to share other versions of 'infographics' with the students. There are many examples on the internet.

Additional activities

You can draw on other real-world data from the website. Ask students to find ways to represent this data.

Students can complete Workbook page 90.

Answers

Student Book pages 172 and 173

Accept any accurate scale which allows students to fit their representations of the countries' populations on a page.

Workbook page 90

Shape	Perimeter	Area
A	18 cm	18 cm²
B	26 cm	19 cm²
C	24 cm	20 cm²
D	34 cm	36 cm²

Explore

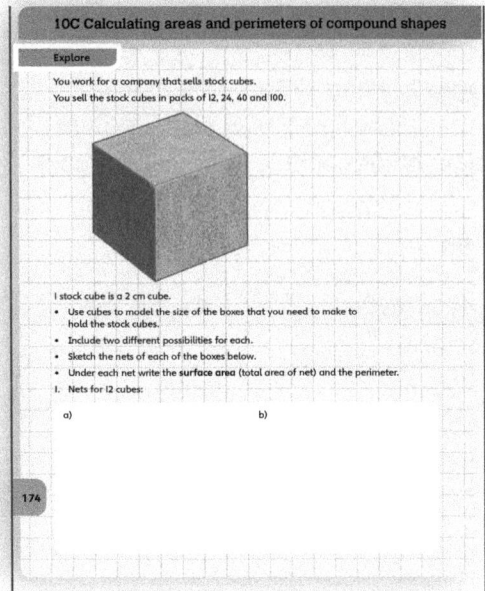
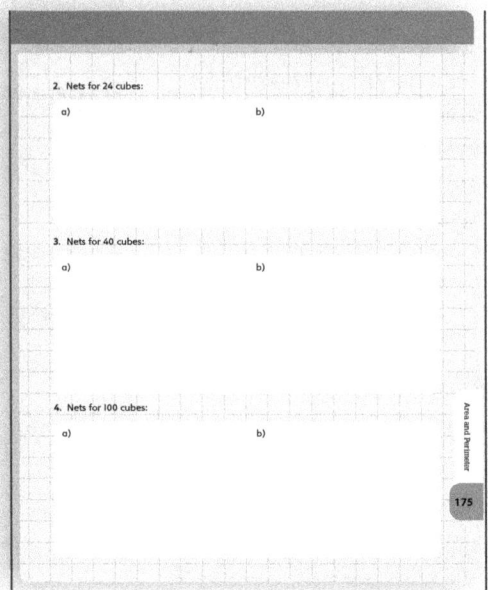

Specific learning focus

- Calculate perimeter and area of simple compound shapes that can be split into rectangles.

Problem solving focus

- Solve simple word problems involving ratio and direct proportion.

Key vocabulary

Length, width, perimeter, area, surface area, square centimetre (cm²), square metre (m²), square millimetre (mm²)

Resources

- Large sheets of squared paper
- Coloured pencils
- Cubes

Links to Student Book

See pages 174–175 in the Student Book.

Links to Workbook

Workbook page 91

Links to Digital Resource Pack

Digital Resource Pack 6 contains two activities which can be used to support students' understanding of calculating the area and perimeter of rectilinear shapes. On the home page, select 'Area and Perimeter'.

Language support

Use students who can act as good role models in the Learning review so that all students hear the appropriate terms and phrases from the Key vocabulary. For example:

- *The surface area of this net is …*
- *The perimeter of this net is …*

Ask students to imagine they need to pack a liquid which has a volume of 36 cm³. Ask: *How many different cuboids can hold this volume of liquid?* Give each pair 5 minutes to find as many solutions as they can. Select one of the answers. Ask a student to sketch the cuboid on the board. As a class decide what the net for this cuboid is. Calculate the **surface area** and **perimeter**.

Note again that while volume is beyond the scope of the Stage 6 framework, it is useful to introduce the concept here in an accessible way as students explore measure.

 Main activity

The Introductory activity allows you to identify students who may need initial support with this activity. You may wish to group these students together and focus on these students at the beginning of this part of the lesson. Some students may find that opening up boxes helps them to understand how to draw the net. Make sure that the students have access to cubes so that they can use practical materials to support them.

Differentiation

Supporting: Support students in finding surface areas and perimeters. Just explore 24 cubes.

Consolidating: Ask students to explain how they are finding areas and perimeters. Make links to factors.

Extending: Ask students to generalise their findings for 12. 24, 40 and 100.

Differentiated outcomes	
All students	should find surface areas and perimeters with support.
Most students	will find surface areas and perimeters and explain their reasoning.
Some students	will find the best solution for the problem.

Ask students to form groups of four or five and compare their answers. Ask: *Which answer do you think is the most efficient design for the stock cube company to work with?* Take feedback from the groups. Agree as a whole class on the solution you would recommend to the stock cube company and why you think this is the best solution.

Additional activities

Students can carry out this activity practically. They can also explore different-shaped containers.

Students can complete Workbook page 91.

Answers

Student Book pages 174 and 175

Answers will vary as students draw their own nets. Check that they have written the correct surface areas for each shape and net.

Workbook page 91

Answers will vary as students draw nets of boxes they have found. Check that the surface area and the perimeter are correct.

10 Area and perimeter

Connect and Review

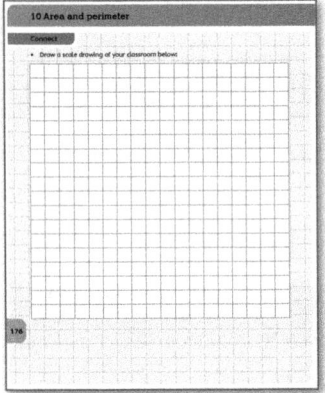 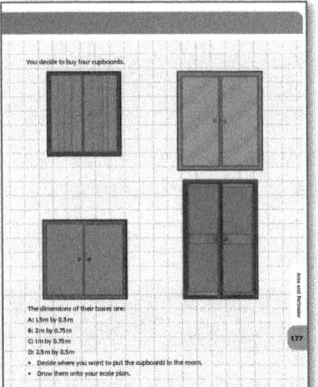 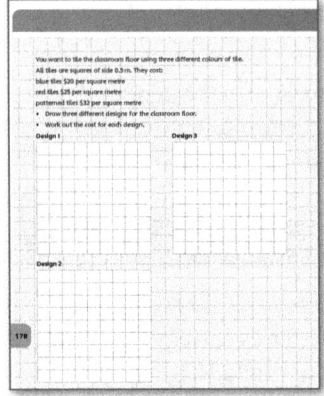 

Specific learning foci

- Measure and calculate the perimeter and area of rectilinear shapes.
- Draw and measure lines to the nearest centimetre.
- Calculate perimeter and area of simple compound shapes that can be split into rectangles.

Problem solving foci

- Understand everyday systems of measurement in length and use these to perform simple calculations.
- Make sense of and solve word problems.

Key vocabulary

Length, width, height, depth, breadth, edge, perimeter, circumference, area, surface, face, surface area, square centimetre (cm^2), square metre (m^2), square millimetre (mm^2), rectilinear, scattergram, correlation

Resources

- Mini whiteboards and markers
- Squared paper
- Rulers and metre rules
- Calculators
- Scissors
- Assessment activity 10 – one per student (Resource sheet 10 – see www.oxfordprimary.com/OIPMteacher)

Links to Student Book

See pages 176–179 in the Student Book.

Links to Workbook

Workbook page 92

Links to Digital Resource Pack

Digital Resource Pack 6 contains two activities which can be used to support students' understanding of the area and perimeter of rectilinear shapes. On the home page, select 'Area and Perimeter'.

Language support

Encourage students to give a clear rationale for the positions that they choose for their classroom arrangement. Ask questions, for example:

- *How much space does that leave for desks?*
- *Should that go on the right-hand side or the left-hand side?*
- *How much longer/wider is that than the other cupboards?*

Introductory and Main activity

Ask students to work in groups of four on the activities on pages 176 to 178 of the Student Book. Encourage them to try to interpret and begin the activity without any teacher input.

If you feel as though the class need additional support, then you could ask students to estimate the length and width of the classroom to the nearest metre. Tell them to write their estimate down on their whiteboard. List all the different estimates on the board. Ask one student to measure the classroom using the metre rule. Work out the dimensions to the nearest metre. Use the measurements in metres and centimetres.

Groups should make cut-outs to represent the cupboards so that they can try them in different locations. Encourage students to see this as a real-life activity and to give good reasons for the choices that they make. During the activity, sketch a scale drawing of the classroom on the board. You can use this in the learning review.

Ask the groups to present their solutions. Ask the class to decide which they prefer and to give reasons for this choice.

Differentiation

Students should work in mixed-attainment groups to support one another in working through the activity on pages 176 to 178 of the Student Book.

For the activity on page 179 of the Student Book, you may want to help write the answers for those less confident with writing or in speaking English.

Differentiated outcomes
This is an activity designed to offer differentiation by outcome.

Learning review

Students should complete the Review activity as individuals as it is a summative assessment.

Additional activities

Students can design layouts for their bedroom or for a space for students to meet in school. They can use furniture catalogues so that prices are realistic.

Students can complete Workbook page 92.

Answers

Student Book pages 176 to 178

Answers will vary as students start with a plan of their classroom and then choose which door and floor tiles they'll use. Check that their calculations are correct.

Workbook page 92

Answers will vary as students draw a plan of a room in their home. Check that their calculations for the area and perimeter are correct.

Assessment activity 10

1. **c)** 84 cm squared
2. **a)** m
3. **c)** 92 cm squared
4. **c)** Length × width
5. **b)** 80 cm
6. **b)** 43 m squared
7. Accept any sensible answer.

Unit 11 Handling Data

Overview

Big Idea

This unit deals with two distinct areas of mathematics. The first, 'Handling Data', is about making decisions about what data represents. Often, students do not know how to interpret data; they learn how to collect and organise the data but do not realise that there may be alternative interpretations that you can draw from the data. It is important that students see the big picture from the beginning. They need to understand that interpretation is just as important as collection and representation of data.

The data handling cycle is:

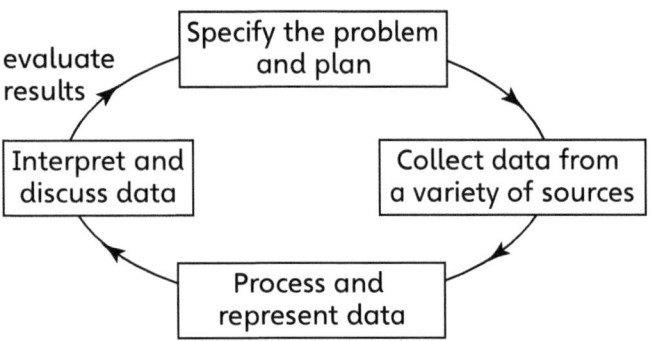

This diagram emphasises the importance of both problem posing and interpretation. It is important to realise that the data handling cycle is continuous. To emphasise this, this unit is not broken down into separate subunits as previous units were. Instead students undertake a single unbroken investigation in which they follow the data handling cycle through one cycle.

The second area dealt with in this unit is that of probability. The Big Idea here is that of 'equally likely outcomes', that is, that we can only calculate probabilities of events that are equally likely.

Possible misconceptions

Some students may be used to simply answering questions based on data. These students probably won't realise that there can be alternative interpretations of the data. This unit asks students to take a critical view of the data throughout. It also encourages them to make their own decisions about which charts to use to represent and interpret the data.

Key vocabulary and language structures

Data, survey, questionnaire, tally; graph, block graph, line graph, pictogram, bar chart, table, frequency table; Carroll diagram, Venn diagram; most/least popular, most/least common; mean, median, mode, range, average; probable, likely, possible, unlikely, most likely/ least likely; event, outcome, probability certain, impossible, equal chance fair, unfair, biased, equally likely outcomes

Coverage in lessons

Learning focus	Learning outcomes
Statistics in everyday life; interpreting data from graphs and tables; finding the mode, median, mean and range of data sets	Do I know how we use statistics in everyday life?
	Can I use data to solve problems?
	Can I use the mean, median, mode and range to help me interpret data?
Probability	Can I explain what is meant by the probability of something happening?
	Can I find the probability of events happening?
	Can I explain what equally likely events are?

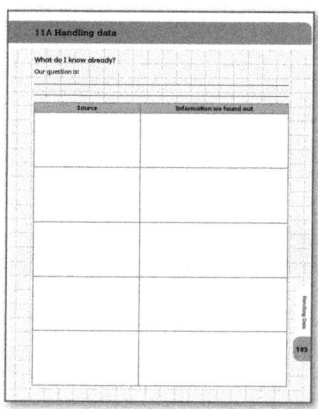
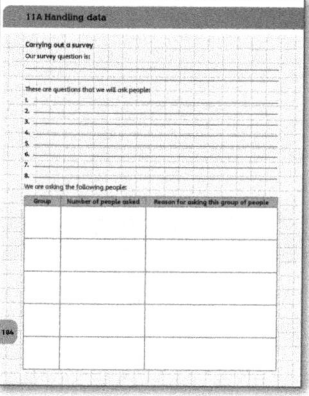

These teacher's notes follow a different pattern from others in this book. The 'Handling Data' section of the unit is written to run as one continuous activity over several sessions. You may choose to allocate a lesson to each part of the process but it is better to allow groups to work at different rates. These notes are divided up so that you can see how to support students within each section of the process. This is the last time that students will study data handling within the programme. The aim is that they draw on and use all their previous knowledge from other stages to follow the data handling cycle as a single continuous experience.

Specific learning foci

- Explore how statistics are used in everyday life.
- Solve a problem by representing, extracting and interpreting data in tables, graphs, charts and diagrams.
- Find the median and mean of a set of data.
- Find the mode and range of a set of data from relevant situations.

Problem solving focus

- Make, test and refine hypotheses, explain and justify methods, reasoning, strategies, results or conclusions orally.

Key vocabulary

Data, survey, questionnaire, tally graph, block graph, line graph, pictogram, bar chart, table, frequency table, Carroll diagram, Venn diagram most/least popular, most/least common mean, median, mode, range, average

Resources

Ideally students need access to the internet for research. If this is not possible, collect together a large number of reference books. Students need access to large sheets of paper and best technology available in school to prepare their presentations. Scrap paper, squared paper, coloured pencils will all be used.

Links to Student Book

See pages 181–188 in the Student Book.

Links to Workbook

Workbook page 94

Links to Digital Resource Pack

Digital Resource Pack 6 contains two activities which can be used to support students' understanding of handling data. On the home page, select 'Handling Data'.

Language support

Write the key words on flip-chart paper. Display them throughout the series of activities. As you work with students during this section of the unit, model the use of these words.

When students plan their presentations, remind them that they need to use this key vocabulary.

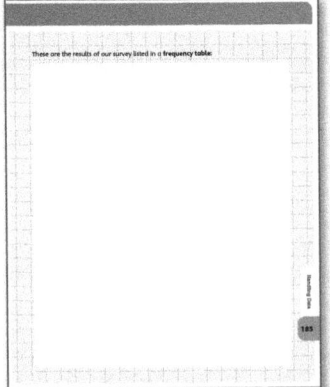
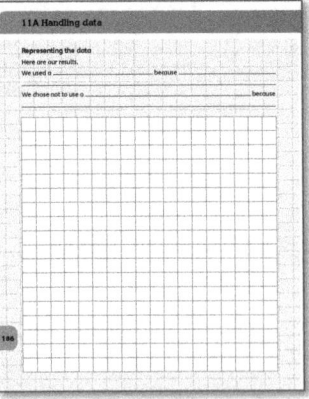
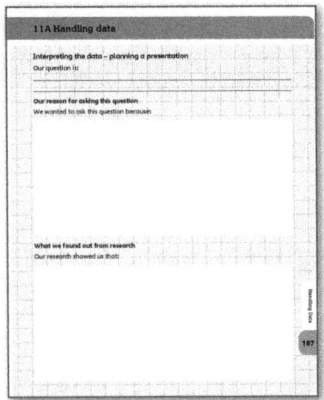
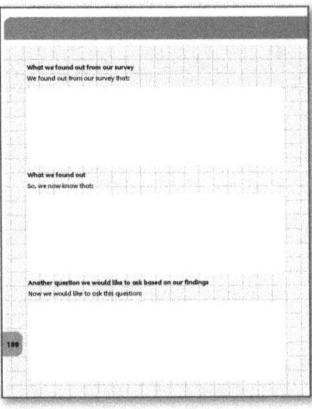

Defining my question

This is the first part of the data handling cycle: 'Specifying the problem'.

Ask students to look at the Engage page in the Student Book. Tell them to work individually and to list all the questions from the page that they are interested in finding out about. They should list these in the Student Workbook. An alternative is to ask students to look at magazines and newspapers and to find all the stories that use data. You can discuss how the journalists might have researched these stories. Common areas that students often like to explore include:

- *How can we improve school dinners?*
- *Is the school environmentally friendly (including recycling and travel to school)?*
- *How does the climate in our country compare with that in other areas?*
- *What programmes are good for a school television/radio station?*
- *Are students at our school getting better at maths?*

When students have prepared their lists of questions, ask them to work in pairs to decide on the three questions that they think are best.

Talk about practicality at this point. Encourage students to choose questions that they are genuinely interested in finding an answer to.

Then ask students to work in groups of four, five or six to decide on a list of three questions for their group. At this point, list all the questions on the board. Ask individual students to pick a question to research.

What do I know already?

Students stay in their groups of four, five or six for the rest of this section of the unit. In this part, ask them to research all the data they can find about the question they are asking. Encourage them to use the internet, newspapers and information texts to carry out this research. For example: a group exploring school dinners can find out what dinners schools in different countries provide, how school dinners have changed over the years in their own country, and what the state or government policy is in relation to the provision of school dinners.

Carrying out a survey

The next stage is 'to collect data from a range of sources'. This involves either carrying out a survey or collecting data that already exists to help with the research question. For example: the school dinners group may put together a questionnaire which asks a range of questions related to satisfaction with school dinners and another questionnaire about what food is available. The group need to make sure that they ask these questions to everyone who has an interest in the answer. This includes parents, students, the dinner staff and teachers.

Groups looking at areas such as climate or athletic performance can collect appropriate data from other sources such as weather websites or world athletics championship results.

Students may use a tally chart to collect the data.

Representing the data

Students need to collect together and analyse their results. It is likely that a frequency table is the most appropriate to show the most/least popular choices of answer. For some questions, however, different data tables may be most useful. For example: athletics results can be presented effectively as a historical list of world record times against the year they were achieved. Differences in climate can be represented in a comparison table. It is also sometimes appropriate to show the data in a graph such as a block graph, line graph, pictogram or bar chart. Venn diagrams and Carroll diagrams are also useful. Encourage students to explain why they have represented the data in their chosen way.

Interpreting the data – planning a presentation

The final part of the cycle is to interpret and discuss the data. As the groups analyse the data they have collected, remind them of how to calculate **mean**, **median** and **mode** if these are appropriate measures, and to work out the **range**.

You can do this by carrying out a survey of shoe sizes of the class and putting the students in the role of shopkeepers. They should use the data and the information they gain to make a decision about the numbers of shoes of each size they would buy for their shop.

Carry out a survey of the students and complete a frequency table. Then calculate:

- The range (the difference between the smallest and the largest shoe size)
- The mode (the most common shoe size)
- The median (the middle shoe size when you arrange all the sizes in order. Note: If there are two sizes in the 'middle' you take the mean of these two sizes)
- The mean (total all the shoe sizes and divide by the number of students)

Refer students back to the key words so that they are mathematically literate in their presentations. Encourage groups to practise the presentation before sharing it with the whole class so that they can refine it.

11B Probability

Discover

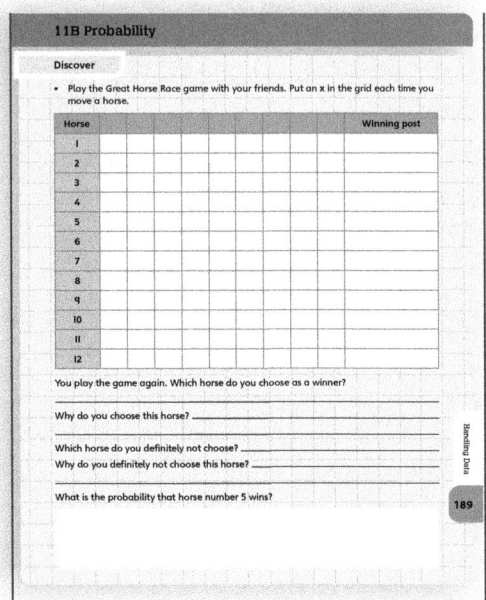

Specific learning focus

- Use the language associated with probability to discuss events, to assess likelihood and risk, including those with equally likely outcomes.

Problem solving focus

- Make, test and refine hypotheses, explain and justify methods, reasoning, strategies, results or conclusions orally.

Key vocabulary

Probable, likely, possible, unlikely, most likely/least likely, event, outcome, probability, certain, impossible, equal chance, fair, unfair, biased, equally likely outcomes

Resources

- Dice
- Counters

Links to Student Book

See page 189 in the Student Book.

Links to Workbook

Workbook page 95

Links to Digital Resource Pack

Digital Resource Pack 6 contains two activities which can be used to support students' understanding of probability. On the home page, select 'Handling Data'.

Language support

Use the following phrases:

- *Are the outcomes equally likely? How do you know?*
- *How many possible ways can you score 7?*
- *What is the probability of an impossible event?*

Ask the students to play the game in mixed-attainment groups of four to six. It is important that students play the game without any prior instruction about how the **probabilities** work. Each group needs two dice and 12 different-coloured counters to represent the horses. Make sure students understand how to play the game. A player rolls the two dice, then moves the horse whose number is the sum of the scores on the dice forward one space on the board. For example, if a 6 and a 4 are thrown on the dice, then horse 10 is moved one space forwards. The horse that reaches the winning post first wins. Let students play the game three or four times until they begin to notice patterns in the results, and identify which horses are most likely/least likely to win. When they have noticed a pattern, allow the groups to complete page 189 of the Student Book before the Learning review.

Ask students:

- *Do you think the game is 'fair' or 'unfair'?*
- *Do you think the results are biased?*

Differentiation

Supporting: Ask the students why they are choosing the horse. Why do they think it will win?

Consolidating: Ask students why the game is unfair. Which horse is most likely to win? Why?

Extending: Ask students to calculate the probabilities of each horse winning.

Differentiated outcomes	
All students	should play the game and notice which horses are most likely to win.
Most students	will notice and explain the patterns – for example, it is impossible for horse 1 to win.
Some students	will make links to probability.

Write the following table on the board. Ask students to complete the table. (The first three rows are completed as an example.) Use the table to remind students that the probability of an event happening is the number of possible ways of that event happening divided by the total number of possible outcomes. Remind students that the individual outcomes must be **equally likely**, and that the sum of the probabilities of all the possible outcomes is 1.

Dice score	Possible ways of making the score	Number of possible ways
1	impossible	0
2	(1,1)	1
3	(1, 2), (2,1)	2
4		
5		
6		
7		
8		
9		
10		
11		
12		

Additional activities

Students can carry out experiments involving probabilities. For example: they can make spinners, or use matchboxes and find the probability of the matchbox landing on its end by tossing it 100 times.

Students can complete Workbook page 95.

Answers

Student Book page 189

Answers will vary as students play the game with other students.

Workbook page 95

Chosen outcome	Equally likely outcomes	Number of possible required outcomes	Probability fraction
Rolling an odd number on a 1–6 dice	There are 6 possible scores.	3 (1, 3 or 5)	$\frac{3}{6} = \frac{1}{2}$
Rolling a total of 9 on two dice	There are 36 possible outcomes	4 (3 and 6; 4 and 5; 5 and 4; 6 and 3)	$\frac{4}{36} = \frac{1}{9}$
Rolling an even number on a 1–10 dice	There are 10 possible scores	5 (2, 4, 6, 8 or 10)	$\frac{5}{10} = \frac{1}{2}$

11B Probability

Explore

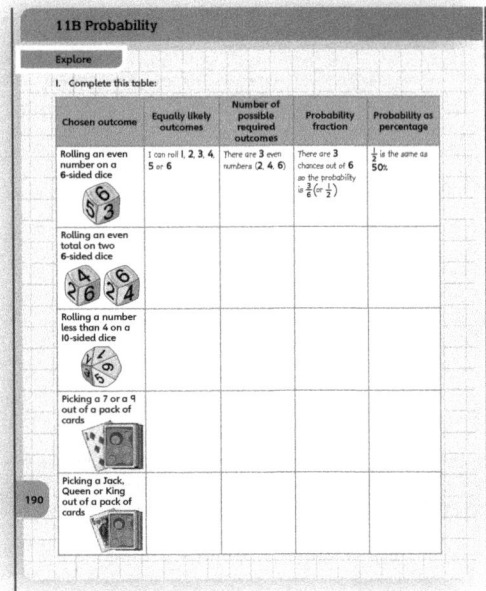

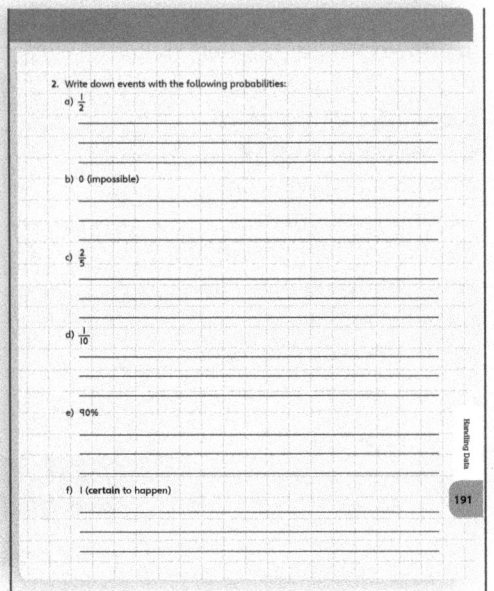

Specific learning focus

● Use the language associated with probability to discuss events, to assess likelihood and risk, including those with equally likely outcomes.

Problem solving focus

● Make, test and refine hypotheses, explain and justify methods, reasoning, strategies, results or conclusions orally.

Key vocabulary

Probable, likely, possible, unlikely, most likely/least likely, event, outcome, probability, certain, impossible, equal chance, fair, unfair, biased, equally likely outcomes

Resources

● Mini whiteboards and markers
● Selection of magazines/newspapers that include stories using probability
● Assessment activity 11 – one per student (Resource sheet 11 – see www.oxfordprimary.com/OIPMteacher)

Links to Student Book

See pages 190–191 in the Student Book.

Links to Workbook

Workbook page 5

Links to Digital Resource Pack

Digital Resource Pack 6 contains two activities which can be used to support students' understanding of probability. On the home page, select 'Handling Data'.

Language support

Model phrases, for example:

● *Are the outcomes equally likely? How do you know?*
● *How many possible ways can you score 7?*
● *What is the probability of an impossible event?*
● *What does a probability of '1' mean?*

 Introductory activity

Write the following phrases on the board:

- *It is very likely that …*
- *It is **certain** that …*
- *There is a fifty–fifty chance that …*
- *It is **impossible** for …*
- *It is **unlikely** that …*

Give each pair a mini whiteboard. Ask them to complete the phrases on their whiteboard. Tell the pairs to write down at least two responses for each statement: one response for each student. Take feedback from students. Make sure that others in the class agree, especially with the statements 'It is unlikely that …' and 'It is very likely that …'. Talk through 'how likely' something has to be before it is 'very likely'. Remind students of the meaning of fifty–fifty or **equal chance**. Talk about their examples – are they exactly 50% or 1 in 2 chances?

 Main activity

Ask students to work in pairs on the activity on pages 190 and 191 of the Student Book. This allows them to discuss the equally likely outcomes and check answers. As they work on the examples, ask individual students: *How are you working out the probabilities?*

Remind them that probability is 'Required outcomes'/ 'Possible outcomes'. They need to use this for question 2. For example: I want to roll an even number on a six-sided dice

Required outcomes are: 2, 4 or 6

Possible outcomes are: 1, 2, 3, 4, 5, 6

$$\frac{\text{Required outcomes}}{\text{Possible outcomes}} = \frac{3}{6} = \frac{1}{2}$$

So the **probability** of rolling an even number on a six-sided dice is $\frac{1}{2}$.

Differentiation

Supporting: Ask students to describe all the equally likely outcomes.

Consolidating: Ask students to tell you how to find a probability.

Extending: Ask students to find probabilities as fractions, percentages and decimals.

Differentiated outcomes	
All students	should find equally likely outcomes.
Most students	will find probabilities as fractions.
Some students	will find probabilities as fractions, percentages and decimals.

 Learning review

Call students to the front of the class at random (you can use a jar of lollipop sticks with students' names on to select students). Ask each student to give one of their chosen events from question 2 in the main activity. Ask the other students to decide what the probability of this event happening is to check that the answer is correct.

Additional activities

Students can explore the language of probability in the media. They can use newspapers to find stories which include the use of probability. You can ask students to assess whether the use of probabilities is accurate.

Students can complete Workbook page 95.

Answers

Student Book pages 190 and 191

Chosen outcome	Equally likely outcomes	Number of possible required outcomes	Probability fraction	Probability as percentage
Rolling an even number on a 6-sided dice	I can roll 1, 2, 3, 4, 5 or 6	There are 3 even numbers (2, 4, 6)	$\frac{3}{6}$	50%
Rolling an even total on two 6-sided dice	1, 1 = 2 1, 2 = 3 2, 1 = 3 2, 2 = 4 1, 3 = 4 3, 1 = 4 1, 4 = 5 4, 1 = 5 3, 2 = 5 2, 3 = 5 3, 3 = 6 2, 4 = 6 4, 2 = 6 1, 5 = 6 5, 1 = 6 1, 6 = 7 6, 1 = 7 2, 5 = 7 5, 2 = 7 3, 4 = 7 4, 3 = 7 4, 4 = 8 2, 6 = 8 6, 2 = 8 3, 5 = 8 5, 3 = 8 5, 4 = 9 4, 5 = 9 3, 6 = 9 6, 3 = 9 5, 5 = 10 6, 4 = 10 4, 6 = 10 5, 6 = 11 6, 5 = 11 6, 6 = 12	18	$\frac{18}{36} = \frac{1}{2}$	50%

Chosen outcome	Equally likely outcomes	Number of possible required outcomes	Probability fraction	Probability as percentage
Rolling a number less than 4 on a 10 sided dice	1, 2, 3, 4, 5, 6, 7, 8, 9, 10	1, 2 or 3 so 3 possible required outcomes	$\frac{3}{10}$	30%
Picking a 7 or a 9 out of a pack of cards	52 cards in a pack	4 possible '7s and 4 possible '9s So 8 possible required outcomes	$\frac{8}{52} = \frac{2}{13}$	15.4%
Picking a Jack, Queen or King out of a pack of cards	52 cards in a pack	4 possible jacks, 4 possible queens, 4 possible kings So 12 possible required outcomes	$\frac{12}{52} = \frac{3}{13}$	23.1%

Workbook page 95

Chosen outcome	Equally likely outcomes	Number of possible required outcomes	Probability fraction
Rolling an odd number on a 1–6 dice	There are 6 possible scores	3 (1, 3 or 5)	$\frac{3}{6} = \frac{1}{2}$
Rolling a total of 9 on two dice	There are 36 possible outcomes	4 (3 and 6; 4 and 5; 5 and 4; 6 and 3)	$\frac{4}{36} = \frac{1}{9}$
Rolling an even number on a 1–10 dice	There are 10 possible scores	5 (2, 4, 6, 8 or 10)	$\frac{5}{10} = \frac{1}{2}$

Assessment activity 11

1. d) Line graph

2. c) It is a good way to show how something changes over time

3. c) 2, 2, 6, 10, 15

4. c) 1, 7, 13, 13, 13, 25, 25, 32

5. d) Look at the test results or **c)** Ask the teachers.

6. c) $\frac{1}{6}$

7. Accept any sensible answer.

6 Glossary

arc part of the circumference of a circle or any curve. You can draw arcs with compasses

average a number that best represents a set of numbers. There are different ways of determining a representative number (average): mean, median and mode

biased if something is unfair it is biased. In probability, a dice or a spinner is biased if there is not the same probability of it landing on any of its faces or sides

centilitre one hundredth of a litre. There are 10 millilitres in 1 centilitre. *Centi* at the start of a word usually means 'one hundredth'

circumference the distance all the way round a circle; the perimeter of a circle

common multiple a number which is in two or more multiplication tables. So 15 is a common multiple of 3 and 5, as it is in the 3 times table and the 5 times table

composite number any positive number greater than 1 that is not a prime number. A composite number is divisible by at least one number that is not 1 or itself

concentric concentric shapes all have the same centre and lie inside each other

correlation any statistical relationship between two sets of data. So the height of a male and his weight will be correlated as, statistically, taller males are heavier

cross-section a cut straight across a 3D shape; a slice of an object

decade a period of 10 years. A century is divided into 10 decades. For example, the 20th century is divided into the 1900s, 1910s, 1920s, 1930s, and so on

decimal equivalent a decimal equivalent of a fraction is a fraction expressed as a decimal fraction: for example, the decimal equivalent of $\frac{1}{2}$ is 0.5

directed numbers numbers that can be positive or negative, with a positive (+) or negative (−) sign in front of them. For example, +4 is positive four, and −16 is negative sixteen. Sometimes the + sign is left off positive numbers, so +6 is the same as 6

dividend the quantity that has to be divided

divisor a number that is divided into another number

dodecahedron a 3D shape that has 12 flat faces. A regular dodecahedron has 12 regular pentagonal faces

equal chance (even chance, fifty-fifty chance) any two events that are equally likely. They have a probability of 50% or $\frac{1}{2}$. For example, if we toss a coin, it is equally likely to come down heads or tails

equally likely any events that have the same probability. For example, if you have 2 yellow balls, 2 blue balls and 2 black balls in a bag it is equally likely that you will pick out a yellow ball, a blue ball or a black ball

event something that can happen when we perform an experiment. When we roll a dice, there are six possible outcomes: 1, 2, 3, 4, 5, 6. If we roll two dice, we can look at different events, such as the event that both dice show an even number, or the event that both dice show prime numbers

factorise find out what the possible factors of a number are, for example we can write: $42 = 2 \times 3 \times 7$

foot (plural feet) an imperial unit used to measure length. A foot is divided into 12 parts called inches. A foot measures about 30 cm

front elevation a 2D drawing of a 3D shape, drawn from in front of the shape

hypothesis a suggested explanation for something, which can be tested by further investigation

Glossary

identical   when two or more shapes are identical, they have exactly the same shape, size, and colour

inch (plural inches)   an imperial unit used to measure length. Twelve inches measure the same as one foot. An inch measures about $2\frac{1}{2}$ cm

interior angle   an angle inside a shape: a triangle has three interior angles; a pentagon has five interior angles

International Date Line   an imaginary line on the surface of the Earth at about 180° longitude, to the east of which the date is one day earlier than the countries to the west

international time zones   the surface of the Earth is divided into 24 long sections (15° of longitude apart) in which a standard time is used. Each zone has a clock time one hour earlier than the zone immediately to the east

intersect   lines intersect when they cross each other. Where they cross is called the intersection. Intersecting lines can be straight or curved

isometric drawing   a representation of a 3D shape drawn on a background triangular (isometric) grid

kite   a four-sided polygon with two pairs of adjacent sides that are the same length and one pair of angles that are the same size

loss   a shopkeeper makes a loss when the selling price is less than the buying price

mean   a kind of average. To find the mean, total the quantities and then divide by the number of quantities

median   a kind of average. To find the median, write out the quantities in order. The median is the middle value

millisecond   a unit used to measure a very small amount of time. There are 1000 milliseconds in 1 second

operation key   the $+$, $-$, $\times$ or $\div$ key on a calculator

ounce (oz) (plural ounces)   an imperial unit of weight or mass. 1 oz is about 25 g

parallelogram   a four-sided shape in which opposite sides are parallel to each other

plan view   a diagram showing what an object looks like from above

plane   a flat surface that can be vertical, horizontal, or oblique

pound (lb)   an imperial unit of weight or mass. A pound is divided into sixteen ounces. A one pound weight is about 450 grams. A kilogram is about $2\frac{1}{4}$ pounds

prime factor   a factor of a number that is also a prime number

prime number   a number that has only two factors, which are 1 and the number itself. The number 1 is not a prime number because it has only one factor

profit   what you make when you sell something for more than you paid for it; the difference between the buying price and the selling price

random   purely by chance. For example, if you choose a number at random, you pick any number that you wish. Random numbers do not have an order

rectilinear   a rectilinear shape is one consisting of or bounded by straight lines

recurring   in a recurring decimal one or more of the digits repeats itself. The recurring decimal goes on and on without end

reflex angle   an angle larger than 180° and smaller than 360°

rhomboid   a parallelogram in which adjacent sides are of unequal lengths

rhombus   a 2D shape with four equal sides. The opposite sides are parallel. Rhombus is the correct name for a diamond shape

Glossary

scattergram   a graph that shows correlation between two things. The graph can show positive correlation, negative correlation or no correlation

side elevation   a 2D drawing of a 3D shape, drawn from the side of the shape

surface area   the total area of all the faces of a 3D object

symmetry   there are different types of symmetry: plane shapes can be symmetrical about a line or have rotational symmetry about a point; solid shapes can have symmetry about a plane or axis

tangram   a puzzle made up of triangles, a square, and a rhombus cut out of a square. The tangram pieces can be used to make new shapes

thousandth   if we divide a value or an object into 1000 parts, each part is worth one thousandth of the original amount

tonne   a metric unit used to measure mass or weight. A tonne equals 1000 kilograms. A tonne is sometimes called a metric ton

transformation   a way of moving a shape or an object, for example: turn (rotation), slide (translation) or flip (reflection)

trapezium   a four-sided shape that has one pair of parallel sides and one pair of sides that are not parallel

volume   the amount of space taken up by a solid shape. When measuring volume, we use cubic units such as cm^3 and m^3

yard   an imperial unit used to measure distance. There are three feet in one yard. A yard is about 90 cm